Girls, Boys, and Language

Language in Education
Series Editor
Michael Stubbs

Language is central to education. Yet very little writing about language is presented in a way that is suitable for teachers to help and guide them in their classroom practice. This series aims to explore in a non-technical way, aspects of language immediately relevant to practising and trainee teachers.

Learning about Writing: The Early Years
Pam Czerniewska

Teaching Grammar: A Guide for the National Curriculum
Richard Hudson

Girls, Boys, and Language
Joan Swann

Girls, Boys, and Language

Joan Swann

BLACKWELL
Oxford UK & Cambridge USA

First published 1992
Reprinted 1993, 1995

Blackwell Publishers Ltd.
108 Cowley Road, Oxford OX4 1JF
UK

Blackwell Publishers Inc.
238 Main Street, Cambridge, Massachusetts 02142
USA

British Library Cataloguing in Publication Data

A CIP Catalogue record for this book is available from the British Libary.

Library of Congress Cataloging-in-Publication Data
Swann, Joan.
    Girls, boys, and language / Joan Swann.
        p.   cm. — (Language in education)
    Includes bibliographical references (p.) and index.
    ISBN 0-631-16469-3 (pbk : alk. paper)

    1. Children—United States—Language. 2. English language-
-Gender. 3. Language arts (Elementary)—United States.   I. Title.
II. Series.
LB1139.L3S88   1992
420'.1'9—dc20
                                                        91–46358
                                                        CIP

Typeset in 11 on 13 pt Palatino
by Photo-graphics, Honiton, Devon
Printed in Great Britain by Athenæum Press Ltd, Gateshead, Tyne & Wear

This book is printed on acid-free paper

Contents

Acknowledgements   viii

1 Introduction   1
   1.1   Language and Equal Opportunities in
            Education   2
   1.2   Biology and Linguistic Destiny   5
   1.3   How this Book is Organized   12

2 Gender and Language Use   14
   2.1   Introduction   14
   2.2   Gendered Expectations   15
   2.3   Girls and Boys Speaking   20
   2.4   Gender Bias in Language   34
   2.5   Conclusion   46

3 Girls' and Boys' Talk in the Classroom   48
   3.1   Introduction   48
   3.2   Gender and Classroom Interaction   49
   3.3   Studies of Classroom Talk – Some Examples   53
   3.4   How do Pupils Get to Talk?   58
   3.5   Gender in Context   64
   3.6   Identifying Imbalances in Classroom Talk   66
   3.7   Conclusion   68

4 Oracy Issues   71
   4.1   Introduction   71
   4.2   Talk and Unequal Relations   72
   4.3   Talk and Learning   74

4.4 Girls' and Boys' 'Communication Skills'   77
4.5 Assessing Speaking and Listening   80
4.6 The Multifunctional Nature of Talk   84
4.7 Some Implications   91
4.8 Conclusion   92

5 Equal Representation?   95
5.1 Introduction   95
5.2 Images in Children's Books   97
5.3 Studies of Children's Books – Some
     Examples   99
5.4 Girl-Friendly Problems?   103
5.5 Images In and Out of School   106
5.6 Identifying Imbalances in Books and
     Resources   108
5.7 Conclusion   111

6 The Literate Female   114
6.1 Introduction   114
6.2 Girls' and Boys' Ability   115
6.3 Reading and Writing Choices   117
6.4 Studies of Reading and Writing – Some
     Examples   120
6.5 The Impact of Schools   127
6.6 Identifying Imbalances in Reading and
     Writing   131
6.7 Conclusion   133

7 Literacy Issues   136
7.1 Introduction   136
7.2 Balancing the Books   137
7.3 Reading, Writing and Assessment   140
7.4 Subjects with a 'Male' Image   143
7.5 Is School Literacy Harmful to Girls?   145
7.6 Reading, Writing and Gender Identity   149
7.7 Resistant Readers and Writers   155
7.8 Some Implications   159
7.9 Conclusion   160

8 Monitoring Language Experience   163
    8.1 Introduction   163
    8.2 Monitoring Classroom Activities   165
    8.3 Looking at Talk   171
    8.4 Looking at Written Texts   189
    8.5 Interpreting Imbalances   197
    8.6 Conclusion   198

9 Introducing Equality   200
    9.1 Introduction   200
    9.2 Contexts for Equality   201
    9.3 Focusing on Pupils' Language   211
    9.4 Making Gender Explicit   220
    9.5 Equality Issues   228
    9.6 Conclusion   234

Further Reading   237

References   243

Index   256

Acknowledgements

Many people have helped me during the writing of this book. I am grateful to Julie Fisher (University of Reading); Janet Maybin, Neil Mercer, and Will Swann (Open University); Michael Stubbs (Universität Trier); and my anonymous reader from Blackwell Publishers for their useful comments on earlier drafts of chapters.

I would also like to thank Norah Arnold (Bedfordshire LEA) for providing me with copies of children's writing quoted in chapter 6; Pauline Bale (Parley First School, Dorset) for providing additional information on the interactions between Ruth and James and Alice and Richard quoted in chapter 4 and for her comments on my original interpretations of these; Hilary Claire (South Bank Polytechnic) for helpful discussion about equality issues and some additions to my Further Reading suggestions; Dorothy Faulkner (University of Warwick) for advice on the notion of verbal ability; John Archer (Lancashire Polytechnic) for his useful comments on my discussion of biological and social explanations of gender differences; Eunice Fisher (University of East Anglia) for advice on gender and computing; Donald Mackinnon (Open University) for much helpful discussion about equality and equal opportunities; Gay Smith and pupils at Stantonbury Campus for allowing me to record and analyse some of their group discussions; and Helen Swann for sharing with me some ideas about girls, boys, and language.

Finally, I wish to thank Michael Stubbs as series editor and Philip Carpenter from Blackwell Publishers for their constant help and encouragement.

The author and publisher would like to thank the following people for permission to reproduce material: Fiona Pitt-Kethley and Shiel Land Associates for the Poem 'Falling Down', from *The Perfect Man*, Abacus, © Fiona Pitt-Kethley, 1989 (cited in chapter 2; Oxford University Press for the entry for 'gossip' from the *Oxford English Dictionary*, 2nd edn, 1989, prepared by J. A. Simpson and E. S. C. Weiner, (cited in chapter 2); Cumbria County Council for the transcripts of talk between Ruth and James and Alice and Richard from the INSET pack *Talking Sense* by Pauline Bales and Robin Acland (cited in chapter 4); the National Association for the Teaching of English for the table showing an analysis of 14 school anthologies of poetry, from NATE Language and Gender Committee (1988) *Gender Issues in English Coursework* (reproduced as table 5.1 in chapter 5); Her Majesty's Stationery Office for figure 6.4 showing the distribution of writing performance measures among 11-year-old girls and boys, from *Language Performance in Schools 1982 Primary Survey Report* (DES/DENI/WO, 1984), reproduced here as figure 6.1 in chapter 6: the figure is reproduced with the permission of the Controller of Her Majesty's Stationery Office; Norah Arnold and the National Curriculum Council for two pieces of children's writing from *What are Writers Made of? Issues of gender and writing*, National Writing Project, 1990 (reproduced here as figures 6.2 and 6.3 in chapter 6); Kate Myers for the schedules 'Classroom interaction/observation, Form A', 'Classroom interaction/observation, Form B' and "Text and picture books, Checklist 3, Modern languages textbooks', from *Genderwatch!* (reproduced here as figures 8.2, 8.4 and 8.9 in chapter 8); D. W. Larche for the poems 'Wee Willie Winkie' and 'Jack be nimble' from *Father Gander Nursery Rhymes* (reproduced in chapter 9); the British Film Institute for slides showing birthday cards sent to a five-year-old girl and a five-year-old boy, from the pack *Selling Pictures* (reproduced as figures 9.1 and 9.2 in chapter 9); the English and Media Centre for the page from *Changing Stories*, by Bronwyn Mellor, Judith Hemming and Jane Leggett (reproduced as figure 9.3 in chapter 9).

1

Introduction

Girls and boys have different experiences of education. Even when they go to the same school, play in the same playground, and take part in the same lessons, they will behave differently, and they will be treated differently by others. Many of those concerned about gender differences have drawn attention to the role of language. Teachers use language as a means of differentiating between girls and boys, and girls and boys themselves use 'gender-typed' language in the classroom and other contexts. In school reading materials children encounter many images of girls and boys that conform to narrow stereotypes. Children's own reading and writing choices are often unnecessarily restricted.

Concerns about such issues became prominent during the 1970s and 1980s, and they remain current today. There are 'equal opportunities' reminders dotted about in the curriculum documents with which we seem to have been deluged since the advent of the National Curriculum in England and Wales, the Scottish Development Programme for pupils aged 5–14 and the Northern Ireland curriculum. But these scattered references have an ambiguous status. Their presence signals official recognition that gender differences and inequalities exist in education and that language plays a part in them; but there is little discussion of these differences and inequalities and virtually no concrete guidance on how to deal with them.

Later chapters in this book look at various aspects of language, gender and education: they consider what evidence we have of differences in girls' and boys' language experiences, and the implications of this for teaching, learning, and assessment. They also consider strategies which teachers have employed to introduce 'equal opportunities' in and through language. In order to provide a context for these issues, this introduction discusses the place of language within concerns about gender inequalities in education. It also reviews the sorts of explanations that have been advanced for differences in girls' and boys' behaviour, including language behaviour, and for differences in girls' and boys' abilities in language.

1.1   Language and Equal Opportunities in Education

Concerns about gender inequalities in education often focus on educational outcomes, such as girls' and boys' subject choices, their performance in different subjects, and the careers they choose. For instance, at the age of 15/16 girls do better than boys in terms of overall numbers of higher grade passes in public examinations, but girls' and boys' subject choices are still somewhat restricted. Particular concerns have been expressed about girls' take-up of the physical sciences and technology, which, although increasing, is still much lower than boys'. Writing in 1985, Patrick Orr argues:

The movement by girls towards equality has so far been mainly associated with the pursuit of examination success, rather than with wider subject choices and the benefits in educational, training and employment prospects that such choices can bring. (p. 8)

Current statistics tell a similar story. In England, slightly more girls than boys attempt GCSE English, and many more girls than boys obtain higher grade passes. More girls than boys also attempt and obtain higher grade passes in French and other modern languages, religious studies, biology, creative arts, business studies, and home economics. On the other hand, more boys than girls attempt and obtain higher grade passes in physics; chemistry; computer studies; craft, design, and technology (CDT); and geography. Slightly more boys than girls take mathematics (DES, 1989, table C10). (What impact the National Curriculum will make on girls' and boys' subject choice and qualifications remains to be seen.) More young women than young men go on to study A Levels, but more men than women still go on to take degree courses (DES, 1989, table C6). Girls and boys also have different career aspirations, and are often encouraged into 'appropriate' careers. Women in employment are less well paid than men, and are found much less frequently in senior positions. (See Central Statistical Office, 1990; the Equal Opportunities Commission publishes a useful digest of statistics showing the position of women and men in Great Britain: EOC, 1991.)

Other concerns have to do with the educational processes that, it is argued, contribute to these outcomes – with how gender distinctions are daily reinforced in school and classroom life. Sara Delamont, in a recent account of gender and schooling, argues that school organization, teachers' strategies for controlling and motivating pupils, lesson organization and content, informal conversations between pupils and teachers, and letting pupils' stereotyping of activities go unchallenged are the five main ways in which gender distinctions are maintained (1990, p. 3). Gender differentiation, argues Delamont, is harmful to both girls and boys; it limits their subject choices, their career opportunities, and their personal and social lives – the ways in which they relate to others both in the home and outside. This is not to suggest that schools are somehow responsible for gender differences and inequalities. Girls and boys are treated differently from birth. When they come to school, they already have a sense of what counts as appropriate behaviour. But children will continually refine their ideas about gender during the school years. While schools can hardly be held accountable for producing gender differences and inequalities, they will contribute to these. Sara Delamont argues that:

schools develop and reinforce sex segregations, stereotypes and even discriminations which exaggerate the negative aspects of sex roles in the outside world, when they could be trying to alleviate them. (1990, p. 2)

Research on school and classroom processes has raised particular concerns about language, because language is one way
in which girls and boys and women and men are differentiated
and in which the values attached to being female or male
are communicated. Sometimes such values are communicated
quite openly:

Mr Flint shouted across at a group of girls, at the back of the class,
to stop talking. He had already succeeded in quietening them with
'I haven't got all day to wait for you lot'. However, he went on very
aggressively, 'ONE THING I HATE AND DETEST IS IGNORANT
FEMALES AND THIS SCHOOL IS LOUSY WITH THEM THESE
DAYS. Suppose I'd better address myself to you lads. Don't want to
see that ugly lot in my lab'. (Science teacher talking to secondary
school pupils about their option choice, cited by Gillborn, 1987,
reproduced in Delamont, 1990, p. 58)

Such explicit examples of sexism may be easy to deal with.
They can be noticed, and talked about; if the opportunity is
there, they can be complained about, simply because they are
so obvious. But the values we attach to being female or male
are present whenever we speak or write. They reside in the
language available to talk about people and in how people are
routinely depicted. Such values are often implicit. They have
been of concern to educationists simply because language,
both spoken and written, is so pervasive in the processes of
teaching and learning.

Much of the interest in language among educationists concerned about gender inequalities has, then, to do with language as a form of social practice: language as something that
embodies and sustains social values, including the values
attached to being male or female in a culture, and that may
also be used to promote change or equal opportunities for
girls and boys. But language is also a means of learning and
a subject in its own right. Differences in girls' and boys'
spoken language have implications for teachers who need to
develop pupils' 'communication skills'; they may also affect
pupils' performance in oral assessment; girls' and boys' reading and writing preferences need to be taken into account in
planning a balanced range of reading and writing activities;

'gender stereotyping' in the language of school texts may affect girls' and boys' perceptions of different subjects; the types of language used in assessment tasks may result in gender bias. The chapters that follow will show how gender-differentiated language use is closely bound up with teaching, learning, and assessment: it affects what is taught as well as how.

1.2 Biology and Linguistic Destiny

> Both men and women agree that what most holds women back at all levels throughout our lives is lack of assert-iveness. For decades we have been told that this is environmentally determined. But now that so much more is known about genetics, and also about hormones, the environmental arguments of the '60s are not so convinc-ing. It may be that most women are just not, by nature, as aggressive and assertive as most men.
> (Minette Marrin, a writer disillusioned with feminism, speaking on the television programme *5th Column*, BBC 2, 25.9.91)

It may seem odd to have a discussion of biology in a book on language use and education, both of them essentially social processes. However, biological factors have frequently been advanced as an explanation of girls' and boys' behaviour, including certain aspects of language behaviour (boys' and men's greater 'assertiveness' is expressed verbally, as well as by other means). Biological factors have also been related to differences in girls' and boys' cognitive ability (such as girls' greater 'verbal ability' and boys' greater 'spatial ability'). The way you explain differences between girls and boys has impli-cations for action. For instance, an explanation that sees girls and boys as *determined* by their biology implies that there is little one can do to promote change. Teachers who wish to introduce equal opportunities may be faced with assertions about girls and boys that assume a biological explanation of difference, such as the idea that differences are 'only natural'.

For this reason, I have included a brief account of biological explanations and how they relate to social explanations.

Biological explanations of difference often invoke the endo-crine (hormone) system. Minette Marrin, for instance, suggests that women's lack of assertiveness and aggression is due to low levels of the hormone testosterone. To evaluate this claim, it is necessary to say something about testosterone and how it operates in human beings. Testosterone is often referred to as a 'male' hormone. In fact, it is found in males and females, but in higher levels in males. Levels of testosterone and other sex hormones, also vary with age. During childhood, girls and boys have low levels of sex hormones, but the hormone testerone plays an important part in the development of the male foetus; during puberty, a wider variety of sex hormones is associated with the development of secondary sexual charac-teristics and, in girls, with menstruation.

There is an association between the presence of testosterone and aggression in certain non-human animals, but causal links between testosterone and aggression in humans are harder to establish. John Archer and Barbara Lloyd (1982) point out that there is a great deal of evidence that boys – even young pre-school-age boys – tend to be more aggressive than girls. Some studies have also found that men or women with higher levels of testosterone are more aggressive than men or women with lower levels of testosterone (though not all studies support this position). However, it is not obvious from this that testos-terone *causes* aggression. Archer and Lloyd suggest that a person's mental state may affect hormone levels, so that the consequences of aggression may themselves contribute to high levels of testosterone (Archer, 1991, gives an up-to-date review of testosterone and human aggression.)

A further problem resides in the definition of 'aggression'. Marrin seems to bundle together the notions of assertiveness and aggression. She sees women's lack of assertiveness/ aggression as underlying their difficulty in speaking out in mixed company, the fact that they obtain fewer first-class degrees and occupy fewer top jobs than men, the problems they face in combining a career and child-rearing, and their enjoyment of romantic fiction in which 'dark masterful men'

dominate 'submissive heroines'. Researchers who have studied aggression have looked at both 'verbal' and 'physical'
aggression. Aggression has included 'rough and tumble'
activity, fighting, and play fighting in pre-school children; a
variety of types of behaviour induced in adults under laboratory conditions; adult self-reports of aggression; and statistics
of 'violent crime'. It is by no means clear that different forms
of aggression, produced in different contexts, can be attributed
to the same specific biological mechanism.

Girls' greater 'verbal ability' has also been related to biological factors, including the hormone system. Verbal ability has
been measured by a variety of tests, including word fluency,
grammar, spelling, vocabulary, and reading. Pre-school girls
have performed better than boys, on average, on several of
these tests. In the primary school years, differences between
girls and boys are not consistent. But during adolescence, once
again, girls tend to perform better than boys (this work is
reviewed by Halpern, 1986). Sex differences in verbal ability
are very slight; nevertheless, biological explanations have
been sought for them. They have been attributed to differences
in the way female and male brains are organized – to the fact
that female brains are less 'lateralized' than male brains. I
shall need to say something about lateralization in order to
address these arguments.

Lateralization refers to the extent to which the left and
right hemispheres in the brain are specialized for different
activities. The argument runs that weaker lateralization (that
is, less specialization between the two hemispheres) is associated with greater verbal ability. Stronger lateralization (where
one hemisphere of the brain is more specialized for language,
and the other hemisphere for certain non-linguistic tasks) is
associated with lower verbal ability, but with greater spatial
ability. Girls and women, whose brains are less strongly lateralized, should therefore do better on verbal tasks; whereas
boys and men, whose brains are more strongly lateralized,
should do worse on verbal tasks but better on tasks requiring
spatial ability.

Diane Halpern (1986) points out that, while there is evidence
that female brains are, on average, less lateralized than male

brains, evidence linking lateralization with cognitive ability is not strong, and is sometimes inconsistent. There are several complicating factors. For instance, people may use different strategies to tackle the same problem. A girl with superior verbal abilities may use verbal strategies to solve a spatial problem. In reviewing this area of research, Halpern comments that the practical significance of sex differences in lateralization still remains unknown (p. 91).

Brain lateralization has been said to be related to the hormone system. One theory suggests that higher concentrations of male hormones in foetuses will result in stronger lateralization in brain functions (and therefore greater spatial ability but lower verbal ability). Much of the evidence in support of this explanation comes from work with animals, with people who have abnormally low levels of male hormones, or people whose mothers have been treated with synthetic hormones during pregnancy. Results so far are inconclusive.

Another theory suggests that the timing of puberty is related to brain lateralization, and so to spatial and verbal ability. The theory is based on evidence that children who mature later have more strongly lateralized brain functions. Since girls tend to mature earlier, they will tend to have less strongly lateralized brain functions, and so lower spatial ability, but higher verbal ability. A problem with this theory is that it depends on an association between lateralization and cognitive ability. I mentioned above that the evidence for this is not strong. Halpern introduces a further complication:

Although adolescence is the time in the life cycle when sex-related cognitive differences clearly emerge as well as the time when dramatic changes in sex hormone levels begin, the coincidence of these two events may be secondary to other salient life changes that occur at the same time, such as the adoption of adult sex roles and different expectations of adolescents with mature bodies. (Halpern, 1986, p.100)

There are certain dangers attached to biological explanations. I suggested earlier that they underlie many people's acceptance of differences and inequalities between girls and boys. Characteristics that are inbuilt may seem impossible to change; so, even if we would like to encourage a wider range of opportunities for boys and girls, in practice, whatever we do is unlikely to be effective. Current research on biological influences on behaviour, however, does not take nearly such a gloomy view. Those who favour some sort of biological explanation tend to see biology as interacting with a range of social factors. As examples of this position I shall look at two 'interactionist' models of differences between girls' and boys' behaviour.

Peter Smith uses the development of 'rough and tumble' play to illustrate his model. He suggests that boys' preferences for rough and tumble activity can be explained in part by hormones, which predispose boys towards rough and tumble; this is responded to by fathers, who engage in rough and tumble with boys; this in turn reinforces boys' preferences for rough and tumble; boys are also inclined to imitate their fathers' behaviour; boys (and their fathers and their peers) are also influenced by media images of gender-appropriate behaviour. (The model is rather more complex than I can describe in a few words. It is set out diagrammatically in P. K. Smith, 1986, p. 136).

John Archer and Barbara Lloyd have put forward an interactionist model that gives greater weight to social factors. They suggest that the human infant is born with the potential to make classifications and to act on the basis of categories such as female and male. This much is biologically given. The child constructs an 'internal system of gender rules' on the basis of his or her experiences. The actual content of the gender rule system depends on the social representations of gender that are available in the child's culture (1982; 1985 edn, pp. 272–3).

It is possible to have social explanations of gender that do not rely on biological sex differences at all. Social explanations point out that gender plays an important part in the way society is structured: it is bound up with the economy, with employment, with how family life is organized, as well as with the education system. At an individual level, it affects the way women and men and girls and boys behave. The existence of gender divisions imposes certain constraints on what people can do. Even when 'gender-typed' behaviour isn't formally prescribed, it is hard to go against the grain of others' expectations and of generally accepted social practices. Social accounts of the development of gender differences point to the different experiences girls and boys have from birth; they suggest that girls and boys learn to behave differently because of these experiences. One of the first questions one asks of a newborn baby is whether it is a girl or a boy. From then on, girls and boys will have different names, different selections of toys, and different clothes. They will also be responded to differently by adults. One or two studies have shown that the same baby is treated differently depending on whether it is thought to be a girl or a boy (see, for example, Smith and Lloyd, 1978). One piece of evidence that has aroused much interest is that fathers differentiate between young girls and boys more than mothers, and are more critical of 'gender-inappropriate' behaviour (for a discussion of these and other findings, see Lewis, 1986). As children grow older, they see girls and boys and women and men behaving differently, and they encounter differing female and male images in books, television, and other media.

The ways girls and boys are responded to by adults and the activities made available to them may have a direct effect on their behaviour and on their cognitive ability (involvement in activities that require greater amounts of verbal interaction may increase girls' early verbal ability; play with construction toys may increase boys' spatial ability). Certain activities may also come to be perceived as feminine or masculine, and so appropriate for girls or boys (for example, activities with a high verbal component may be perceived as feminine and therefore appropriate for girls). (Halpern, 1986, Singleton, 1986; and Lewis, 1986, discuss the possible effects of girls' and boys' upbringing on cognitive ability.)

In dealing with (educational) language use, this book is necessarily concerned with some of the social processes that contribute to children's developing gender identity and their educational aptitudes and preferences. This is not to suggest that biology is irrelevant, but I do not think it can provide a convincing explanation of the range of differences between girls' and boys' behaviour, many of which are culturally specific. For those with a practical concern about gender differences and inequalities, it is particularly important to look at social processes that contribute to these, to see how they may be challenged.

It is worth pointing out, however, that while social explanations of gender do not rely on 'inbuilt' differences between girls and boys, they can still be just as determinist as some biological explanations. Children have been seen as passive recipients of social messages, moulded by their upbringing and their exposure to media images. There is also a form of linguistic determinism which suggests that a person's view of the world is determined by the structures of the language they speak. This is relevant to a consideration of gender issues, since some feminists have argued that the sexist structure of English and other languages leads to a view of the world that is distorted by sexism. Social and linguistic determinism are just as dangerous as biological determinism. They can suggest that external forces are so powerful that there is little possibility of change. But we know that change does occur. Accepted customs and practices change over the years; individuals change, and they behave differently on different occasions.

It is partly through spoken and written language use and through encounters with linguistic and non-linguistic images that children learn how they are expected to behave. But, in using language, children are also (re)negotiating relationships with others and (re)interpreting the images they encounter; they are not simply recipients of messages. Nor are children's language experiences uniform: there is some degree of diversity, and even contradiction. Children need to make sense of diversity and contradiction, and diversity and contradiction can be exploited by those who wish to promote change – to widen the range of opportunities open to girls and boys. These issues are explored further in later chapters.

1.3 How this Book is Organized

I have tried to organize this book so that it can be read by people with a range of interests. It may, like most books, be read straight through in sequence. But the chapters are relatively self-contained, and can be read in isolation. It is possible to take a variety of routes through the book, and I have indicated, at the beginning and end of each chapter, how it builds on or paves the way for ideas in other chapters.

Chapter 2 considers, in a very general way, the relationship between gender and language use: how gender is routinely constructed in daily acts of speaking. The bias in the chapter towards spoken language is because sociolinguistic research and research from other academic traditions that look in any detail at social differences in language use have tended to focus on speech. Whenever possible, I have drawn on research involving children and young people, but the evidence comes mainly from outside schools. I intend this to provide a context for the more specifically educational studies mentioned in subsequent chapters.

Chapter 3 looks at spoken language in the classroom, chapter 5 at how females and males are represented in children's reading matter, and chapter 6 at girls and boys as readers and writers. These chapters consider the evidence of difference and discrimination in educational language use that has been collected over the past two decades and at how such evidence may be interpreted. The division into spoken language, representation, and reading and writing reflects differences in the types of research that have been carried out by educationists with an interest in gender and language use.

Chapters 4 and 7 focus, respectively, on oracy and literacy. Each chapter asks whether it is reasonable to be concerned either about girls' and boys' language use or about the gendered images, linguistic and non-linguistic, that inhabit schools and classrooms. Some of the concerns addressed in these chapters are social, and have to do with the perceived role of schools in sustaining gender differences and inequalities. Others have to do more directly with teaching, learning, and assessment.

These earlier chapters stress that the way language is used and interpreted is highly context-dependent. One cannot simply assume that patterns of difference and discrimination found by researchers will be replicated in each and every classroom. Teachers and others with a practical concern about gender and language use need to monitor what is happening in their own particular context. Chapter 8 provides guidance on observing and analysing language use for those who wish to investigate gender imbalances.

It is not immediately obvious what to do about gender imbalances in practical terms. Early 'anti-sexist' strategies designed to change pupils' language behaviour and to inoculate or insulate them against the effects of sexist images have been recognized as too blunt an instrument, and one that is, at any rate, unlikely to be successful. While there is sometimes a need to challenge sexism head on, teachers have also identified a need to understand at a more subtle level, what is going on when pupils talk, read, and write – how pupils use language to establish, maintain, and change relationships with others; and how, in interpreting spoken and written texts, they construct a set of viable meanings. Chapter 9 considers strategies for dealing with gender imbalances in classroom talk and in girls' and boys' reading and writing. I hope these strategies will provide ideas for teachers who wish to carry out similar work; but they are not presented simply as practical tips. Several different approaches have been taken to the provision of equal opportunities, and these can be subjected to critical appraisal in the same way as the research considered in earlier chapters.

Each chapter in the book represents an introduction to a topic or set of topics. At various points I have suggested books and articles that provide further information or that explore some of the issues discussed in greater depth. There are also suggestions for further reading at the end of the book.

2

Gender and Language Use

Language reveals and conceals much about human relationships. There are intimate connections, for example, between language and social power, language and culture, and language and gender.
Language in the National Curriculum: Materials for Professional Development, p. 1)

2.1 Introduction

By the time they come to school, girls and boys have already begun to learn gender-differentiated language; they have begun to learn how to speak differently *as* a girl or a boy, how to speak *to* other girls and boys, and how to speak *about* them. Such learning continues throughout the school years and afterwards. Language use is not static: people will, to some extent, change the way they use language, either intentionally, as when a writer consciously begins to use *she or he* rather than 'generic' *he*, or even without such conscious planning, in order to adapt to new contexts.

The way people speak and write is important, both socially and educationally. It affects how they are perceived and evaluated. It is through language, particularly spoken language, that relationships with others are negotiated. In talking in a certain way a speaker is saying something about the kind of person they are, as well as about their perceptions of the listener and the task in hand. The accumulation of individual acts of speaking also contributes to longer-term relationships between groups of people, to how girls and boys and women and men habitually relate. To the extent that relationships between the sexes are unequal, spoken language use will contribute to this inequality.

The language habitually used to talk or write *about* people is also bound up with gender differences and inequalities, in the sense that different words and expressions are used to refer to and describe girls and boys and women and men. It has been argued that the vocabulary of English and the way words are routinely used systematically discriminate against girls and women.

I mentioned in chapter 1 that such issues have been of particular concern to educationists because of the pervasiveness of written and spoken language in schools. The language used by pupils and teachers and in books and other resources necessarily plays its part in reproducing gender differences and inequalities. It is in recognition of this that language is often a focus of equal opportunities policies in schools. The language used in schools and classrooms is discussed in more detail in later chapters. This chapter deals with language use in a very general sense: with the patterns of language that are prevalent in the community and that children bring with them to school.

2.2 Gendered Expectations

People have quite clear perceptions of how women and men and girls and boys use language – and how they ought to use language. An increasing interest in gender and language during the 1970s prompted several studies that investigated these perceptions. Studies have tended to focus on spoken language. I shall discuss below some perceptions of 'female' and 'male' speech and also some prescriptions about what is appropriate speech for females and males.

Perceptions

How hard it is for women to keep counsel!
Shakespeare, *Julius Caesar*

Whimsey, not reason, is the female guide.

George Granville, *The Vision*

Imagine a man and a woman both looking at the same wall, painted a pinkish shade of purple. The woman may say (2):

(2) The wall is mauve,

with no one consequently forming any special impression of her as a result of the words alone; but if the man should say (2), one might well conclude he was imitating a woman sarcastically or was a homosexual or an interior decorator.

(Robin Lakoff, 1975, *Language and Woman's Place*, p. 8)

Gender is clearly perceived as an important social category that affects how we speak: when asked, people are quite willing to specify sets of 'male' and 'female' speech habits. Cheris Kramarae provided students in US high schools and a university with a list of 51 speech traits. She asked students to indicate the extent to which these were characteristic of different types of speaker, including 'female speaker' and 'male speaker'. The students said that male speakers were more likely to have deep and demanding voices; their speech was louder and more confident, militant, authoritarian, aggressive, forceful, and dominating; they showed anger rather than concealing it, and came straight to the point; they were more boastful, tended to lounge and lean back while talking, used slang, and had a sense of humour in speech. Female speakers, on the other hand, were said to have a high speaking pitch and also a wide range in rate and pitch; their speech was fast, gentle, and smooth; they were friendly, smiled a lot when talking, showed concern for the listener, were open and self-revealing, enthusiastic and emotional; they enunciated clearly, and used good grammar and polite speech; they used their hands and faces to express ideas; they gave many details; and they tended to talk a lot, to gossip, to talk about trivial topics, and to talk gibberish. (This research is reported in Kramer, 1977.)

One or two studies have investigated the development of such perceptions in young children. Carole Edelsky (1976) gave adults and 6–11-year-old children a set of sentences, and asked them which would be more likely to be said by a man, by a woman, or by both. Some sentences contained stereotypically masculine usages such as direct commands or expressions such as 'damn': for example, 'Get me that pencil.' 'Damn it, the TV set broke!' Others contained 'feminine' usages: indirect requests or expressions such as 'adorable and 'Oh dear': 'Won't you please get me that pencil?' 'Oh dear, the TV set broke.

There was a high degree of consensus among adults on what constituted 'male' and 'female' speech. Children's perceptions were found to become increasingly like those of adults as they grew older. Six-year-old children showed little agreement among themselves or with adult speakers. They also tended to base their judgements on the topic of the sentence, saying that a sentence would be said by a man because, for example, 'My dad watches the TV'. By the time they were 11, children's judgements were more consistent and more likely to be in agreement with those of adults.

Asking people to respond to a list of speaking traits by no means guarantees that you will tap their 'true' attitudes towards women's and men's speech. What people say about their beliefs will vary, depending upon how they perceive the task they have been set. What studies such as those carried out by Kramarae and Edelsky do illustrate is the nature of stereotypes of female and male speech, stereotypes that can be drawn on when needed and that are reproduced in everyday discourse (jokes, cartoons, even books by academic linguists).

Prescriptions

Let your women keep silence in the churches: for it is not permitted unto them to speak . . . And if they will learn any thing, let them ask their husbands at home: for it is a shame for women to speak in the church.

I Cor. 14: 34–5

Swete of speche schalt thou be . . .
How the Good Wife Taught her Daughter, a 14th-century
'courtesy book', cited by Bornstein, 1978

Let fewe se her and none at all here her. There is nothynge
that so sone casteth the mynde of the husbande from his
wife as dothe moche scoldynge and chidyng, and her
mischeuous tonge.
Vives (1523), *De Institutione Christianae Feminae*, cited by
Bornstein, 1978

Her voice was ever soft, gentle, and low – an excellent
thing in woman.

Shakespeare, *King Lear*

The woman who has a receptive ear not only can provide
great comfort and release for her husband – she possesses
a priceless social asset as well. The quiet, unpretentious
woman who is fascinated by another's conversation, who
asks questions which show she is digesting every word,
is the girl most likely to succeed socially, not only with
the menfolk, but also with her fellow females.
Mrs Dale Carnegie, 1957, *How to Help Your Husband Get
Ahead*

The hero in a television film has just been killed:
Girl (aged 8): Oh, that's just bloody! . . . Bloody!
Mother: I don't think you need to swear about it.
Girl: Why not? I didn't say 'ff. . .' (extending the 'f').
Mother: Even so, it's still swearing. Anyway, don't let
Grannie hear you say it.
Girl: Why not?
Mother: She doesn't think girls ought to swear like that.

There has been, and still is, a plethora of advice given to
women and girls about how they should speak. Diane
Bornstein (1978) analysed the advice given to women about
their speech in several manuals written from the Middle Ages
to the Renaissance. She found that women were advised to
speak little and, when they did speak, to be 'meek, sweet,
gentle and polite' (p. 133). They were not to express anger,

but were to suffer patiently any intemperance on the part of their husbands. They were to curb their natural instincts to gossip. They were not to curse or swear. Bornstein notes that in some respects the advice given to women was similar to that given to children and servants. She also argues that the double standard, by which the sort of language men were allowed to use was proscribed for women, acted as an effective form of social control, one that was still in operation when she wrote, since contemporary etiquette books for young women still counselled against talking too much and swearing.

FALLING DOWN

I fell on the shallow sharp stone main stairs
of the British Museum. Two men who'd paused
looked shocked and hurried off when I yelled 'Fuck!'

I sat there shaken, nursing bruised fingers,
and wondered why my Anglo-Saxon shout
had lost me sympathy from that prim pair.
They must have done it in their time and yet
could not take a reminder of the root of life
in such a place and from a woman.

Soon, the entrance hall returned to normal –
conversations restarted – schoolchildren
and tourists trekked in search of mummies, cards,
the Elgin marbles.
                    (Fiona Pitt-Kethley, *The Perfect Man*, p. 17)

Not only should women themselves not swear, they're often thought to need protection from swearing by others.

McEnroe then turned on my wife. What he said was utter obscenity and I would not repeat it. . . . It is scored on her mind. (Chairman of an exclusive London club, from which John McEnroe had been expelled for using obscene language. Cited in *Daily Mirror* 26.7.85)

Perceptions of female and male speech and prescriptions about how female speakers in particular ought to speak are two sides of the same coin. Our perceptions seem not to be idiosyncratic.

Many jokes rely upon an understanding, if not an acceptance, of stereotypes about language. Cheris Kramarae identified a set of perceptions that were reasonably consistent among those whom she interviewed. Such perceptions tend to have a basis in fact – they would be unlikely to survive if they bore no resemblance to reality – but they may be exaggerated, and some are unfounded.

Prescriptions counsel against 'unattractive' features thought to be prevalent in female speech. But there is also a 'double standard', as Bornstein mentioned. Some features that are acceptable in male speech are proscribed for females.

Ideas about appropriate behaviour, including language behaviour, for girls and boys and women and men form one way in which gender is maintained as a social division. But there are more than gender *differences* involved; the speech encouraged in girls and women is of the sort that would keep them polite, deferent, and subservient to males.

In the following section I shall look at the evidence for gender differences in language: what differences have been found between female and male speakers and how far these correspond to our perceptions and prescriptions?

2.3   Girls and Boys Speaking

> Whenever we speak we cannot avoid giving our listener clues about our origins and the sort of person we are. Our accent and our speech generally show what part of the country we come from, and what sort of background we have. We may even give some indication of certain of our ideas and attitudes, and all of this information can be used by the people we are speaking with to help them formulate an opinion about us.
>
> (Peter Trudgill, 1983, *Sociolinguistics*, p.14)

Language use is highly variable. People use different kinds of language depending upon the social groups they belong to, the person or people they are talking to, and the context –

for instance, whether formal or informal. As Peter Trudgill suggests, such variability is functional: it conveys information to others.

Gender is only one of a number of social groupings related to language use. The way anyone speaks on any one occasion will depend on several factors. Because of this, gender differences in language, or at least in the English language, are always differences of degree. Female speakers tend to speak in one way and males in another, but there are no forms that are exclusively female or male; there is always an overlap between the sexes.

Studies of gender and language use have looked, in the main, at spoken language. There is little evidence available of systematic linguistic differences in girls' and boys' or women's and men's writing. I shall consider such differences as have been found under three headings: pitch and voice quality, language variety, and language in interaction. In each case, I shall provide a relatively brief account, concentrating on those aspects of gender difference that are most relevant to education. I shall mention, where possible, research that has looked at the speech of children and young people, although most research has focused on adult speakers. Studies of gender differences in language use have been discussed in considerably more detail in a book I wrote with a colleague (Graddol and Swann, 1989). I shall occasionally refer readers to this book for a more comprehensive account of issues I discuss here.

Pitch and voice quality

It may seem odd to include pitch of voice in a discussion of gender differences, because there is an anatomical basis to speaking pitch. However, people can vary their speaking pitch, and it has been suggested that female and male speakers tend to speak in a way that accentuates the differences between them. In other words, we could sound more similar to one another, but we choose not to. Evidence for a social basis to pitch of voice comes from studies involving cross-cultural comparisons, which have found that the average pitch for male speakers varies between different countries, and that the extent to which women's and men's pitch differs is also culturally variable (see, for instance, Majewski *et al.*, 1972; Loveday, 1981).

There is also evidence that girls' and boys' voices sound different before they reach the age of puberty. In a study that has now become something of a classic, Jacqueline Sachs, Philip Lieberman, and Donna Erickson (1973) asked adult listeners to identify the sex of young (pre-pubertal) children after listening to tape recordings of their voices. The children's ages ranged from 4 to14 years. The adult listeners were, in most cases, able to judge the children's sex accurately. Sachs, Lieberman, and Erickson made an analysis of the children's voices. They discovered that the boys' 'fundamental frequencies' (that aspect of perceived pitch that derives from the vibration of the vocal folds in the larynx) were slightly higher than the girls'. But the boys' 'formant frequencies' (the aspect of pitch determined by the size and shape of the vocal tract) tended to be lower. This could not be attributed to any difference in size between girls and boys. But the vocal tract is quite flexible; it is possible to alter its size and shape (we do this to make the different sounds of language), and it may be that boys are able to 'enlarge' their vocal tracts to produce lower formant frequencies. Sachs, Lieberman, and Erickson suggest that this difference in voice may, at least in part, explain why listeners in their study were able to distinguish accurately between the sexes.

Whether a voice sounds feminine or masculine is affected by factors other than speaking pitch. Henton and Bladon (1985) discovered that in two groups of (British) English speakers they studied, women used more 'breathy voice' than men. Unfortunately, there is a dearth of similar studies looking at the distribution of such aspects of voice quality in relation to gender.

So far, I have suggested that female and male speakers speak in ways that make them sound more feminine or more masculine, so that pitch of voice, for instance, is one way of establishing a gender distinction. But female and male voices carry other connotations:

There was always a thought that women didn't carry the authority in their voice that a man did, and this was the important part when it came to reading news. (Anne Every, first woman to read the news on the BBC World Service)

One might suggest that female voices 'carry less authority' simply because they are female voices, rather than because of any particular aspects of voice quality. But this cannot be the whole story. Loud, deep voices are associated with greater physical size and therefore power in animals as well as people. And listeners are willing to assign a whole range of personality attributes to people on the basis of their voices alone. For instance, higher pitch is associated with being less competent and generally less powerful, for male as well as female speakers.

In learning to speak in a 'feminine' way, girls take on board a whole set of other characteristics, many of which have become stereotypically associated with femininity. Girls and women may face a choice between, say, sounding competent and sounding feminine.

Language Variety

We were reading a story called *'Orrid John*. Helen, aged 7, asked what the apostrophe was for. I said it meant there was a letter missing. Helen thought for a minute:
H: It's *h*, it's *h*, isn't it? I know why it's like that. Boys would say *'orrid, It's 'orrid, ye knaa*. [*An attempt at Tyneside pronunciation*]
J: Goodness. What would girls say?
H: [*Very refined*]: *It's horrid, you know*.

I have interpreted the quotation from Peter Trudgill at the beginning of this section rather broadly to refer to all aspects of spoken language; but in fact much of Trudgill's own work has been concerned with the ways in which features of accent and dialect vary between different social groups. This aspect of language variation has been particularly well researched. Several earlier studies, carried out in the 1960s and 1970s in the USA and the UK, focused on differences between speakers from different social classes. But many also compared the speech of women and men. One consistent finding across these studies is that female speakers, all other things being equal, tend to use more 'prestige' or standard forms of language than their male counterparts.

We have only limited evidence of how and when such social differences are acquired. It is clear, however, that, even among primary school-age children, girls will use more 'prestige' forms than boys, though the differences will be less systematic than between adult speakers (some of these findings are reviewed in Romaine, 1984).

One or two more recent studies have looked at gender differences in the speech of young people. Jenny Cheshire (1982) studied the speech of two groups of girls aged from 9 to 13 and one group of boys aged from 11 to 17 in Reading, Berkshire. All speakers were white and from working-class backgrounds. Cheshire looked at features of dialect (such as whether a child said 'I does' or 'I do'). In this study, boys used non-standard forms more often than girls. But such non-standard usage was also associated, for boys, with how closely integrated they were into their peer group (the girls' groups were generally less close-knit than the boys'). For both girls and boys, use of non-standard forms was associated with participation in what Cheshire called 'vernacular culture' (illicit activities such as swearing and petty crime). An interesting finding here is that sometimes girls and boys used different forms to signal their allegiance to 'vernacular culture'.

Another study highlights the importance of taking a range of social and contextual factors into account when interpreting girls' and boys' speech. Viv Edwards (1986, 1988) describes a study of the speech of young British Black people in Dudley, West Midlands. The study looked at the speakers' use of Patois, as opposed to a local vernacular variety of English.

The choice between Patois and English has important social implications, as the following extract from an interview shows. Here, Carol is Carol Tomlin, a member of the research team who is Black; Nora and Patty are two young women being interviewed:

CAROL: You reckon nearly all the Black people can speak Jamaica talk or Patois?

NORA: Yes, of course. Some people can but they don't think it right, you know. Like my sister, right. She's a right little snotty ... Anyway, she ... like if she came here now, right, she'd talk plain English. But she can speak Patois better than me.

CAROL: Really?

PATTY: Yes, I've heard.

NORA: But she wouldn't have spoke it here though.

CAROL: No, probably because she doesn't know me or whatever.

NORA: I don't know you either. But everybody else would – but she wouldn't, even if the whole of them were speaking Patois, she wouldn't speak it.

CAROL: And if they know her ... but does she speak it at home?

NORA: Not to my parents.

CAROL: So who does she speak it with?

NORA: She speaks it to me, to some of the coloured friends who she knows speak Patois but to her snotty coloured friends she speaks English and she speaks it to these lot if they're having a joke, but if they're talking normally ...

PATTY: I've heard her ...

NORA: She talks Queen's English brebber. She's the snotty one of the family!
(Open University, 1987)

Edwards found that Patois was used more often by speakers who were closely integrated within the Black community and by speakers who were more critical of mainstream white society. There was no overall significant difference between the Patois usage of young men and women in this sample, although there was an interaction between sex and education: young men with a higher level of education used fewer Patois features, but level of education was not associated with the use of Patois in young women.

Edwards is cautious in interpreting these results, but she does suggest that

The popular stereotype of the Patois speaker is male, underachieving and hostile to white society. The findings of the present study suggest that this view is, at the very least, a gross oversimplification . . . For the purposes of the present discussion it is also important to note that many of the most competent Patois speakers were women. (Edwards, 1988, p. 47)

Edwards contrasted only speakers' use of Patois and English features: she does not report whether the young women in her sample used more standard English features than young men. It may be that since Patois is so closely bound up with integration into the Black community, there are other ways in which female and male speech is differentiated.

Language in Interaction

The mummies on the bus go chatter, chatter, chatter
Chatter, chatter, chatter
Chatter, chatter, chatter
The mummies on the bus go chatter, chatter, chatter
All around the town

The daddies on the bus go nod, nod, nod
Nod, nod, nod . . .

Nursery song

Children need to learn not only how to use appropriate accent and dialect forms, but also how to make conversation appropriately with others. One of the most pervasive images of female speakers is that of the talkative sex; women are the gossips and nags, whereas men are the strong, silent sex. Yet those who have investigated the amount spoken by female and male speakers tend to find the contrary. Studies have been carried out in a variety of public contexts – 'laboratory' studies, classrooms, meetings, analyses of television chat shows – all with similar results: it is male speakers who talk more (see Graddol and Swann, 1989, for a review of this evidence). One may wonder, then, why the stereotype of the talkative female persists. One explanation provided by Dale Spender (1985) is that there is a double standard in operation; women and girls, Spender argues, are meant to talk very little (hence the various prescriptions reminding them of the virtues of moderation). If they go beyond the limits - even if they talk less than men and boys – they are perceived as hogging the floor.

Amount of talk has been associated with conversational dominance. It is suggested that, in talking more, male speakers are better able to get their points across and have their 'say', – so that they are in control of the conversation and it serves their interests more than women's. But talking more will not always have this effect. Imagine a gangster forcing an unwilling captive to spill the beans or, more mundanely, a person desperately trying to get another to put down the newspaper and pay attention to what they're saying. In neither case does the person doing most of the talking seem 'in control'. To know how to interpret amount of talk, it is necessary to know something about the kind of talk that is being produced.

The amount people talk varies considerably. Carole Edelsky (1981) examined talk in informally organized university committee meetings. She identified two types of talk: more formal, 'one person at a time' talk, which she called F1 (for 'Floor 1'); and collaboratively developed talk, in which there was much more overlapping speech, termed F2. Edelsky found that

In F1s, the men held forth, took longer turns though not more of them – dominated the construction of the floor by virtue, at least, of the time they took talking. In F2s, men talked less than they did in F1s and occasionally even less than the women in F2s, a rare finding given the usual one of men as the 'big talkers'. (Edelsky, 1981, p. 415)

Edelsky's work suggests that the type of talk engaged in affects how much people speak. But this will be influenced by a variety of other factors, including the context (for example, a meeting or a chat with friends at home), who people are speaking to, the purposes of the talk, and how speakers perceive their own role.

Investigations of language in interaction have looked not just at how much people speak, but at how conversations are put together and speaking turns organized. Researchers have identified several conversational features that, in the contexts studied, are used more often by female or male speakers. Examples include the following:

- Male speakers tend to interrupt more than female speakers. In mixed-sex talk, female speakers receive interruptions from male speakers.
- Male speakers use more 'direct speech' than female speakers; for example, they make direct rather than indirect requests.
- Female speakers give more conversational support than male speakers – they use 'minimal responses' such as *'Mmh'*, *'Yeah'* and *'Right'* to encourage another speaker to continue and questions that enable another speaker to develop their topic.
- Some studies have suggested that female speakers, more than male speakers, use features that indicate tentativeness, such as 'tag questions' ('That's good, isn't it?'), hedges (*'I wonder, 'sort of', 'I guess'*), and other expressions that make them sound hesitant or uncertain. Other studies have failed to find evidence to support this. Some research suggests that, rather than being associated directly with female speakers, 'tentative' features are used by speakers of either sex in a relatively powerless position.

For examples of these studies, see Eakins and Eakins, 1976; Fishman, 1983; Leet-Pellegrini, 1980; O'Barr and Atkins, 1980; Preisler, 1986; West and Zimmerman, 1983; Zimmerman and West, 1975. Findings such as these have given rise to the idea that female speakers, in general, are more collaborative when they talk and male speakers more competitive. This might disadvantage female speakers in mixed-sex conversation.

These findings need to be interpreted with caution. Interaction studies, like other studies of language use, identify average differences between the sexes. Not every female or male speaker behaves in a typically feminine or masculine way. People's behaviour also varies in different contexts, and depends upon who they are interacting with and how they perceive the purposes of the interaction. For instance, a study of interaction in university tutorials found that women students in this context interrupted as often as male students (Beattie, 1981).

In interacting, speakers are doing things with words. It is important to take into account the meaning of interaction features, what functions they're serving on any occasion. To take interruptions again, these enable someone to cut off the current speaker and introduce their own topic. Like amount of talk, they have been associated with conversational dominance, enabling the perpetrator to have more say in what is going on. Not all overlapping speech has this function, however. In Edelsky's study of university committee meetings, 'collaboratively developed' talk contained a great deal of overlapping speech, but Edelsky did not feel this constituted an interruption. The need to interpret functions of talk in context means that such interpretations will always be subjective ones.

Some gender differences in conversational styles have been found in children and young people. Anita Esposito (1979) looked at conversations between pairs of nursery school children (aged 3.5–4.8 years). She focused on interruptions such as:

A: And my Mommy's gonna take me and ⎰ Mimi to go to . . .
B: ⎱ My Mommy's goin
  to Florida with me.
(Esposito, 1979, p. 216)

where the second child, B, came in at an inappropriate point before A could be expected to finish. Esposito found more of these interruptions in mixed-sex than in single-sex pairs, and that boys interrupted girls more than twice as often as the other way round.

Marjorie Harness Goodwin (1980) analysed conversations between black working-class children in Philadelphia. The children were aged between 8 and 13. They were playing and talking in single-sex groups. The boys were making slingshots from old coathangers, while the girls made rings from bottle tops. The boys carried out their tasks as two competing teams. Their talk was organized hierarchically, with speakers negotiating their position in the hierarchy. Goodwin gives the example of one boy, Michael, staking out a claim for himself as leader by using explicit commands:

> 'Gimme the pliers!'
> 'Give me that man. After this after you chop em give em to me.'

Although Michael used such forms routinely, he received indirect requests from others. Michael also established his authority by contradicting proposals from others and responding on behalf of others.

Interaction among the girls was more collaboratively organized, with joint decision making and minimal negotiation of status. Girls tended to frame their directives as requests for future action rather than commands: for example, 'Let's ask her.' They sometimes weakened requests by using terms such as 'maybe': for example, 'Maybe we can slice them like that.' Goodwin points out that this does not mean girls are unable or unwilling to use explicit commands. They can use these when the occasion demands, as when a girl tells a younger child: 'Don't put that down. Put that back up! It's supposed to be that way.'

Despite some evidence of gender differences in the use of interaction features among young children, we don't know enough yet about how and when such differences develop.

Talking to Women and Girls

> Helen and I go out of the house and pass the milkman. I pay him the money we owe. He says: 'Thanks, love.' Helen turns to me:
> H: Do you know that man?
> J: Not really. Why?

H: He called you 'love'.
J: Mmh.
H: He must be a Geordie.
J: Why's that?
H: A Geordie would say 'love'. At least, he'd say it to a woman. Well, perhaps to a young woman or a middle-aged woman. But especially to a little girl.

While much of the discussion above has dealt with differences in language used *by* female and male speakers, there are also differences in the ways language is used *towards* women and men and girls and boys. Women often complain that they are treated differently from men and that they are talked to in a belittling way. But there have been few systematic studies of the language used towards the two sexes. A US study carried out by Nessa Wolfson and Joan Manes (1980) analysed the terms of address used by service personnel towards customers and clients. They found, predictably, that adult customers could be referred to as 'Sir' or 'Ma'am', or without a term of address, but that women were also frequently addressed by a term of endearment: 'Dear', 'Hon', and so on. As we might expect to find among speakers of English in the UK, terms of endearment were more often used towards customers who were younger than the speaker, and such usage varied in different parts of the country.

In another US study, Wolfson (1984) found that women received more compliments than men. Furthermore, while men tended to be complimented by someone older or a superior (for example. a boss complimenting an employee on his work), women could be complimented by anyone. Many compliments to women concerned their appearance. Wolfson gives examples such as a male professor who interrupted a female professor's class to whisper loudly: 'Can I whisper in your ear? I didn't have the chance to tell you this morning how lovely you look' (p. 243).

Compliments, terms of endearment, and comments on someone's appearance are normally intended to be pleasant, but they also serve as a reminder that a woman's appearance is available to be commented upon and that the person giving the compliment is in a position to pass judgement.

Explanations and Implications

I mentioned that pitch of voice and aspects of voice quality could be used to signal femininity or masculinity, although they also had other connotations. Similar explanations have been given for gender differences in the use of accent and dialect features. We have some evidence that working-class speech is associated with masculinity. Peter Trudgill (1972, 1974) investigated speakers' speakers' use of different pronunciations; he also asked speakers how they *thought* they pronounced certain words. Speakers were often accurate but, when they weren't, it tended to be because women overestimated, and men underestimated their use of prestige pronunciations. John Edwards (1979) asked adult listeners if they could identify the sex of 10-year-old children from tape recordings of their voices. Half the children were working-class, and half were middle-class. Although the children's voices hadn't broken, listeners were normally able to identify their sex correctly (this is similar to Sachs, Lieberman and Erickson's study of children's speaking pitch (1973)). But when mistakes were made, these formed a regular pattern: middle-class boys tended to be misidentified as girls and working-class girls misidentified as boys. Working-class children were also thought to have lower, rougher, and more masculine voices than middle-class children.

If there is an association between vernacular speech and masculinity, then, in selecting more vernacular forms of speech, male speakers may be attempting to sound more masculine. Similarly, female speakers may sound more feminine if they adopt more 'prestige' variants. In adopting 'gender-appropriate' ways of speaking, speakers will also be helping to re-create them, to establish such gender distinctions as normal.

A second explanation of accent and dialect differences relates to the fact that women and men and girls and boys lead rather different life-styles; women and men have different jobs, and may be expected to interact with different sets of people. Gender differences in language may be, in part, an incidental effect of these other differences. Many accent and dialect studies have shown how other attributes of speakers that might be related to gender could affect language use. And some studies (of adult speakers) have shown that the ways in which womens' and men's language differs depends upon the roles they engage in in the community (Milroy, 1980; Nichols, 1979).

These two explanations aren't incompatible. Speakers may use a variety of language to establish a particular gender identity both directly and also indirectly by signalling the kinds of behaviour that are appropriate for a girl or a boy or a woman or a man in any community.

Turning now to interaction features, if these are used more commonly by female than by male speakers, they will, like accent, dialect, and voice quality, become indicative of femininity, and a speaker may use them to sound feminine. Also like accent, dialect and voice quality, interaction features have other connotations: for instance, in sounding feminine, a female speaker may also sound more tentative. Interaction features will therefore play their part in the continual re-creation of gender as a social division, as well as contribute to the connotations attached to being female or male. The situation is complicated by the fact that speakers are likely to 'play the system', to make a trade-off between the use of different features. For instance, a professional female speaker may use certain features to signal competence and others to show that she has 'retained her femininity'. Since one may signal gender and other forms of social identity through a variety of means, non-verbal systems may also be drawn on. A speaker could, for instance, use clothing to convey an impression of competence or to 'tone down' an otherwise forceful manner.

Features such as interruptions and questions are also the means by which the interaction itself is accomplished. In teacher-led question and answer sessions in the classroom, teachers' questions allow them not only to find out what pupils know, but also to control the subject-matter and direction of the talk and to nominate those whom they want to speak. In less ritualized interactions, other devices are available. By interrupting, a speaker may be able to take a speaking turn away from another. The first speaker may give way or try to stand their ground. A variety of interaction features affects how the conversation is organized, who gets to speak, and whose topic is pursued. It is in this sense that the use of certain conversational techniques has been said to allow boys and men to 'dominate' mixed-sex conversation. For this to happen effectively (to keep the conversation smooth and avoid minor breakdowns) female speakers must also comply – say, by using techniques that support the contributions of others. It is in this sense that female speakers have been said to 'give away power' in conversations.

2.4 Gender Bias in Language

So far, I have concentrated on gender differences in spoken language. But a considerable amount of linguistic research has focused on language as a resource: the language that is available to talk about girls and boys and women and men. Such research has concentrated on the vocabulary of language (mainly English). It suggests that language contains a gender imbalance, in that females are linguistically 'hidden', or excluded; and that linguistic images of females and males are often stereotyped, with females treated in pejorative terms. Such research has given rise to claims that language contains a systematic 'bias', and several 'anti-sexist' guidelines have been produced advocating the use of language that includes girls and women and takes account of their interests. Despite increased awareness of gender bias and attempts to counteract this, the problem persists, within education as in other contexts. Many analyses of gender bias in language were carried out in the 1970s, but the examples I give below come, in the main, from more recent sources.

Gender and Generics

English makes a (linguistic) gender distinction in certain common words for people (and some animals). There are separate words for *he* and *she, man* and *woman, girl* and *boy, uncle* and *aunt, manager* and *manageress,* and so forth. Where gender-neutral terms exist (*person, child*) we still often prefer to specify someone's sex if this is known: we use expressions such as 'Good girl!' or 'Good boy!', rather than 'Good child!' Such linguistic distinctions highlight the importance of gender as a social category. They also allow for the possibility of linguistic sexism: of inequality between female- and male-referring terms.

One of the most frequently documented examples of sexism in the English language has been the use of *he* and *man* as both masculine and gender-neutral terms, to refer to males and to human beings in general. *He* and *man* are often referred to as 'generic masculine' terms. Many women feel excluded by 'generic' usages. There are also signs that *he* and *man* are not really used generically, phrases such as 'prehistoric man' tend to engender male images; and when people talk about *he* and *man,* they sometimes let slip that they actually have males in mind.

Anti-sexist language guidelines argue that *he* and *man* should be used exclusively to refer to males. Where the intention is to refer to people of both sexes, alternative, gender-neutral terms should be used. Since there aren't universally agreed alternatives, many writers adopt an individual policy:

I have used two devices to combat the sexism which is widespread in the English language. In some places, I have used *she* as well as *he* when a neutral between-sexes pronoun is required. In other places, I have followed the increasingly common practice of using *they* and *their* as singular forms after a neutral noun.
(Jean Aitchison, 1987, Preface to *Words in the Mind,* p. viii)

The problem of the 'generic masculine' isn't confined to *he* and *man.* Virtually any gender-neutral term can slip into a masculine use:

They said that over the previous days, paramilitary border police had been taunting the villagers by insulting their womenfolk from the hills above the village.
(*Independent*, 14.4.89)

To make love, a dinosaur had to get his leg over. Even if he happened to be a 160-ton brontosaurus, the female could bear his weight. (*Guardian*, 29.8.87.)

Of course, it's possible to use gender-neutral terms as feminine:

To make love, a dinosaur had to be able to bear the weight of the male.

But this is rarer, and is normally found only in contexts in which we expect a particular word to refer to a female. In other contexts, it's common to mark a term explicitly as feminine: *female dinosaur, women in the village,* and so on. We rarely feel the need to mark terms as masculine in this way, unless they refer to activities habitually carried out by women: for example, *male midwife.*

Semantic Pejoration

'Masculine' and 'feminine' forms of a word tend not to have equivalent meanings. Compare *master* and *mistress, bachelor* and *spinster, governor* and *governess, manager* and *manageress, lord* and *lady,* and so on. Words referring to women may have connotations of lower status; other pejorative connotations; and sometimes sexual connotations.

Examples such as these have been frequently cited; but I think that any masculine and feminine pairs are likely to carry stereotypical associations. The meanings of *man* and *woman* have been analysed respectively as 'adult male human being' and 'adult female human being'. The *Oxford English Dictionary* gives these meanings, but also specifies other connotations: *woman* may be used 'with allusion to qualities attributed to the female sex, as mutability, proneness to tears, or physical weakness; also to their position of inferiority or subjection'. The police officer who complained that Arsenal and Norwich football-players scrapping on the field were behaving 'like a bunch of women' presumably had in mind certain character-istics associated with *women* (bitchy? emotional? scratching someone's eyes out? or just generally derogatory?), rather than any narrower definition of the term (this example was cited in several newspapers, including the *Weekend Guardian*, 11–12.11.89).

Some research has documented a historical process, termed 'semantic pejoration', or 'derogation', whereby negative con-notations 'stick' to words for women and girls. The meaning of such words suffers a systematic historical decline (Schulz, 1975). *Mistress* and *governess*, for instance, started life as roughly parallel to *master* and *governor*, then changed their meaning. *Hussy* used to refer to the mistress of a house; it has the same root as *housewife*. *Wench* used to refer simply to a young girl. *Gossip* was a gender-neutral term that sub-sequently became associated with women, and then acquired negative associations (see *OED* entry for *gossip*, reproduced overleaf).

Semantic pejoration is not confined to words for women and girls. It also happens to words that refer to other socially powerless or disparaged groups, such as people with a dis-ability or of low social status (Leith, 1983).

Lexical Gaps

Researchers have identified systematic gaps in the vocabulary of English: for example, there is an absence of words to refer to girls' and women's experiences. What is the feminine equi-valent of *virility*, for instance? Or of *emasculate*? Many of the gaps seem to be in areas related to female sexuality. A survey of North American English found very few words to refer to women's experience of sex. Most verbs referring to sexual intercourse required a male subject or were gender-neutral (Stanley and Robbins, 1978). On the other hand, there were several words for a promiscuous woman and very few for a

GOSSIP

gossip ('gɒsip), *sb.* Forms: 1 godsib(b, 4 godsyb(be, -zyb(be, 4-5 gossib(be, 4-7 godsib(be, 5-6 gos(s)y(p)p(e, 5-7 godsip, gossipp(e, gos(s)op(e, 5-8 gossep(pe, 6-7 goship, (5 godsep, -sypp, gossyb(e, 6 ghosseppe, gossup, goshyp(p, godcept, 7 godsepte, ghossip), 6- gossip. [OE. *godsibb* masc. (f. *god* GOD + *sib(b* adj., akin, related: see SIB *a*.) = ON. *guð-sefe* masc., *guð-sifja* fem., OSw. *guzsowir* masc., *gupziff, gudzsöff* fem. In ME. a single example is found of a fem. *godzybbe* corresp. to masc. *godzyb* (see quot. 1340 in 1).]

1. One who has contracted spiritual affinity with another by acting as a sponsor at a baptism.

a. In relation to the person baptized: A godfather or godmother; a sponsor. Now only *arch.* and *dial.*

1014 WULFSTAN *Serm. ad Anglos* (Napier) 160 Godsibbas and godbearn to fela man forspilde wide gynd þas þeode. 1340 *Ayenb.* 48 þe zeuende is.. of godsone to þe children of his godzyb oþer of his godzybbe. 1590 GREENWOOD *Collect. Sclaund. Art.* G, The rashe, vndiscreete, and vnpossible vowe of the saide gossipps. 1649 EVELYN *Diary* (1827) II. 16 The parents being so poore that they had provided no gossips. *a* 1654 SELDEN *Table T.* (Arb.) 90 Should a great Lady, that was invited to be a Gossip, in her place send her kitchen-maid. 1711 HEARNE *Collect.* (O.H.S.) III. 194 Fully designed to come and stand gossip in person to Dr. Hudson's child. 1770 FOOTE *Lame Lover* I. 12 Do you know that you are new christen'd, and have had me for a gossip? 1819 S. ROGERS *Hum. Life* 34 Now, glad at heart the gossips breathe their prayer. 1856 MISS YONGE *Daisy Chain* I. ix. (1879) 79 I'll find gossips, and let 'em be christened on Sunday. 1876 FREEMAN *Norm. Conq.* V. xxv. 560 The Englishman whose child was held at the font by a Norman gossip..cast aside his own name. 1886 *S.W. Linc. Gloss.* s.v., I suppose the same gossips will do for both.

fig. 1581 J. BELL *Haddon's Answ. Osor.* 407 b, And this place yᵉ Catholicke gossæppes have Christened by the name of Purgatory. 1607 MIDDLETON *Michaelm. Term* III. iv, I would never undertake to be gossip to that bond which I would not see well brought up. 1673 [R. LEIGH] *Transp. Reh.* 8 Who would be Gossip to all the nameless Off-springs of the Press.

† b. *transf.* With reference to the christening of a bell. *Obs.*

1563 FOXE *A. & M.* 380 The bel hauing a new garment put vppon it..they goo vnto sumptuous bankets, where-vnto also the Gossips are bidden. 1778 PENNANT *Tour in Wales* (1883) I. 47 A bell..was also christened..The gossips.. were doubtlessly rich persons.

† c. In relation to the parents: (One's) child's godfather or godmother. *Obs.*

c 1325 *Lai le Freine* 42 He schal mi gossibbe be. 1475 SIR J. PASTON in *P. Lett.* No. 766 III. 145 He was fayn to sue to the said Duc..by the meanes of his godsip the Bisshop of Wynchestre. [He was sponsor to the Duke's daughter.] 1494 FABYAN *Chron.* vii. 561 Which Wyllyam..was gossyp vnto the quene. *c* 1610 SIR J. MELVIL *Mem.* (1683) 70, I requested her majesty to be a gossip to the Queen. 1612 DAVIES *Why Ireland*, etc. (1747) 113 The English were forbidden to marry, to foster, to make gossippes with the Irish. 1625 B. JONSON *Staple of N.* Induct., And those Mothers had Gossips (if their Children were christned) as we are. 1698 M. MARTIN *Voy. Kilda* (1749) 76 The Officer ..condescended to be the Impostor's Gossip, i.e. Sponsor at the Baptism of one of his Children. 1893 P. W. JOYCE *Short Hist. Irel.* 88 When a man stood sponsor for a child..he became the child's godfather, and gossip to the parents.

† d. In relation to one who acts as godfather or godmother on the same occasion: A fellow-sponsor.

c 1386 CHAUCER *Pars. T.* ⁋835 A womman may in no lasse synne assemblen with hire godsib, than with hire owene flesshly brother. *c* 1440 *Promp. Parv.* 204/2 Gossyp, mann, *compater.* Gossyp, woman, *commater.* 1563 BECON *Acts Chr.*

& Antichr. Wks. III. 416 Christen Gossippes.. those men and women that haue bene Godfathers and Godmothers together of one childe at Baptisme. 1622 FLETCHER *Sp. Curate* II. i, *Lean.* I have heard him say you were gossips too. *Lop.* You did not heare him say to whom. 1666 PEPYS *Diary* 2 Dec., I took my pretty gossip to White Hall with us.

† e. *gen. Obs.*

c 1315 SHOREHAM 69 In that cas thou myȝt weddy To thyne wyfes gossibbe. *c* 1386 CHAUCER *Pars. T.* ⁋834 Parentele is in two maneres, outher goostly or fleshly; goostly, as for to delen with hise godsibbes.

2. a. A familiar acquaintance, friend, chum. Formerly applied to both sexes, now only (somewhat *arch.*) to women. (A sense apparently derived more immediately from 1 c.)

The expression in quot. 1641 is app. the name of some rustic game or dance.

1362 LANGL. *P. Pl.* A. v. 152 'Ic haue good ale, gossib', quod heo. 'Gloten, woltou assaye'? 1393 *Ibid.* C. VII. 47 What ich gaf for godes loue, to god-sybbes ich tolde. *a* 1450 *Knt. de la Tour* (1868) 79 There was a false bauude that was her godsib. *a* 1529 SKELTON *E. Rummyng* 356 Lo, gossyp, I wys, Thus and thus it is. *c* 1560 INGELEND *Disobedient Child* F ij b, She is to her Gossypes gone to make mery. 1641 BROME *Joviall Crew* II. (1652) D 2 b, He makes us even sick of his sadness, that were wont to see his Ghossips cock to day; mould Cocklebread; daunce clutterdepouch [etc.]. 1766 H. BROOKE *Fool of Quality* (1809) II. 11 Barnaby Boniface, his next neighbour and gossip. 1820 KEATS *Eve St. Agnes* xii, Ah, Gossip dear, We're safe enough; here in this arm-chair sit. 1857 C. BRONTE *Professor* I. xi. 180 The old duenna—my mother's gossip. 1873 OUIDA *Pascarel* I. 65 His mother too, was a gossip of her own.

b. *esp.* Applied to a woman's female friends invited to be present at a birth.

1590 SHAKS. *Mids. N.* II. i. 47 Sometime lurke I in a Gossips bole, In very likenesse of a roasted crab. 1620 *Swetnam Arraign'd* (1880) 44 Bidding of Gossips, calling to Vpsittings. *a* 1661 FULLER *Worthies* (1840) I. xx. 75 They are as good evidence to prove where they were born, as if we had the deposition of the midwife, and all the gossips present at their mothers labours. 1721–1800 BAILEY, *A gossiping*, a merry Meeting of Gossips, at a Woman's Lying in. 1764 *Low Life* 29 Poor labouring Men.. are obliged to.. go a Nigiting, i.e. fetching Midwives, Nurses and Gossips. 1805 *Med. Jrnl.* XIV. 258 The officiousness of nurses and gossips. 1858 M. PORTEOUS *Souter Johnny* 31 Whan your nieve the gossip streikit.

transf. 1664 BUTLER *Hud.* II. i. 90 To do the office of a Neighbour, And be a Gossip at his Labour.

3. A person, mostly a woman, of light and trifling character, esp. one who delights in idle talk; a newsmonger, a tattler.

1566 [see 6, *gossip-like*]. 1579 LYLY *Euphues* (Arb.) 52, I will..bring..a visard on my face, for a shamelesse gossippe. 1600 DEKKER *Fortunatus* Wks. 1873 I. 97, I wonder what blind gossip this minx is that is so prodigall. 1614 T. ADAMS *Devil's Banq.* 320 There arise in the end.. as many Gospels as Gossips. 1687 DRYDEN *Hind & P.* III. 003 The common chat of gossips when they meet. 1709 HEARNE *Collect.* (O.H.S.) II. 212 John Stevens.. a negligent, busy, prating Gossip. 1716 ADDISON *Freeholder* No. 26. 144 A Gossip in Politics is a Slattern in her Family. 1833 HT. MARTINEAU *Loom & Lugger* I. i. 6 If he did not mean the girls to grow up the greatest gossips in the neighbourhood. 1854 EMERSON *Soc. Aims* Wks. (Bohn) III. 176 Why need you, who are not a gossip, talk as a gossip? 1884 MRS. EWING *Mary's Meadow* 13 The Weeding Woman is a great gossip.

4. The conversation of such a person; idle talk; trifling or groundless rumour; tittle-tattle. Also, in a more favourable sense: Easy, unrestrained talk or writing, esp. about persons or social incidents.

1811 *Sporting Mag.* XXXVII. 11, I was up to his gossip, so I took him. 1820 W. IRVING *Sketch Bk.* II. 358 A kind of travelling gazette, carrying the whole budget of local gossip from house to house. 1833 HT. MARTINEAU *Loom & Lugger* I. i. 6 All this gossip about their neighbours. 1849 LD. HOUGHTON in T. W. Reid *Life* (1891) I. 2. 439 A sort of focus of political gossip. 1870 E. PEACOCK *Ralf Skirl.* I. 27 We are fond of topographical gossip. 1889 BARRIE *Window in Thrums* 177 My presence killed the gossip on her tongue.

man. Of the small number of words for such men, many had jovial or positive connotations (Stanley, 1977).

Gender Bias in Use

While it is possible to analyse the meanings of individual words like this, words do not normally occur in isolation. There have been complaints that the phrases and expressions conventionally used to describe girls and women are often demeaning. Women are seen as appendages of men:

The hens live here. They lay big brown eggs each day. The farmer's wife collects them in a basket. (*On the Farm*, Ladybird Toddler Books)

There is also a focus on girls' and women's appearance:

One of those MPs, Emma Nicholson, is here today, in a red dress, with a handbag, so well armed. (Interview with Emma Nicholson, about to lobby Mrs Thatcher for compensation for haemophiliac victims of AIDS; BBC Radio 4 *Today Programme*, 22.11.89)

Clare Burstall – five foot nothing, blond hair, animated manner – has been the director of the National Foundation for Educational Research since 1983. (*Times Educational Supplement*, 8.3.91, p. 4)

And women and men and girls and boys are frequently described in stereotyped ways. Sometimes texts that look as if they're addressed to readers of either sex turn out to be oriented towards male readers; but this can't be attributed to 'gender bias' in the meaning of a particular phrase or expression:

The current charge to be woken up by Beattie is £2.47 of real money. For which you get an adenoidal earful and that's your lot. Isn't it time some enterprising pornophone offered an alternative? At 44p a min, Zeitgeist or one of its sultry-voiced sirens guarantees to get you up. Whether out of bed is up to you. (*Guardian*, 2–3.3.91, p. 3)

Language guidelines offer advice on ways of avoiding stereo-typed usages in books and newspaper articles and in advertis-ing and similar material. But they tend to focus on single words or phrases. It's much harder to tackle the general 'orien-tation' of a text.

(There is a fuller account of sexism in language in Graddol and Swann, 1989. See also Miller and Swift, 1981, for an example of guidelines for its avoidance.)

Explanations and Implications

> In a society where women are devalued the words which refer to them – not surprisingly – assume negative conno-tations. But because the options for defining women are confined to negative terms, because their meanings are primarily those of minus male, women continue to be devalued. By such an interrelated process is the subordi-nation of women in part created and sustained. It is a semantic contradiction to formulate representations of women's autonomy or strength and so it remains unenco-ded and women are deprived of the opportunity to for-mulate positive representations of themselves.
>
> (Dale Spender, 1985, *Man Made Language*, pp. 23–24)

> The introduction and legitimation of *he/man* was the result of deliberate policy and was consciously intended to promote the primacy of the male as a category. If there are people today who are unaware of the significance of *he/man*, I do not think that some of the male grammarians who promoted its use were quite so unaware.
>
> (Ibid., p. 150)

> In a man's world, language belongs to men.
>
> (Julia Penelope, 1990, *Speaking Freely*, p. 1)

The existence of sexism in language has led to allegations that men are somehow in control of language, that they have encoded 'male meanings' that discriminate against women. A further claim is that (sexist) language affects its speakers' perceptions, thereby reproducing sexism in society. I shall argue that there are problems with both of these notions and that, rather than linguistic bias *per se*, it is (situated) language use that is implicated in the reproduction of gender inequalities.

Part of the evidence for 'male control' of language comes from the fact that men have been more public language-users (as writers, public speakers, and so on) and that men have been responsible for codifying the language by writing dictionaries and grammars. Dale Spender (1985), for instance, cites the case of the prescriptive grammarians from the 18th century onwards, who stipulated that using *he* and *man* was the 'correct' way to refer to people of either sex or those whose sex isn't specified.

While certain meanings can be said to serve men's interests, it is debatable whether they can legitimately be referred to as 'men's meanings'. Words and meanings don't reside in the language by virtue of grammarians' prescriptions, but because they are used by speakers and writers. While women have traditionally communicated less in public than men they have undoubtedly used the language, and there is no evidence that, as a group, they have systematically ascribed different meanings to words than men have.

There are also problems with the notion that linguistic bias limits the perceptions of a language's speakers. Concerns about sexist language motivated several experiments devised to test the effects of texts containing examples of sexism. These focused mainly on the use of 'generic' *he* and *man*. The experiments showed that, when presented with sentences containing 'generic' *he* or *man*, readers tended to interpret these as referring to males (see, for instance, Moulton *et al.*, 1978; Silveira, 1980, reviews 15 studies).

Such findings have implications for those who prepare materials and resources for use in schools and other contexts. But they are concerned with the interpretation of specific utterances. They do not show that sexist bias in the vocabulary of a language constrains the thoughts of language-users in any general sense.

Other aspects of sexism – such as the negative connotations

attached to words for women and girls or the existence of lexical gaps – have also been said to affect a language's speakers. In the case of lexical gaps, it's been argued that the absence of a word to refer to a particular concept makes it difficult to think about that concept. Female experiences that aren't encoded in the language therefore go unrecognized.

Some early experimental work looked at the potential effects of linguistic forms on speakers' perceptions – for instance, contrasting the perceptions of speakers of languages that differ in terms of how they categorize objects. But the results of such work have been inconclusive (Clark and Clark, 1977, review several studies in this area). There are major problems in any such experimental work: it simply cannot assess the potential long-term and cumulative effects of systematic biases (such as sexism) in language; nor can it take account of the fact that social values, including the values that attach to being female or male, are bound up with a whole set of social practices, of which verbal language is only one. Similar problems beset experimental work on media effects, which I shall discuss in chapter 5.

Many women have complained about the difficulties caused by the absence of words to refer to important female experiences. The fact that such absences can be discussed is an indication that lexical gaps don't constrain thought. But the absence of appropriate terms probably makes it more difficult to communicate certain experiences, in that speakers need to resort to circumlocution. Further, the presence of appropriate words might legitimize women's experiences, as seems to have happened with the introduction of expressions such as 'male chauvinism', 'sexual harrassment', and 'girl-friendly'.

From a linguistic point of view, the notion of sexist language is not unproblematical. Word meaning is notoriously difficult to analyse. I mentioned above that words for women and the word *woman* itself have attracted negative connotations. But, as with any word, the connotations of *woman* vary in different contexts:

'He's a bit of an old woman'
She's warm and womanly.

'Suits do help separate the women from the girls.'
The women's shoe department.

Although it's tempting to say that sexism resides in 'the language', this allegation may be misleading. It is common in linguistics to distinguish between language as a system, a resource that speakers or writers draw on ('the English language'), and instances of actual language use. But the words and meanings that constitute the vocabulary of a language are actually generalizations derived in some way from language use.

Language, in the sense of a resource, is not static: it changes through time. The introduction of expressions that legitimate girls' and women's experiences (such as those mentioned above) provides evidence of this. Sometimes words are consciously revalued – using *woman* rather than *lady*, for example (compare the revaluation of the term *Black*). Nor are words and meanings fixed at any one time; speakers use words to particular effect in particular contexts, and listeners take account of a whole range of factors (the physical context, who the speaker is, their relationship with the listener, their perceived intentions) in interpreting what is said. Listeners may be uncertain as to how to interpret an utterance. Different listeners may disagree. In terms of sexist language, what seems to be at issue is how language may be used to try to carry out sexist acts, and how such attempts may be supported, condoned or resisted.

An example of this process can be found in the practice of sexist name calling, something which has concerned many teachers:

One of the main themes I am concerned about at the moment is people being pushed into sexual relationships earlier than they actually want to be, because there is peer-group pressure. I discuss comments boys might make - if the girl does she's a 'slut', if the girl doesn't she's 'frigid' – and I tell girls they should not give in to these sorts of comments. (Norma Neeson, a secondary school teacher, discussing her approach to sex education; cited by Holly, 1989, p. 22)

Sue Lees (1986) carried out a study of adolescent girls, part of which documented the way insulting expressions could be used against them. The commonest term, used by both boys and girls, was *slag*; but all terms reported by the girl informants in this study related to a girl's sexual reputation. Many, like *slag*, stigmatized her as 'easy', or sexually available. But a girl could also be put down for being cold, a 'tight bitch'. A problem for girls who were called names, particularly if the insult came from a boy, was that there weren't equivalent insult terms to use against boys. One of Lees' informants commented:

One thing I noticed is that there are not many names you can call a boy. But if you call a girl a name, there's a load of them. You might make a dictionary of names you can call a girl. (p. 32)

Of the insult terms that were used specifically against boys, terms such as *prick* and *wanker* seemed milder than *slag*. Others, such as *poof*, clearly stigmatized boys who appeared effeminate – and were rarely used by the girls of boys. There were no derogatory terms for promiscuous boys.

Lees relates this disparity in name calling to the social pressures on girls (and boys), and, most important, to girls' need to protect their reputations: 'The girls tread a very narrow line. They musn't end up being called a slag. But equally, they don't want to be thought unapproachable, sexually cold - a "tight bitch"' (p. 37).

In a study of boys' sex talk in a school 'sin bin', Julian Wood (1984) also documents boys' tendency to categorize girls according to their sexual attractiveness and sexual availability (using expressions such as 'dogs', 'horny birds', and 'right whores'). Boys also used slang expressions to provide a catalogue of parts of the female body, which Wood refers to as 'a literal naming of parts' (p. 58). But the importance of such terms, for Wood, resides less in their existence as part of the language than in the use to which they are put by the boys. He comments:

In terms of the developing sexism of the centre boys it is the use of terms for parts of the body *combined with* the intent to assess girls in crude and superficial ways that constitutes the element of attempted domination. (p. 58)

Such attempts at domination could be, and were, resisted by the girls:

TIM: I like them with great big tits with great big nipples!
LORRAINE: (*aggressively*) What?
TIM: I, er . . .
LORRAINE: Just shut up, OK Tim?
TIM: Alright humpy.

(Wood, 1984, pp. 57–8)

In this case Wood notes that Lorraine misconstrues Tim's comment as one that applies to her; she is responding to a personal remark, rather than to Tim's sexism in a general sense. Her rebuke is also effective because of her superior physical strength.

Wood's study focuses on boys' talk, and doesn't document any use of parallel terms by girls. However, Barbara Risch (1987), in a study carried out among women college students in the USA, reports that her informants have a rich array of 'dirty words' they can use against men. Some of these are masculine, some neutral, and others terms that were formerly thought to apply only to women, such as *bitch*, *whore*, and *slut*. Risch's study suggests either that some young women are changing and are adopting a particular language usage – 'dirty words' – hitherto used by men or that women have always had access to such expressions, but that this was never publicly acknowledged. Whichever interpretation seems most plausible, it is clear that, if girls such as those in Lees's study feel unable to insult the boys, this is not just because suitable terms do not exist. It is social processes that are important – processes in which boys (or girls) attempt to represent girls in certain ways, and girls accept or reject such representations - rather than 'inherent' biases in the language.

This takes us back to gender differences in language use, discussed in section 2.3. The dearth of 'crude' insult terms that girls may use to target boys (or men) *as males* may be a function of girls' tendency to swear less in general – which may be changing. Differences in the availability and use of 'gendered' epithets also suggest that girls and boys are using language to establish their respective gender identities and to categorize others, to acquiesce in such categorization or to resist it.

2.5 Conclusion

In this chapter I have discussed some examples of research into gender and language use. The examples come, in the main, from outside school. The main points I have made are:

- We have certain perceptions and expectations about the ways female and male speakers use language and about the ways they *should* use language; many negative connotations are attached to female speech, and several prescriptions exhort girls and women to speak in ways that would render them subservient to men.
- Gender differences have been found in several aspects of language: female speakers use a higher speaking pitch than males, more standard varieties of language, and more 'supportive' interaction features.
- Gender differences in language have been found in young children (often less consistently than in adult speakers); but we don't yet have a clear picture of how, or when, gender differences develop.
- By adopting 'gender-typed' forms of language, speakers are signalling gender and helping to re-create this as a social division. They are also signalling other attributes of gender-appropriate behaviour. The use of certain interaction features is said to contribute to male 'dominance' in mixed-sex talk and to females 'giving away power' in such talk.
- There is evidence that language, considered as a resource, exhibits a 'gender bias'. Such bias may be detrimental to girls and women; but it is in language use that gender inequalities are maintained (or

challenged) rather than in the existence of gender bias *per se*.

- Language is dynamic. Its meanings vary according to context, and it is subject to change.

Such evidence is relevant to teachers, because gender differences in language will be maintained or challenged in the classroom, as in other contexts. Teachers need to decide how to respond to girls' and boys' language: to what extent and how girls and boys should be encouraged to adopt different ways of speaking and how gender differences in language should be taken into account in teaching and learning. Knowledge of gender differences can also inform work on language awareness. Comparatively young children are likely to have their own views about appropriate speech for women and men - and probably for girls and boys. It's possible to explore popularly held beliefs with children in school, to question where these come from and how far they correspond to the ways children feel they and their friends actually speak.

This chapter has considered gender and language use in a general sense, drawing on studies from a range of contexts. Educational implications of gender differences are explored in later chapters. The following chapter focuses more narrowly on a subset of 'interaction' studies that have documented girls' and boys' participation in classroom talk.

3

Girls' and Boys' Talk in the Classroom

> [In planning for speaking and listening] the need for equal opportunities for boys and girls should receive consideration.
> (NCC, 1989a, English Key Stage 1: non-statutory guidance,
> p. C4)

3.1 Introduction

Classrooms are different from many of the contexts for talk discussed in chapter 2, in that one participant, the teacher, has a formal status that gives greater 'rights' to speak than other speakers. Sometimes, for instance, in formal question and answer sessions, or in whole-class discussion, talk is organized through the teacher, who nominates pupils to speak. Even in more informal, or 'child-centred', classrooms, it is the teacher who sets the agenda for interaction. It is therefore important to consider not just how girls and boys interact, but also how teachers interact with girls and with boys. Evidence suggests that teachers help to reinforce gender differences in the classroom, including differences in language use.

Researchers have argued that girls' and boys' interaction styles are not just different but that, in various ways, they favour one sex at the expense of the other; normally, they favour boys at the expense of girls. There is inequality in the straightforward sense that girls tend to talk less than boys, inequality also in that girls and boys contribute in different ways to classroom talk. Such evidence from the classroom is consistent with evidence from other contexts discussed in chapter 2.

Gender differences and inequalities in classroom talk need to be considered not only in the light of unequal relations between girls and boys, but also in the light of the increasing attention paid within education to the development of pupils' 'communication skills', the recognition of the role played by talk in pupils' learning, and the requirement for pupils' spoken language to be assessed. Such issues have become increasingly important in the UK with the advent of the National Curriculum for England and Wales, the Northern Ireland Curriculum and the Development Programme for pupils aged 5–14 in Scotland.

This chapter will look at the nature of girls' and boys' participation in classroom talk. I shall examine some of the evidence for gender differences and inequalities. This involves considering the kinds of research that have been carried out in classrooms and the different research methods that have been employed. It is necessary to consider the methods used by researchers, since these effect how studies may be interpreted. I hope also that giving some consideration to the pros and cons of different types of research will be useful to teachers who wish to monitor talk in their own classrooms.

Chapter 4 will consider some of the practical implications of gender differences in spoken language for teaching, learning, and assessment, drawing on evidence discussed in chapter 2 as well as in this chapter.

3.2 Gender and Classroom Interaction

Observations in middle schools

Miss Tweed announces, 'I'm still waiting for most of the boys to do that measuring'. (Later) Yvette has finished measuring her worksheet. Miss Tweed says, 'Another girl finished'. . . . (Later when Tammy and Stephanie are up) Miss Tweed says, 'Only seven girls to go.' Someone asks how many boys and the answer is lots . . . Later when Kenneth is up for marking, Miss Tweed says, 'Only five girls to go now.' 'How many boys?' 'Nearly all of them.'

In a cookery lesson the home economics teacher said: '*Boys* – is it boys who are making so much noise or is it a bunch of girls? . . . Be careful boys that you get your tables all nice and straight.'

In Mrs Hind's class, pupils are writing their own sentences, each one including three words from the board. The word trios are:
boy   football   window
gorilla   cage   keeper
monkeys   coconuts   hunters
soldier   army   tank
Several ask her about the words, so she reads through them. Says of 'soldier army tank': 'That's one for the boys really, I suppose.'

Observations in secondary schools

After break go to Technical Drawing with Mr Quill. He lines them up at the back and the side of the room, and allocates seats in alphabetical order. Boys first – leaving spaces for absentees. There are twenty-eight children on the class list – and only twenty-three proper drawing tables – so five girls get left without proper desks and are given slots on the side benches. Then they are told that when anyone is absent, they can sit in the absentees' seats.

At Waverley Miss Southey had a class in the school library and when she saw most of the girls had borrowed books but none of the boys she said 'All the girls are taking out books but not one boy yet. Can't the boys read in this class?'

It is 3.30. Mrs Leithen says 'Nobody is going from here till you are all quiet.' When they are quiet they are allowed to leave a small number at a time, girls first, then the boys in small groups.

(Observations cited by Sara Delamont, 1990, *Sex roles and the School*, pp. 29–60)

Katherine Clarricoates, in a review of two decades of research on gender and classroom interaction, concludes that interaction between teachers and pupils, and between pupils themselves is 'suffused with gender' (1983, p. 46). Studies have found a range of ways in which gender differentiation is maintained in the classroom. The major findings include:

- While there are quiet pupils of both sexes, the more outspoken pupils tend to be boys.
- Boys also tend to 'stand out' more than girls. Michelle Stanworth (1983) notes that in her study teachers initially found some girls 'hard to place'. Boys also referred to a 'faceless' bunch of girls.
- Boys tend to be generally more assertive than girls. For instance, a US study of whole-class talk (Sadker and Sadker, 1985) found boys were eight times more likely than girls to call out.
- Girls and boys tend to sit separately; in group work, pupils usually elect to work in single-sex rather than mixed-sex groups.
- When they have the choice, girls and boys often discuss or write about gender-typed topics.
- Boys are often openly disparaging towards girls.
- In practical subjects, such as science, boys hog the resources.
- In practical subjects, girls 'fetch and carry' for boys, doing much of the cleaning up, and collecting books and so on.
- Boys occupy, and are allowed to occupy, more space, both in class and outside – for example, in play areas.
- Teachers often make distinctions between girls and

boys – for disciplinary or administrative reasons or to motivate pupils to do things.

- Teachers give more attention to boys than to girls.
- Topics and materials for discussion are often chosen to maintain boys' interests.
- Teachers tend not to perceive disparities between the numbers of contributions from girls and boys. Sadker and Sadker (1985) showed US teachers a video of classroom talk in which boys made three times as many contributions as girls – but teachers believed the girls had talked more.
- Teachers accept certain behaviour (such as calling out) from boys but not from girls.
- Female teachers may themselves be subject to harrassment from male pupils.
- 'Disaffected' girls tend to opt out quietly at the back of the class, whereas disaffected boys make trouble.

(This list is adapted from one that appeared originally in Swann, 1991.)

For examples of this work see, for instance, Clarricoates, 1983; Delamont, 1990; Lees, 1986; Sadker and Sadker, 1985; Spender, 1982; Stanworth, 1983; Whyte, 1986.

Many studies also report that teachers prefer teaching boys, though some studies, particularly in primary schools, have found a preference for girls. Clarricoates suggests that there is a dichotomy between teachers' 'professional values' about how pupils should behave in class and their 'personal values' about appropriate behaviour for girls and boys. Noisy, boisterous boys may be exhibiting appropriate 'boy-like' behaviour, although this violates 'school' norms. Teachers may dislike boys as pupils, but like them as boys. If, as is suggested, 'feminine' behaviour is more consistent with school norms, then 'noisy, active and aggressive girls would be least liked, as they violate *both* sets of values' (p. 57, emphasis original).

The list I've given draws together patterns of behaviour from several studies. But it needs to be interpreted with caution. Points to bear in mind include:

- Differences between the sexes are always average ones, as I mentioned in Chapter 2. Clearly, in classrooms you do get some talkative girls and quiet boys. Girls and boys also behave differently in different contexts.
- Factors other than gender affect how pupils behave and how they are responded to. Perceptions of, and behaviour towards, pupils are likely to be coloured by other social factors (for example, class, ethnicity), by personality, and by perceived ability.
- The studies from which the list derived were carried out indifferent contexts; they used a variety of methods; and they focused on different aspects of talk; not surprisingly, not all studies produce identical results.

I shall look at some studies of classroom talk to illustrate these points. First, to give an idea of the kinds of studies that have been carried out, the methods of enquiry commonly adopted, and the concerns that motivate researchers, I shall look at studies of talk around the computer and talk in science and in design and technology lessons.

3.3 Studies of Classroom Talk – Some Examples

Talk round the Computer

The studies mentioned above looked at talk in several several subject areas; Sadker and Sadker (1985), for instance, looked at lessons in the 'language arts', English, maths, and science in primary and secondary schools. But there has been particular concern about gender inequalities in areas of the curriculum in which girls traditionally do less well or in which they have less confidence. Computing is one such area. Educationists have been concerned at the 'male image' of computing: boys have more positive attitudes towards computing, they make greater use of computers out of school; and they dominate what resources there are in school.

Lorraine Culley (1988) reports on a study of girls, boys, and computers in secondary schools. Culley's observations of classroom interaction during computing lessons reveal some familiar patterns:

In the discussion part of lessons boys dominated the lesson, consistently asking more questions of the teacher and making more comments on the content of the lesson. Girls were also marginal to the class in a physical sense, often seated in groups at the back or sides of the room. In the practical part of lessons boys would typically acquire the newest computers, those with disc drives and *colour* monitors. Often girls would be left standing in the rush, without access to a computer at all. (Culley, 1988, p. 6)

In the primary school, pupils often work at computers in pairs or small groups. Such arrangements may have their origins in the relatively small numbers of computers available for general use in primary schools, but it's also claimed that there are educational benefits in pupils working together at the computer, collaborating on problems, and so on. Teachers also show a preference for mixed-sex pairs or groupings at the computer. Some concerns have been expressed at boys' tendency to take over or dominate small-group work at the computer, but researchers have also focused their attention on girls' and boys' different interaction styles – with the computer and with each other. Celia Hoyles and Rosamund Sutherland recorded and analysed the interactions of pairs of pupils (single-sex and mixed-sex) when working with Logo at the computer. They report:

The girls were less likely to fight for control than the boys – who often seemed concerned to establish their autonomy and impose their problem representation and solution. Boys used few verbal supports of their partner's contributions. They appeared to be trying hard to convince each other, which led to a competitive style of speech. Boys tended to be more careful with the exact local detail of their designs, which were often very carefully planned in advance. Their interactions were therefore often simply suggestions for actions which were not negotiable as they had already been worked out in advance. (Hoyles and Sutherland, 1989, p. 175)

Other research has focused on whether girls and boys learn better when carrying out computing activities in single-sex or mixed-sex groups. Geoffrey Underwood, Michelle McCaffrey, and Jean Underwood (1990) compared pupils' performance on a language task when working as individuals and when working as members of a pair. They found that pupils in single-sex pairs performed better than when they worked alone, but that pupils in mixed-sex pairs showed no such improvement. They also made 'informal' observations of the pupils' talk. They found that both boys and girls collaborated in single-sex pairs, sharing tasks with one another. In mixed-sex pairs, however, there was little collaboration. One partner tended to take over the computer, while the other gave them instructions.

Not all studies have found that pupils perform better in single-sex pairs. For instance, Hughes, Brackenbridge, Bibby, and Greenhaugh (1989) found that in a task that involved steering a 'turtle' round an obstacle course, girls performed better in mixed-sex pairs. It is likely that features of the particular task set, as well as how pupils are grouped or paired, will affect the quality of pupils' talk, as well as how well they perform.

Talk in Science, and Design and Technology

The physical sciences and technology, like computing, tend to have a male image. Educationists have been concerned at the low take-up of these subjects by girls. The Girls into Science and Technology project (GIST) tried to find out why so few girls in Manchester secondary schools took up the physical sciences and technology. GIST researchers used ethnographic research methods; they observed science lessons in eight secondary schools over four years, making field notes of their observations. They were able to look at school and classroom organization; when observing classroom interaction, they noted non-verbal, as well as verbal, behaviour. They found patterns of gender differentiation that are consistent with those identified in section 3.2 (Whyte, 1986).

Other studies have focused more narrowly on classroom talk, often coding and counting different types of talk from teachers and from girl and boy pupils. In a study carried out in the USA Linda Morse and Herbert Handley (1985) examined classroom talk in 'traditional, teacher-directed' secondary science lessons. The researchers tape-recorded and analysed six 30-minute sessions. They found that teachers spoke more with boys than with girls; they asked boys more questions than girls, and spent more time reinforcing or rewording questions for boys than for girls; boys gave more unsolicited responses than girls; they also received more feedback from teachers, which served to prolong the amount of teacher–pupil talk.

In a UK study, Gay Randall (1987) examined talk between a teacher and secondary school pupils engaged in practical work in craft, design, and technology lessons. She worked in one school in which the teacher, the head and the local authority were all strongly committed to equal opportunities for girls and boys. Because Randall focused on practical work, the teacher she observed was not directing class discussion but walking round speaking to individual pupils as they worked. Talk was private rather than public, and there was more opportunity for pupils to initiate conversation.

Randall made a close analysis of two lessons, and found that girls took more speaking turns than boys. These findings contradict the general patterns found elsewhere – though it's worth noting that many of the girls' turns were questions about their work of the 'What do I do now?' type. Randall suggests three interpretations: this teacher has succeeded in eliminating gender bias, at least from this type of lesson; girls aren't confident at speaking up in 'public' discussion, but prefer to talk to the teacher 'privately'; or girls are less independent, and seek more reassurance from the teacher.

Leonie Rennie and Leslie Parker (1987) investigated pupils' talk in single-sex and mixed-sex groups in primary school science lessons in Australia. They looked at classes taught by 18 teachers, all of whom had completed an in-service course on teaching electricity. Ten of the teachers had also completed a course on gender awareness, focusing on girls' and boys' attitudes and achievements in science and how to develop skills in, and positive attitudes towards, physical science. The teachers taught six lessons on electricity following the syllabus, approach, and procedures advocated during the in-service course. Rennie and Parker describe the observations made in one lesson taught by each of the 18 teachers. In this lesson the pupils were involved in group work (making a switch).

Rennie and Parker found that there were few differences in boys' behaviour in single-sex or mixed-sex groups. Boys also behaved similarly whether or not their teacher had been on the 'gender awareness' course. Girls, on the other hand, behaved differently in different contexts; they tended to spend more of their time watching and listening in mixed-sex groups. In lessons taught by teachers who hadn't been sensitized to gender, girls also spent less time manipulating equipment in mixed-sex groups. Rennie and Parker conclude: 'There is a danger that girls in mixed-sex groups may miss out on their share of the 'hands-on' experiences' (p. 71), but that sensitizing teachers to gender differences could have a positive effect on girls' participation, at least in the short term.

Another study from Australia has produced evidence that conflicts with findings from previous studies. Barry Dart and John Clarke (1988) looked at teacher–pupil talk in 24 science lessons in a Brisbane secondary school. It is not clear from Dart and Clarke's account what form these lessons took, but the examples of teacher and pupil speech that are quoted suggest that some lessons or some portions of lessons involved whole-class talk while others involved talk between teachers and pupils during practical work. Overall, teachers talked more with boys than with girls, but the differences were not statistically significant (in other words, they were not greater than could have been expected to occur by chance). Boys responded more to teachers' questions but girls initiated more contact with teachers (again, neither of these differences was statistically significant).

It's hard to evaluate Dart and Clarke's evidence without knowing more of the context in which the talk took place. It may be, for instance, that talk was differently distributed during class discussion and practical work. It would be consistent with the other studies I have mentioned if boys contributed more during class discussion, though not necessarily (to the teacher) during practical work.

There is a further general point here, which applies also to the studies by Morse and Handley, Randall, and Rennie and Parker. These studies categorized different types of talk, then counted the amount of talk produced that fell into each category. While this method allows one to make comparisons between talk in different lessons or with different teachers, in reducing talk to a set of categories, the original meaning of the talk is lost – what prompted a pupil to 'initiate contact', for instance, and how this was responded to by the teacher. To understand what is going on with respect to gender differences and inequalities (or, for that matter, other aspects of classroom talk), it is necessary to look more closely at examples of talk in context. I shall look at one or two studies that have done this, in an attempt to discover how girls and boys obtain speaking turns.

3.4 How do Pupils Get to Talk?

Jane French and Peter French (1984) analysed a recording of a lesson in a primary classroom, a teacher-led discussion on the topic 'What I do on Mondays and what I would like to do on Mondays'. This lesson showed an imbalance in the number of turns taken by girls and boys, with the boys taking 50 turns between them and the girls 16 turns. French and French also give a breakdown of the turns taken by individual pupils, which shows that there was considerable variability within groups: the boys' greater participation could be accounted for by three particularly talkative boys. One of these boys took 17 turns, and the other two took 10 turns each. French and French seek to explain how the more talkative boys obtained so many speaking turns. They suggest that though the teacher was directing the discussion (asking the questions and selecting pupils to respond), there were strategies available to pupils that enabled them to contribute more. One such strategy was to give an answer that was out of the ordinary, and

so invited further probing by the teacher. French and French
give an example:

1	*Teacher*:	what time do you get up Tom?
2		(0.7)
3	*Tom*:	half past four
4	*Teacher*:	what?
5	*Tom*:	half past four
6	*Teacher*:	(what do you get up at that time for?)
7	*Pupils*:	[exclamations etc.]
8	*Tom*:	(no) I've got to feed the a-animals and (clean all the aviary)
9	*Teacher*:	what?
10	*Tom*:	I've got to clean the (aviary) and feed all the animals and (.) all that
11	*Teacher*:	what animals?
12	*Pupils*:	⎰ all the animals, ⎱ he's got a (hamster) [various pupils call out - difficult to distinguish individuals]
13	*Teacher*:	(I think) half past four perhaps is a little bit early I mean that's half way through the night Tom
14		(1.9)
15	*Teacher*:	what animals have you got?
16	*Tom*:	erm
17	*Teacher*:	you've got your parakeet
18	*Tom*:	two cats (.) two dogs (.) hams- no hamster (.) two rabbits
19	*Wayne*:	birds
20	*Tom*:	erm (1.0) parrot (1.0) that's all (.) I've got about (0.5) two rabbits (.) (I've) got about(.) fifty-three birds something like that
21	*Teacher*:	what (.) have you got them in an aviary have you (.)(have you got them in the garden)?
22	*Tom*:	yeah
23	*Teacher*:	well it must take a long time to feed so you'll have to get up a bit before eight o' clock that's true (.)what happens on a Saturday then?
24	*Tom*:	I cleans 'em all out
25	*Teacher*:	yeah but what time do you get up on a Saturday then you've still got to feed them

26   (0.5)
27   *Tom*:   I gets up about (.) half past eight
28   (1.0)
29   *Teacher*: half past eight (.) what time do you get
             up early? [to Rachel]
30   *Rachel*: quarter to eight
31   *Teacher*: quarter to eight (.) what about you Laura?
32   *Laura*:   half past seven
33   *Teacher*: half past seven [nods to Jason]
34   *Jason*:   quarter to eight
35   *Teacher*: quarter to eight [points to Rowena]
36   *Rowena*: seven o' clock
37   *Teacher*: seven o' clock

(Adapted from French and French, 1984, pp. 128–9)

(Note: the following transcription conventions are used in this transcript: (I think) = likely wording; [nods to Jason] = description of some relevant activity; (1.0) = 1 second pause; (.) = brief pause; { = overlapping speech.)

Tom's answer clearly surprises his teacher, and wins him a succession of speaking turns in which he talks about his animals. By contrast, pupils who give more conventional answers simply have these acknowledged before the teacher passes on to the next person. French and French suggest that pupils' use of such strategies, ensures that, even in teacher-directed question and answer sessions, the allocation of speaking turns to pupils is a collaborative business.

A study that I carried out with a colleague (Swann and Graddol, 1988) tried to explore the mechanisms by which speaking turns were allocated in the classroom, looking at non-verbal as well as verbal behaviour. We analysed video recordings of two interactions between teachers and small groups of pupils in primary classrooms. In both cases, boys talked more on average than girls, though there were some quiet boys and one particularly talkative girl. Because our sample size was very small, differences between boys and girls were not statistically significant; besides, our study focused less on who talked more than on how more talkative pupils obtained turns at speaking.

Like French and French, we found we had to look at the behaviour of both teacher and pupils to understand what was going on. Boys in one class seemed to obtain more speaking turns simply by 'chipping in' more often in response to the teacher's questions. But a close analysis of the teacher's patterns of gaze showed that she more often looked towards the boys when formulating a question, thereby encouraging them to respond. In the other class, pupils were normally selected to speak from those who had their hands raised, and the talk seemed to be more directly under the teacher's control. When selecting a pupil in this way, however, the teacher nearly always selected the pupil whose hand was raised first. The transcript below shows how this works for Kate, the particularly talkative girl. The teacher is asking questions about the rescue of miners trapped down a pit.

At the beginning of this sequence the teacher is looking at the boys. Kate's hand goes up and draws her attention. By the time the boys' hands are raised, the teacher is already beginning to turn towards the girls. By the time Anne's hand rises, the teacher's gaze is directed towards Kate. The whole process is very rapid: the video recording shows a flurry of hands, and a frame by frame analysis is required to determine the precise order of hand raising. Presumably the teacher is reacting to additional non-verbal cues, such as posture, in responding so accurately to the first hand raised.

                                 K J M E A

      .... _____
Mrs A.:   How did they know that those men were alive(.)yes
      _____
Kate: Miss they were knocking
      _____
Mrs A.:   They were knocking . . .

(Note: *in this transcript, lines above the speech are used to indicate the direction of the teacher's gaze:* .... = *teacher's gaze towards boys;* _____ = *teacher's gaze towards girls; capital letters above the line denote order of hand raising: Kate, John, Mark, Emma, Anne.*)

In this lesson, then, it seemed that although the teacher formally selected pupils to speak, pupils themselves could influence the selection by managing to get their hands up first. Kate was the only girl who used this strategy, but the boys obtained most of their speaking turns this way.

The teacher also looked towards the boys more overall during the lesson – during exposition, as well as when asking questions. When the teacher began a question looking towards the boys, her gaze tended to stay with them (unless attracted by a girl's raised hand, as in the case of Kate above). But when the teacher began a question with her gaze towards the girls, she either switched to the boys half way through or darted about between girls and boys. This pattern of gaze seemed, then, to favour the boys.

In both the sequences we analysed, teachers and pupils contributed jointly to a selection procedure that favoured the boys, but the cues used were quite subtle and probably operated below the level of conscious awareness.

One very interesting study was carried out by Julie Fisher (1991), a head teacher who also taught an infant class part-time. She had spent a term monitoring small-group work in her infant class, noticing that girls seemed more responsive in single-sex than in mixed-sex groups, but also that children responded very differently during different activities. She decided to compare one group of children, two boys and two girls, over several tasks to see how their contributions differed. She looked at five tasks, all based on the book *The Jolly Postman*. All tasks involved discussion; some also involved drawing or collaborative model-making. In addition, she monitored the girls' and boys' talk in one activity in which they worked in single-sex groups with other pupils.

In the mixed-sex group the boys spoke, overall, much more than the girls. This difference is consistent with other studies, but the tiny sample makes its interpretation as a gender difference problematical. The important point, though, is not the difference between girls and boys but the fact that girls' and boys' levels of participation varied dramatically in different contexts. For instance, in one context (building a Wolf-proof house) girls spoke only 5 and 7 words each, compared to boys' 615 and 373 words; in another context (building a coach for Cinderella) girls spoke 336 and 69 words, and boys 240 and 274 words.

Fisher carried out a detailed qualitative analysis of each context, showing how ideas were initiated by pupils, supported, or dismissed. Overall, the two boys controlled the mixed-sex discussions, and the girls allowed them to do so, remaining supportive and passive; but the ways in which girls and boys interacted varied from one context to another, and there were also differences between girls and between boys.

Fisher's analysis of the pupils' talk while building Cinderella's coach illustrates the limitations of focusing purely on the amount pupils speak. One girl, Elizabeth, was particularly talkative during this activity, but her contributions had little effect:

My field notes and the video reveal that Elizabeth was particularly excited. This became noticeable when the children, quite naturally it seemed, paired off as they began construction, so that Elizabeth was working with David, and Nadia with Simon. David is considered the class leader and is extremely popular with the girls. I think a major part of Elizabeth's verbosity stemmed from the fact that David had chosen *her* to work with, and the excitement got the better of her . . .

I was very surprised to see the pairings because it was the first time that the group had fallen into boy/girl partnerships. However, my pleasure was quickly dispelled as I realised that the boys were organizing the construction of the coach and were using the girls to fetch, carry and hold the various parts they needed:

David: [*to Elizabeth*] Get them.
Simon: We need four. Where are they? Get four Nadia.
David: We'll need some bits for the window, Elizabeth.
Simon: Nadia, put one of those in here.

(Fisher, 1991, pp. A109–110)

Fisher points out that the girls readily accepted the helper role required of them by the boys.

Small-scale studies such as the three I have described are

useful in that they allow researchers to examine closely what is going on. A limitation is that one cannot make generalizations (that is, claims about how girls or boys *generally* behave) on the basis of evidence from small numbers of pupils in one or two lessons. For a critique of French and French, 1984, and Swann and Graddol, 1988, in this and other respects, see Hammersley, 1990.

3.5   Gender in Context

I mentioned earlier that, clearly, neither girls nor boys are homogeneous groups. Factors other than gender will affect the way people behave. This is one reason why there will always be exceptions to any gender difference. In their examination of male dominance of talk in US schools, Sadker and Sadker (1985) did not find any systematic difference between Black and white pupils, those from different age-groups, or those from urban and rural communities. But it is undoubtedly true that girls' and boys' experiences of school will differ depending on factors such as their social class, ethnic group, whether they have a disability, and so on.

To take ethnic group as an example, Grace Evans (1988) writes of white teachers' complaints about 'those loud black girls' who didn't conform to expected norms of 'good' behaviour. Cecile Wright (1987), in her account of a study of two multiracial comprehensives in the Midlands, notes that interaction between white teachers and Afro-Caribbean pupils was frequently characterized by antagonism and conflict, more so than between teachers and white or Asian pupils. Black pupils also experienced overt racism from a few teachers in the form of disparaging remarks about their ethnicity and physical appearance. While there has been a complaint that girls receive too little teacher attention, Wright notes that Black pupils of both sexes complain of receiving too much – mainly negative. Such experiences have lead some Black women to argue that racism has played a more important part in their school lives than sexism.

There has been relatively little detailed analysis of the way in which girls and boys from different ethnic groups interact in the classroom. In one paper produced in 1989 for the Ealing Gender Equality Team, Hilary Claire and John Redpath provide an account of gender and ethnic imbalances in classroom discussion in four nursery and primary schools in Ealing. Redpath found that boys averaged three times as many speaking turns as girls. As in other studies, however, there were some quieter boys and some more vociferous girls. Claire, in a follow-up analysis of Redpath's data, suggests that there may have been an interaction between pupils' gender and ethnic group. Boys who dominated class discussion, for instance, were white and Black Afro-Caribbean. Asian boys took little part in class discussion. Furthermore, dominant white boys were perceived as 'bright' by their teachers, whereas the Black boys were 'constantly in trouble for attitude and unacceptable behaviour' (p. 13). White and Black (Afro-Caribbean) girls took an equal part in discussion, but Asian girls participated least of all pupils. Quieter pupils, including Asian girls, did participate more in carefully selected small groups. Claire speculates on the extent to which factors such as teachers' attitudes and behaviour and lesson content might affect pupils' participation in class discussion:

Suppose . . . that white boys appeared more interested in topics like Romans or dinosaurs, what effort is there to find topics in which black and Asian boys and girls of all ethnic groups are equally involved? How are topics chosen and by whom? Are pupils themselves ever asked their opinion about 'boys'' or 'girls'' topics? Are their responses in discussion ever monitored to check whether their perception of gendered subject matter makes a difference? (1989, p. 14)

These observations are in line with the prevailing view of Asian girls as quiet and passive. But 'Asian girls' don't constitute a single unified category. Roger Hewitt warns of the danger of seeing ethnicity as fixed and static. He comments on the results of some research on pupils' group talk in oral assessment:

Part of our research involves interviewing teachers about their oral work and, although not uniformly, certainly with the confidence of long-established daily contact, we have been warned of the stark contrast between the oral performances of Asian boys and Asian girls, whose shyness is invincible. But what we have found most difficult to explain is the contrast between this account and what actually finds its way on to our classroom video recordings. These reveal some shy girls, it is true, but many more who are happy to interrupt other speakers, to take long turns, who know how to take the floor and muster arguments and who are well able, even eager, to challenge boys, patriarchy and a range of value systems often with considerable - and clearly practised – articulacy. (Hewitt, 1989, p. 12)

More work is needed on the interaction between gender and other social factors such as pupils' ethnic origin, as well as on the effects of lesson content, classroom organization, and so forth. But the work I've mentioned does at least suggest that generalizations about girls' and boys' behaviour may sometimes obscure important contrasts between contexts and between different sets of people.

3.6   Identifying Imbalances in Classroom Talk

The studies I have described in this chapter have used a variety of methods to collect and analyse evidence. Each of these methods allows researchers to focus on different aspects of talk, and each has its own advantages and disadvantages:

- Studies such as those carried out by Sara Delamont (cited at the beginning of the chapter) and the Manchester GIST team (see section 3.3) are ethnographic, and researchers spent a considerable amount of time observing and trying to understand what was going on in classrooms. Observation was open-ended; researchers did not usually go into classrooms deliberately looking for particular types of talk. The researchers jotted down their observations as field notes. They were able to include non-verbal and con-textual information and to provide an overall picture of classroom life.

With open-ended observation, however, there's a danger of recording isolated events and attaching too much significance to them. Researchers often try to counteract this by including an observation only if it has occurred more than a certain number of times or in more than one context or if it's been recorded by more than one observer. But there's still the risk that observers 'see what they want to see'.

- Other studies (for example, those of Morse and Hand-ley, Randall, Rennie and Parker and Dart and Clarke discussed in section 3.3) have relied on more struc-tured observations, with researchers noting how often speakers use particular categories of talk. Such studies provide data that look more objective and reliable. It's possible to make systematic comparisons between talk produced by different pupils and in different contexts. But looking simply at categories doesn't tell you about the meaning of the talk or about how it fits in with the rest of the discourse. For instance, categorizing and counting speaking turns doesn't tell you how these were obtained; classifying something as 'pupil initiation' doesn't tell you what purpose that initiation fulfilled or what preceded it and how it was responded to.

- Studies such as those of French and French, Swann and Graddol, and Fisher (see section 3.4), looked in detail at relatively small amounts of talk, using a mixture of quantitative and qualitative methods. They were able to show how discourse is organized, and transcripts allowed their data to be re-examined (and reinterpreted) by other researchers. But such studies are highly specific, and it's debatable how far one can generalize from them.

No method is perfect, each highlights different aspects of

talk. It's important to be aware of the sources of evidence about gender inequalities and classroom talk, since this will affect how such evidence is interpreted and what practical implications it has.

3.7 Conclusion

Many studies have claimed that classroom talk is discriminatory: boys dominate mixed-sex talk, and girls give away power, in the classroom as in other contexts. Such arrangements are supported, often unconsciously, by teachers. This chapter has examined evidence for these claims. The points I have made include the following:

- There is considerable evidence that girls' and boys' behaviour, including language behaviour, differs in the classroom. This might be summarized by saying that boys take up more 'verbal space' than girls, have more say in what goes on, and receive more attention from teachers.
- Some research studies have focused on talk in isolation. In practice, other aspects of classroom interaction, including girls', boys', and teachers' non-verbal behaviour, are equally important in ensuring boys' dominance of classroom life.
- Gender inequalities (verbal and non-verbal) have been found in several subject areas. They are of particular concern in areas in which girls tend to have less confidence or do less well, such as science, design and technology, and computing.
- Pupils will talk differently in different contexts: Girls' and boys' participation is likely to be affected by teachers' attitudes and behaviour, the way the classroom is organized, and the activities engaged in.
- Girls and boys are not homogeneous groups; other aspects of a speaker's personal and social identity will affect the way they talk. I mentioned pupils' ethnic

group as a social factor that might interact with gender, affecting the way pupils participate in classroom talk and how pupils are responded to by teachers.

- When looking at gender and classroom talk, it's important to look at how all participants behave. Several studies have suggested that boys' dominance is the outcome of strategies employed by boys *and* girls *and* teachers. If gender-typed talk is regarded as normal, it is likely that it will be supported by all participants in an interaction.

- Several different types of study have been made of classroom interaction. I mentioned, as examples, ethnographic studies that look at talk in context, studies that categorize and count different types of talk, and small-scale, detailed studies often involving transcription of relatively small amounts of talk. There are pros and cons attached to each method. The methods used in a study also affect the interpretations that can be placed on its findings.

Evidence of boys' dominance of classroom interaction has attracted concern from many teachers and researchers. This is because talk is one way in which relationships between people are established and maintained. Few would claim that classroom talk is *responsible* for the establishment of unequal relationships between girls and boys; but unequal relationships in the classroom may build on or support those established in other contexts. A corollary of this is that the classroom is a place where inequalities between girls and boys can be explored and challenged. Challenging and changing unequal patterns of interaction can improve working relations in the classroom. Promoting equal opportunities for classroom talk may also have the wider aims of changing girls' and boys' behaviour and how they relate to one another both inside and outside school.

This chapter has focused on the different kinds of research that have been carried out into gender and classroom talk. The implications of such research for the use of talk in teaching, learning, and assessment are considered in chapter 4. Chapter 8 provides guidance for those who wish to monitor talk in their own teaching context. Chapter 9 considers strategies designed to introduce equal opportunities in classroom language.

4

Oracy Issues

4.1 Introduction

In discussing gender differences in spoken language in chapters 2 and 3 I have been primarily concerned to document the evidence for such differences. I have also mentioned some implications. These include social implications, to do with the fact that language use is one way in which relationships between the sexes are negotiated and maintained, and in which social divisions and inequalities are reinforced. I have looked at such implications because teachers must clearly be concerned about language and social inequalities. I have also mentioned other, more directly 'educational' implications of gender differences in language use, to do with teaching, learning and assessment. These different implications are considered further in this chapter.

I have distinguished four issues to which gender differences in spoken language seem particularly relevant: the fact that relationships between girls and boys are established in the classroom, as in other contexts, and the classroom is one place in which unequal relationships may be challenged; the importance of pupils' talk for learning; the need for all pupils to develop a range of communicative strategies; and the requirement for pupils' spoken language to be assessed. Gender differences could disadvantage girls or boys in each of these areas, but the way in which such a disadvantage might operate is not at all straightforward. I shall consider these issues separately below.

4.2   Talk and Unequal Relations

> Teachers should be prepared to draw older pupils' atten-
> tion to the contribution of language generally to the cre-
> ation and maintenance of inequalities between the sexes
> and invite them to discuss the issue and offer solutions
> to the problems and concerns they can identify.
>
> SED, 1990, *English Language 5–14*, p. 20)

Studies of gender and language use have suggested that language use is inextricably bound up with speakers' personal and
social identities: with how speakers present themselves, with
how they are perceived by others, and with how they relate
to one another. Language use, it is argued, supports asymmetrical relations between the sexes. At a local level, using
certain features of language may lead to a speaker being
perceived in a certain way (as feminine, working-class, hesitant, and so forth). The way a speaker uses language also
contributes to the outcome of an interaction (for instance, in
a particular mixed-sex interaction, a female speaker may have
difficulty getting her point across). In a wider sense, certain
ways of speaking become established as normal; they affect
the way women and men conventionally relate; and it is partly
through talk that children learn to behave appropriately *as*
girls and *as* boys. One reason why educationists have been
concerned about differences in girls' and boys' spoken language is that gender differences and asymmetrical relationships
between girls and boys are fostered in schools and classrooms,
as in other contexts.

Teachers have a legitimate interest in setting relationships
between girls and boys on a more equal footing, and this is
likely to involve tackling the ways they use language towards
girls and boys and the ways girls and boys use language
towards one another. But language use in schools and
classrooms is only one of a number of means by which
relations between the sexes are structured. It will play its part
alongside girls' and boys' language in other contexts, and also
alongside factors other than spoken language. While language

use is an important focus of attention in the promotion of equal opportunities in the classroom it cannot be tackled in isolation.

The fact that differences between girls and boys are *average* ones is also relevant to teachers who wish to tackle relationships between pupils: a whole variety of relationships is likely to be negotiated through classroom talk, and many of these will interact with gender (in chapter 3 I mentioned pupils' ethnic group as an example of this); on any occasion, some are likely to assume greater importance. Teachers need therefore to be sensitive to differences among girls and among boys.

A further point to take into account is that relationships between girls and boys (and other social relations) are not static. In the longer term, they are subject to change. But, as I mentioned in chapters 2 and 3, they also vary in different contexts (so that a female speaker may be more confident in some contexts, for instance, but less so in others). Teachers concerned to promote equal opportunities need to pay attention to the contexts in which girls and boys interact, to what their goals seem to be, and to the strategies they use to achieve these goals.

The role of talk in establishing and maintaining or challenging a whole variety of social relationships seems to have been marginalized in the National Curriculum for England and Wales, though it has received recognition in materials developed by the Language in the National Curriculum project. In the National Curriculum programmes of study and non-statutory guidance, 'speaking and listening' tend to be viewed as apolitical: as a valuable aid to learning or as a set of useful skills, but not as a means of 'dominating' others or 'giving away power'. This applies to the notion of the standard language in education and to the role of English in relation to minority languages as much as to language and gender. But, in practice, the political aspects of language cannot sensibly be omitted from any consideration of language in education; they are inevitably interlinked with other roles and functions of classroom language. This is a point I shall return to below.

4.3   Talk and Learning

[Oracy is] a condition of learning in all subjects.
Andrew Wilkinson, 1965, *Spoken English*, p. 58

It is as talkers, questioners, arguers, gossips, chatterboxes, that our pupils do much of their most important learning. Their everyday talking voices are the most subtle and versatile means they possess for making sense of what they do and for making sense of others, including their teachers.
Harold Rosen, 1969, 'Towards a language policy across the curriculum', p. 127

Throughout the primary and middle years the change of emphasis from teaching to learning has meant that talk now occupies a position of central importance.
DES, 1975, *A Language for Life* (the Bullock Report), para. 10.10

The value of talk in all subjects as a means of promoting pupils' understanding, and of evaluating their progress, is now widely accepted.
DES/WO, 1989, *English for Ages 5–16* (the 'Cox Report'), para. 15.2

[Pupils'] learning is supported and extended through discussion with peers and adults. Through talk and informal writing they are able to make their ideas clearer to themselves as well as making them available for reflection, discussion and checking.
NCC, 1989b, *Science: non-statutory guidance*, p.A8)

An enormous amount of research has been undertaken which establishes the primary importance of learners being able to talk about their own experience as a starting point for learning. Yet we have an education system where not only is it extremely difficult for half the population to find an opportunity to talk – particularly to the teacher – but where the experience about which they

could talk is seen as inappropriate, as not sufficiently
'interesting' to be talked about.

Dale Spender, 1982, *Invisible Women*, p. 60

Over the past 20–30 years increasing attention has been paid
to talk among pupils and between teachers and pupils as
a means of encouraging active learning. The 1980s saw the
introduction of new forms of oral assessment (such as the
GCSE in England, Wales, and Northern Ireland and Standard
Grade in Scotland); the establishment, in 1987, of a National
Oracy Project in England and Wales; the inclusion of an
Attainment Target for Speaking and Listening in English in
the National Curriculum and for Talking and Listening in
the Scottish programme for English Language 5–14; and the
recognition of the value of talk in curriculum guidance in other
subjects. Such developments have given official recognition
to the place of talk in both the primary and the secondary
curriculum. Given this preoccupation with talk for learning,
one important reason for concern about gender differences
and inequalities, highlighted by Dale Spender, is that if talk
is an important aid to learning, both girls and boys should
have their fair share of it.

The notion of talk for learning and the consequent disadvantage to girls, who, in mixed-sex classes, don't get the chance
to talk, has to be handled with some caution. Girls' educational
disadvantage isn't in terms of some generalized academic
deficiency. On current measures of attainment, girls do as well
as boys overall, often better, in the school years. There is a
host of ways in which we can learn about things, one of
which, clearly, is talking them through with others. But you
can also learn a lot by listening, and maybe by making fewer,
but well-thought-out and well-timed, contributions. It's not
necessarily the case that, merely by talking less, girls are
academically disadvantaged.

Concerns about differences and inequalities in girls' and
boys' talk need to be related to the types of talk that have been
observed and analysed. Many studies discussed in chapter 3
counted the number of turns taken by different participants;
but this tells us nothing about the nature of those turns. For

instance, brief answers to a teacher's question may enable the teacher to check that a pupil has understood something, but whether this is valuable 'talk for learning' is another matter (Douglas Barnes, one of those who has done most to encourage exploratory, problem-solving talk in the classroom, has been quite critical of tightly controlled question and answer sessions (Barnes, 1969)).

Other studies have coded pupils' talk in terms of different categories; but such coding systems still provide only limited information about the quality of pupils' talk, and leave open the question of how valuable an aid to learning this is.

Finding that boys occupy a disproportionate amount of speaking time in the classroom or that certain categories of talk are differentially distributed between girls and boys suggests that something is going on that requires further investigation, but it also suggests that teachers concerned about equal opportunities need to take into account the types of talk in which girls and boys engage as well as girls' and boys' talk in different contexts. Some small-scale studies, such as that conducted by Julie Fisher (see section 3.4), have attempted to examine the quality of girls' and boys' talk. Perhaps further, similar studies will help shed light on the extent to which, and the ways in which, gender differences in language affect pupils' learning in small-group and other types of discussion.

I have argued that one needs to be cautious about interpreting gender differences in language in terms of 'impediments' to girls' learning in any general sense. But this is not to suggest that such differences need give rise to no concern. It seems reasonable to suggest that the opportunity for all kinds of learning should be open to all pupils (the allegation has often been that girls *can't* get to speak). When classroom learning is organized around group discussion and joint exploration of ideas, pupils do need the space to rehearse these ideas and to have them responded to by others; they also need practice in this for more pragmatic reasons, since it is one way in which they will be assessed. In subjects in which many girls lack confidence, such as computing, technology and the physical sciences, class discussion and practical work need to be organized in such a way that girls can take an active part, without being 'crowded out' by boys. At a practical level, it is necessary to monitor talk among pupils and between teachers and pupils and to introduce strategies to ensure that quieter pupils have the chance to participate.

4.4 Girls' and Boys' 'Communication Skills'

English is there, in use all the time, by different groups, in a variety of situations. Let us show children what there is: and, showing them, help them to a wider control and a greater tolerance over other registers, other styles.

Alan Davies, in Wilkinson, 1965, *Spoken English*, p. 38

School could be a place where pupils enriched their resources, because it would be there that they encountered new verbal strategies and were inspired to more ambitious uses of language than those provided outside.

Harold Rosen, 1969, 'Towards a language policy across the curriculum', p. 126

Children should be helped to as wide as possible a range of language uses so that they can speak appropriately in different situations and use standard forms when they are needed.

DES, 1975, *A Language for Life* (the Bullock Report), recommendation 110

In addition to its function as a crucial teaching and learning *method*, talk is also now widely recognised as promoting and embodying a range of skills and competence – both transactional and social – that are central to children's overall language development.

DES/WO, 1989, *English for Ages 5–16* (the 'Cox Report'), para. 15.4

Communication skills, including the ability to talk, listen, explain, understand and develop respect for the views of others, and creative activities involving children in formulating novel ideas and using their imagination, can be encouraged and developed through science.

NCC, 1989b, *Science: non-statutory guidance*, p. C1

Schools have long had an interest in developing pupils'
capacity to use oral language effectively. What this actually
means in practice has varied considerably, from elocution
lessons, for instance, to learning to participate in formal academic debate. More recent preoccupations with pupils' oral
language have been based on the notion of 'communicative
competence': the idea that people vary their speech so as to
speak appropriately in a range of different contexts. Such a
model of adult speech suggests that, during the school years,
pupils need to acquire competence in speaking in a variety of
ways and in a variety of contexts. The model underlies both
attempts to monitor pupils' spoken language (for example,
the Assesment of Performance Unit's national monitoring of
pupils' spoken language at ages 11 and 15) and guidelines
for developing speaking and listening in the classroom (for
instance, in English in the National Curriculum). Within the
National Curriculum it has been translated into the notion of
'communication skills'.

Preoccupations with the need for schools to develop pupils'
'communication skills' have given rise to a second concern
about gender differences in talk: if there are differences in
girls' and boys' speaking styles, both sexes may be unnecessarily restricted; all pupils need to develop a range of ways
of speaking and listening that are appropriate in different
contexts.

Children come to school with certain language varieties and
ways of speaking at their disposal. Some of these will be
further encouraged and extended in school, while others will
be discouraged, or at least disregarded. Deciding which types
of language use to encourage amongst pupils involves making
a value judgement;it involves considering what kinds of language use are most appropriate for pupils in class, in certain
out-of-school contexts, and in preparation for adult life.

Teachers following an examination syllabus or basing their
work on Statements of Attainment such as those specified in
the National Curriculum for England and Wales may seem to
have had such judgements made for them. But the guidance
given to teachers and the criteria themselves tend to be vague.
Statements of Attainment such as

- Participate as speakers and listeners in a group engaged in a given task (*English in the National Curriculum*, Attainment Target 1: Speaking and listening, Statement for Level 2a)

leave a lot of discretion to the teacher to decide what level and type of participation count as appropriate.

Even statements that look more precise, such as

- Take an active part in group discussion, contributing constructively to the development of the argument

and

- Take an active part in group discussion, contributing constructively to the sustained development of the argument (*English in the National Curriculum*, Attainment Target 1: Speaking and listening, Statements for Level 7c and 8c)

leave open what counts as 'active' and 'constructive' and what distinguishes a 'sustained development' from a 'development'. Similar points can be made about statements of attainment for English language in the Scottish Development Programme and the Northern Ireland Curriculum. Teachers' own judgements about the value of different types of talk are still important, therefore, and this is likely to include judgements about the types of talk deemed appropriate for girls and boys.

English for Ages 5 to 16 (the 'Cox Report') sees some features associated with girls' speech and others associated with boys' speech as beneficial to each sex, depending on the context:

In some tasks, the more direct way of speaking that is more common to boys will be advantageous; in others, the more tentative approach more frequently found in girls will be more appropriate. (DES/WO, 1989, para. 11.15)

This is an additive model of competence: it implies that speakers can simply add on new skills or new ways of speaking to those they already have. It also implies that girls and boys will use the same ways of speaking to similar effect. But the situation is less straightforward than Cox suggests, and poses something of a dilemma for teachers. If they encourage 'gender-appropriate', talk they will necessarily be restricting the range of ways of speaking available to pupils. But in encouraging a similar range of speaking styles for both sexes – the 'androgynous' approach advocated by Cox – they may be departing from social conventions. It is not clear that girls' 'direct' speech will be perceived in the same way as boys', or that it will have the same communicative effect. A similar point applies to 'tentative' speech. The same expressions are likely to be perceived differently, depending on who utters them. An expression that is 'hesitant' or 'uncertain' in a girl may be defined as 'cautious' when uttered by a boy. The point can be extended to other aspects of language; a boy's working-class accent may be accepted as normal, for instance, whereas a girl's is more negatively evaluated. A girl's interruption may be regarded as pushy whereas a boy's escapes attention.

Teachers clearly do need to extend pupils' communicative abilities; but this has to be handled sensitively, in the knowledge of the social meanings attached to language. A 'communication skills' approach suggests that language can somehow be tackled in isolation, as a discrete parcel of skills that speakers have at their disposal. It neglects the fact that, in extending the range of speaking styles available to girls and boys or changing the way they talk, teachers are also challenging the ways girls and boys conventionally relate to others. The issue goes far beyond language.

4.5   Assessing Speaking and Listening

Children should be judged on what they can do and on what they know, not on who they are.
But
The possibility of bias arises especially in the assessment of oracy, because of the difficulty of separating pupils' spoken language from perceptions of their personality and background.
DES/WO, 1989, *English for Ages 5 to 16* (the 'Cox Report'),
paras 11.9 and 11.11

The fact that we tend to set a different value on different types of talk has implications for how girls' and boys' spoken language is assessed. On the one hand, the speaking styles conventionally adopted by girls or boys may advantage or disadvantage them in oral assessment. Conversely, if the *same* expression or choice of accent or conversational technique is differently evaluated in girls and boys, this again may affect the way girls' and boys' talk is assessed. Some forms of oral assessment involve children talking in groups or pairs. There are problems in assessing an individual as a member of a group; the fact that speakers have to work together to construct a sequence of talk makes it difficult to allocate responsibility to any individual for the way the talk develops. And some forms of contribution, while vital to the development of a discussion, may receive less attention from assessors. This gives rise to a third concern about gender differences: that differences in girls' and boys' spoken language use and differences in the evaluation of girls' and boys' spoken language may lead to injustices in assessment.

We have as yet little evidence of the relationship between girls' and boys' language use and their performance in oral assessment. The Assessment of Performance Unit (APU) monitored the language performance of pupils in England, Wales, and Northern Ireland from 1979 through the 1980s. At first, the Unit confined its attentions to reading and writing, but from 1982 surveys of spoken language were carried out. Looking at the results across all tasks, these surveys have found no significant difference between the performances of girls and boys. This contrasts with writing, in which every survey has shown a significant difference in favour of girls, and reading, where several surveys have shown a significant difference in favour of girls.

While the APU surveys found no overall differences between girls' and boys' spoken language performance, some individual tasks did show a gender difference. For instance, in the 1982 survey a task requiring an 'adversarial' style of speaking favoured boys; but this finding was not replicated consistently in subsequent surveys. One task produced a gender difference consistently in all surveys; this was a task with a high 'technological' content, which favoured boys (Gorman *et al.*, 1988). It is likely that the content of an assessment task will affect girls' and boys' performance; for talk is always about something, and in practice it is difficult, if not impossible, to separate someone's communicative ability from their knowledge of a particular topic. We need more evidence of the extent to which girls' and boys' performance differs on different tasks and in different contexts.

A problem in interpreting the APU surveys is that much of the assessment was carried out on pairs of pupils, and pairs were normally single-sex (since they were self-selected). For some tasks, groups were produced by combining two pairs, and in this case half the groups were single-sex and half mixed. Published accounts of the surveys don't make any comparison between pupils' performance in single-sex or mixed-sex groups. Nor was any analysis undertaken of the speaking styles adopted in different groups.

One more recent study of oral assessment in a GCSE English examination suggests that girls' speaking styles put them at something of a disadvantage in this context. Jenny Cheshire and Nancy Jenkins looked at differences in girls' and boys' performance in the interpersonal skills component of oral assessment (their study is reported in a two-part paper: Cheshire and Jenkins, 1991, and Jenkins and Cheshire, 1990). 'Interpersonal skills' in this context meant being able to manage a conversation effectively: listening and responding to others, helping to sustain the talk, being able to follow another's argument, and so on. Some of the interaction features more commonly found in female speakers seemed particularly suited to this aspect of oral assessment, so Cheshire and Jenkins felt that girls might be at an advantage in this part of the oral examination. They analysed the talk in three mixed-sex groups, focusing on pupils' use of minimal responses, such as 'Yes' or 'Mmh', which signal attention; interruptions; questions used to draw other speakers into the discussion; contributions that build on the contributions of others; ways of introducing new topics; and remarks that tend to close down discussion.

Looking simply at the forms of speech used, Cheshire and Jenkins found that girls tended to use more features associated with female speakers and that might be expected to support the conversation; thus they used more minimal responses and questions, and when introducing new topics, they frequently framed these as questions, inviting others' participation. Boys, on the other hand, interrupted more frequently, and used more remarks that closed down conversation. Both girls and boys made contributions that built on the contributions of others. These general findings, however, mask the variability that Cheshire and Jenkins also found between girls, between boys, and between different groups. Use of minimal responses provides an example of this variability.

In two groups, girls used significantly more minimal responses, such as 'Yes' or 'Mmh', than boys. In the other group, minimal responses were more evenly divided between girls and boys, but boys used them to different effect – as a prelude to their own contribution, which frequently came in the form of an interruption.

Cheshire and Jenkins also asked teachers to assess and comment on girls' and boys' performance in their oral discussion groups. They found that teachers' marks did not always reflect the degree of support girls had given to conversations. On the basis of their research, Cheshire and Jenkins suggest that:

- The ability of a candidate to do well in group discussion depends as much on the other members of the group as on his or her own contribution.
- The girls in these groups played a key role in maintaining the discussion, supporting each other and the boys, but these skills were not always reflected in the marks they received; instead they benefited the group as a whole.
- Teachers appeared to expect the girls to play a sustaining role in discussion, and they penalized them if they did not do so. The teachers seemed to judge the girls by very strict criteria which they did not always apply to the boys.

Cheshire and Jenkins's study is small scale and looks at oral assessment in only one context; more evidence is needed of assessment in other contexts. But the study does suggest that teachers need to monitor carefully how girls and boys contribute to talk designed for oral assessment, as well as the values set by assessors on different types of talk.

4.6   The Multifunctional Nature of Talk

So far I have treated separately the role of talk in establishing and maintaining relationships; the role of talk in learning; and talk as a set of communication skills that need to be developed and that may be assessed. But in practice the different functions of talk are more closely integrated. I mentioned above the impossibility, in assessment, of separating a speaker's 'communication skills' from his or her knowledge of a particular subject. When people speak, they are normally doing several jobs at the same time. Pupils engaging in problem-solving talk, or talk that leads to the completion of a task are also relating in a certain way to one another, perhaps getting on well together or trying to take control or acquiescing in someone else's control. When considering the educational value of pupils' talk, there may be conflicts of interest between the different roles that talk fulfils.

The transcripts of talk below provide an example of this. They come from a video recording made by the Cumbria Oracy Project (1988) for their in-service materials *Talking Sense*. The video recording shows two pairs of children: an older pair, Ruth and James, and a younger pair, Alice and Richard. Both pairs of children have been set a task: to build a crane together. Alice and Richard collaborate well, and produce quite an impressive crane. Ruth and James, on the other hand, collaborate less well; they fall out, and their crane is far less impressive.

TRANSCRIPT 1: RUTH AND JAMES

Ruth: Now what do we need? (*really talking to herself*)
James: Bring it over here, then I can reach.
Ruth: Alright . . . bring it over here . . . How many of them do we need?

James: Er . . . How big do we want it? . . . About that high?

Ruth: I think a bit bigger.

James: OK.

Ruth: Only if you want it . . . Whoops . . . (*as she tries to join a piece and it slips*)

James: (*mumbles*) . . . Ruth . . . get two er . . .

Ruth: Shall we make it bigger . . . How big do you want it? (Is this where she gives him the green light to become the 'boss'?)

James: About that high.

Ruth: I'll see what I can find.

James: It keeps falling down.

Ruth: About there I think.

James: Mm . . . one layer higher.

Ruth: You're beating me . . . There that high I think . . . now we need the roof on . . .

James: I need one of those.

Ruth: How do you stick the thread? . . . You have to tie it . . . You have to tie it onto the . . .

James: Snap it.

Ruth: No you don't.

James: Yes we do . . . you snap it when you've decided how long you need it.

Ruth: I'm not . . . he is (*in answer to a question about arguing from the other pair*)

James: Put it here about.

Ruth: (*whispered*) Oh you're daft.

James: (*whispered*) Now we need . . . (*normal voice*) We need that . . . right . . . snap it.

Ruth: What'll you do?

James: Snap it.

Ruth: How are we going to get the cog wheel to turn it round?

James: Aw . . . (*in disgust*) Turn it onto that.

Ruth: We need . . . we need the thread . . . cause . . .

James: There you are.

Alice: (*from the other pair*) Are you helping him, Ruth?

James: Not really.

Ruth: Now we need . . . Is it one way? . . . Come here.

James: (*petulantly*) Well I'd like to see you do it any better.

Ruth: You don't put that . . . in . . . to that . . . cos it doesn't go in. You need one of . . .

James: Does . . . does, does, does.

Ruth: You need one of these . . . you need . . . you need one of these.

James: OK clever clogs, it does doesn't it?

Ruth: No, one of these.

James: Then you get . . . Don't do it like that.

Ruth: Then how do you get . . . They're getting on well (*looking at the other two*) . . . We need one of these things to go in there.

James: (*disdainfully*) Oh yes . . . an axle . . . Clever . . . Very, very clever.

Ruth: (*seemingly ignoring the tone of voice*) How do you get that out? Hey . . . How?

James: Easy . . . you do that . . . and you've got it out.

From this point, things got worse, with comments like 'Stop moaning' and 'You're useless' and pieces getting broken off the crane.

TRANSCRIPT 2: ALICE AND RICHARD

Alice: We need those green bars don't we? What else do we need?

Richard: Not those screws . . . you need . . . We need the big screws.

Alice: Oh dear.

Richard: Yes we do.

Alice: Those bits.

Richard: (*showing her what he is doing*) Do that . . . you've got to do that . . . Do that . . . Right . . . Then we get this bit so you can make . . .

Alice: Richard . . . I've got those.

Richard: Good . . . A big screw.

Alice: There should be lots of them . . . Ah here's one.

Richard: Thanks . . . I need another one.

Alice: I'll screw this side . . .

Richard: Good . . . let's just . . . Take that . . . take that one again . . . I don't think we need that.

Alice: I put that in the wrong way round, I did.

Richard: The one in the wrong way round.

Alice: (*laughs*)

Richard: You've got to put them that way . . . you've got to put them that way.

Alice:	Oh . . . Richard.
Richard:	Screw them on tight.
Alice:	Oh, now to do that . . . one done . . . now we need that one undone.
Richard:	Put the screw on tight.
Alice:	Oh dear . . . What am I doing? . . . Are you helping him Ruth? . . . Are you putting the wheels on already?
Richard:	Yes . . . I'm putting the wheels on.
Alice:	Now what do I need? . . . I need . . .
Richard:	You . . . you need one of those and then you can screw . . . a little screw . . .
Alice:	Those?
Richard:	Yes . . . a little screw.
Alice:	One of those?
Richard:	Yes.
Alice:	Well I can't find one . . . Those . . . I know . . . Those . . . OK . . . Is this one? Do you need to put that on?
Richard:	Wrong way round.
Alice:	Oh . . . is it? . . . Now what do I do?
Richard:	You put that through there and screw it on with this box.
Alice:	Oh dear . . . I can't get this stupid thing on . . . Oh . . . gone wrong . . . I can't do this.
Richard:	Just do it.
Alice:	Oh yes I can . . . Now what do I do? . . . Do I do it? . . . Oh dear . . . I've put the big screw in.

Richard was always patient and explained to Alice without complaint when she needed help. They made a lovely crane together. (Cumbria Oracy Project, 1988, pp. 63–5)

In their brief opening commentary on the video extract, Cumbria Oracy Project (1988) notes:

It is interesting in this extract to compare the very different ways in which the two pairs work and the very different attitudes of the two boys to the girls.

The younger pair work together well and when Alice says, 'Oh dear, I can't do this,' Richard says, 'You can.' With his encouragement, she succeeds. The older pair don't work so well together. James seems to think that he can do better than Ruth, who is determined to prove him wrong. When things don't go exactly to plan, they immediately blame each other, while Richard and Alice continue to talk their way through the work and help and encourage each other. (p. 63)

The transcripts seem to me to be particularly interesting in their own right, but the comment provided by the Cumbria Oracy Project, which seems to set a higher value on Alice and Richard's talk is also interesting. Initially, I shared the assessment of the authors; in terms of using talk to help construct their crane, Alice and Richard do get on very well. Alice is often uncertain of what to do. She questions Richard, and Richard provides guidance. Ruth and James, on the other hand, are sometimes in competition with one another, and quarrel over how to attach certain pieces to build their crane.

On closer examination, however, there seem to be similarities as well as contrasts between the two pieces of talk. The Cumbria Oracy Project comments on the fact that James becomes 'the " boss" '. There's also a suggestion that Ruth 'gives [James] the green light', but that later she tries to stop him from taking control. There does seem to be a tension in the way that Ruth participates in the interaction. She is willing to give way to James: 'I think a bit bigger,' but 'Only if you want it.' She also tries to collaborate: 'Shall we make it bigger? How big do you want it?' 'I'll see what I can find.' But she puts forward her own suggestions for constructing the crane: 'About there I think'; 'We need . . . we need the thread.' She also challenges James when she thinks he is doing something wrong: 'You don't put that . . . in . . . to that . . . cos it doesn't go in.'

In the Alice and Richard extract, it seems to me that Richard is firmly in control; he is a more effective 'boss' than James, perhaps because his control is maintained collaboratively. Alice frequently asks Richard for advice or assistance (13 of her contributions are questions that seem to have this function). Other contributions reflect Alice's lack of confidence: 'Oh dear'; 'I put that in the wrong way round, I did'; 'Oh dear . . . I can't get this stupid thing on . . . Oh . . . gone wrong . . . I can't do this.' Richard takes the lead, responding to Alice's questions and advising her, but also using her as a helper.

So far, I have considered the talk on its own, but because the sequence was video-recorded it is possible to look at some of the non-verbal interaction. The positioning of the camera was such that this is easier to observe consistently for Ruth and James than for Alice and Richard. Below is a brief extract – the first few seconds of the interaction between Ruth and James – in which I have added two 'non-verbal' columns to the transcript. These show the activities engaged in by Ruth and James alongside their talk.

TRANSCRIPT 3: RUTH AND JAMES SHOWING NON-VERBAL BE-HAVIOUR

Dialogue	Action	
Ruth and James	Ruth	James
	Watching J.	Holding base + 1 Lego piece.
Ruth: Now what do we need?		
		Attaches piece to base.
James: Bring it over here, then I can reach.	Turns to box, picks up piece.	Turns to box, holds out hand.
Ruth: Alright.		Takes piece from R.
Ruth: Bring it over here.	Points to floor near her.	Attaches piece to base to start crane.
		Pushes crane to R.
	Takes crane. Other hand in box.	Puts hand in box.
	Watches J., one hand on box and one on floor.	Takes crane. Attaches another piece.
Ruth: How many of them do we need?	Feels in box for more pieces.	
	Hand on crane, turns towards her.	One hand on crane, the other in box.
	Attaches piece at opposite end to J's.	Adds another piece.

James initially takes the flat Lego piece that will form the base of the crane, and begins adding pieces to one side. He takes one piece from Ruth to help him. Ruth has to ask firmly for the base to be put nearer to her (emphasizing the request with a gesture towards the appropriate spot) so that she can reach it. The base is now between the two children, each of whom has access to one side. But James has already added four pieces to his side before Ruth is able to begin on hers. This means not only that James is in the lead (at a later point in the transcript, Ruth comments that he is beating her), but also that he has set a pattern for the construction that Ruth begins to mirror on her side of the base. All this happens very quickly, but it shows that James's attempts at control and Ruth's acquiescence, as well as her attempts at resistance, are exercised non-verbally as well as verbally.

I find it very hard to set a value on these two extracts of talk. Alice's and Richard's talk is collaborative, and they produce a better crane. Alice has probably learnt something about using construction materials. But she has also learnt, in a small way, to act as an apprentice. Ruth's and James's talk is much less collaborative. It is not clear how much they have learnt about constructing cranes, although trying things out and getting them wrong may be an effective means of learning. The children are undoubtedly frustrated; but Ruth has made some attempt to resist James's control of the construction activity.

The extracts of talk suggest that one cannot consider certain aspects of talk (the use of talk for learning or talk as 'communication skills') in isolation from everything else that goes on when children interact. Nor, ideally, should one consider talk in isolation from the non-verbal component of a communication, though in practice it is difficult to take full account of non-verbal behaviour. One might also wish to question the value set on collaborative talk and 'successful' completion of an activity. Collaboration, or at least an absence of conflict, seems to underlie many Statements of Attainment in English in the National Curriculum. Perhaps we need to reconsider the value of talk as a means of resistance.

4.7 Some Implications

The variety of functions that girls' and boys' talk fulfils in the classroom has a number of practical implications for teaching and learning, as well as for assessment, to do both with contextual factors that affect talk and with the need to pay attention to talk itself. Below are implications that occur to me. I have phrased these as questions, as points to consider in planning classroom activities that involve talk.

Planning contexts for talk

- How are pupils grouped for collaborative work or discussion? Can pupils be grouped so that quieter pupils have the confidence to contribute? On the other hand, it may be important for pupils to learn to work in a range of different groupings.
- How is the content of group discussion decided? Can this be made interesting to all pupils? Can discussion take account of the full range of pupils' experiences? Can contexts be monitored so that different pupils have the chance to be 'experts'?

Focusing on teacher and pupil talk

- How do teachers respond to girls and boys? How much time and attention are given by teachers to different pupils? But also, what *type* of attention is given? Does 'attention' for some pupils relate mainly to discipline, for instance?
- What different teaching and learning strategies are used in class? How can all pupils have access to a range of ways of learning?

- What types of talk take place in different subject areas? Do some of these seem to favour girls or boys? How/when should girls and boys be encouraged to adopt alternative speaking styles?
- What values are set on different types of talk? How are criteria for speaking and listening interpreted? Do criteria seem to favour girls or boys?

These implications are, necessarily, couched in rather general terms. How one actually responds to girls' and boys' talk will vary from one context to another. Several teachers have made attempts to introduce equal opportunities for girls and boys both in and through classroom talk. I shall discuss such strategies in chapter 9, as a more concrete illustration of some of the implications I have mentioned.

4.8 Conclusion

This chapter has considered gender differences in spoken language in relation to four important educational issues that have been highlighted by recent curricular developments in the UK: the role of talk in establishing (often unequal) relations between girls and boys, the importance of talk for pupils' learning, the requirement that all pupils develop a range of 'communication skills', and the requirement for teachers to assess pupils' speaking and listening. The points I have made include the following:

- Asymmetrical relations between girls and boys are established in the classroom, as in other contexts; the classroom is one place in which they may be challenged.
- Given the importance of talk for learning, there is a concern that girls may be disadvantaged because they participate less in mixed-sex discussion. We

need more evidence on how gender differences in talk relate to pupils' learning; but it is clear that a range of learning styles should be open to all pupils.

- There is a fear that girls' and boys' speaking styles may be too restrictive and a concern that all pupils should develop a range of 'communication skills'. In encouraging pupils to develop a range of ways of speaking, teachers need to take account of the social meanings and social functions of talk.

- Another concern is that differences in girls' and boys' speaking styles may lead to inequalities in oral assessment. Different types of assessment may discriminate against girls or boys; there is limited evidence that girls' 'supportive' styles may disadvantage them in certain contexts. More evidence is needed on explicit and implicit criteria in oral assessment that may favour girls or boys.

- In practice, talk is 'multifunctional', it fulfils a variety of functions (learning, maintaining a relationship, and so forth) simultaneously. Setting a value on talk is difficult because there may be 'conflicts of interest' between these different functions.

I have emphasized the need for teachers to monitor what goes on in their own classrooms. Such monitoring is necessary, because more detailed evidence is needed on girls' and boys' speaking styles in certain classroom contexts, such as small-group discussion; on precisely how gender differences affect children's use of talk for learning; and on the value set on girls' and boys' talk. Some sort of monitoring of what is going on is a necessary precursor to the introduction of equal opportunities initiatives. Monitoring is also necessary to evaluate the success of such initiatives. Guidance on observing and monitoring girls' and boys' speaking is provided in chapter 8.

The issues raised in this chapter also have implications for teachers who wish to promote equal opportunities in classroom talk. I have suggested some points to bear in mind when planning talk activities. Specific equal opportunities initiatives are discussed in chapter 9.

5

Equal Representation?

> To secure implementation of the programmes of study,
> schools will need to ensure that materials are varied,
> come from a wide range of sources and comply with
> policy on equal opportunities.
>
> NCC, 1989a, *English Key Stage 1 non-statutory guidance*,
> p. B3

5.1 Introduction

Previous chapters have focused on differences and inequalities
in girls' and boys' spoken language. This chapter turns to
children's reading material: to the words and images that
confront girls and boys in school-books and other print
resources. In chapter 3 I discussed ways in which spoken
language in the classroom might be said to be discriminatory
(in the main, there has been concern that it discriminates
against girls). School-books are also discriminatory in that
there is an (unjustifiable) imbalance in the way women and
men, and girls and boys are represented. Many analyses of
books have looked at language use: for instance, how female
and male characters in stories are described. But there is a
variety of other ways in which female and male images are
represented in books.

When considering imbalances in books and printed
material, it is necessary to take account of how females and
males are represented on several levels; for instance, in stories
it is important to consider the number and type of female
and male characters and how they are represented visually
as well as in the printed word. Just as, in the classroom,

verbal language is only one way in which relations are negotiated, so language in children's books works alongside other ways of representing people. These can also be thought of as communicating systems, communicating sets of social values.

I've referred to books *and printed material* because of the obvious point that children don't just read books. Most studies of gender imbalances have looked at books – a large number have focused on reading books and story-books – but there is evidence of very similar imbalances in other print resources used by children. In this chapter I shall focus on children's books, the sorts of books that are available in school, because that is where much of the evidence comes from. I shall also draw a parallel between gender imbalances in children's books and in other print resources, using assessment material as a main example.

I mentioned that gender imbalances are often unjustifiable and discriminatory. People normally write about imbalances in terms of 'sexism' or 'sexist bias' in books. I shall look at the different types of study that have been carried out and at what aspects of books and resources have been identified as sexist. As in chapter 3, it seems worth raising such methodological issues; for teachers concerned to introduce equal opportunities will need to make a decision about what counts as sexist, both in selecting new resources and in monitoring resources that are already available.

Educationists have been concerned about sexism in print resources because of the local, or immediate effects this may have; for instance, the predominance of male examples in science textbooks may suggest to girls that science isn't really for them; in assessment tasks, girls or boys may be disadvantaged, depending on whether 'male' or 'female' experiences are drawn upon. But there is also a concern about continuing, more general effects: that the female and male images conveyed to pupils contribute to their sense of what is normal for girls and boys and women and men in our society; that children's reading material helps reinforce gender as a social division, and perpetuates inequalities between girls and boys and women and men. Such concerns underlie the studies of reading material discussed in this chapter and also several studies of children's writing discussed in chapter 6. I shall consider the educational implications of stereotyped imagery in reading and writing in more detail in chapter 7.

5.2   Images in Children's Books

The department had just spent a large sum on a 'new' maths scheme, which although claiming to be 'good maths' had not been monitored for racism or sexism. The new books portrayed very few girls or black pupils; the strong message being given was that maths is a subject studied by white boys.

Geraldine Scanlan, 1986, 'Was your mother good at maths?', p. 15

Cinderella took off her apron and ran to see the prince. As soon as the glass slipper was slipped on Cinderella's foot, she became a lovely princess once more. 'Will you marry me?' asked the prince, delighted to find his love. 'Oh, yes,' replied Cinderella, her heart filled with joy.

Studio Publications, 1988, *Cinderella*, pp. 21–2

There was Prince Ronald. He looked at her and said, 'Elizabeth, you are a mess! You smell like ashes, your hair is all tangled and you are wearing a dirty old paper bag. Come back when you are dressed like a real princess.'

'Ronald,' said Elizabeth, 'your clothes are really pretty and your hair is very neat. You look like a real prince, but you are a toad.' They didn't get married after all.

Robert Munsch, 1980, *The Paper Bag Princess*

If picture books portrayed all women as weight lifters or bus drivers, that would be silly, but we could all benefit from a wider and more realistic view of women's roles.

Julia Hodgeon, 1985, 'Holding a mirror: considerations of book provision', p. 40

Any survey of the print resources available to children, both in school and out, will show an imbalance in the representation of females and males that is consistent with the imbalance found more generally in the mass media. During the 1970s and 1980s several analyses were carried out of children's stories, reading schemes, textbooks, and information books used in schools across a variety of subjects. The overall pattern that emerged was:

- Males simply feature more often than females as characters in stories and as illustrations and examples in textbooks. There are more men than women and more boys than girls; there are even more male than female animals. Some stories have no female characters. There are rarely stories with no male characters.
- It tends to be males who take on leading roles or feature as main characters; females often play secondary roles.
- Males are more active than females. They simply do more things; in stories they have more adventures, and they go further away from home. Females are more passive; they are often dependent; in stories they often need to be helped or rescued and so on.
- Males feature in a wider range of activities than females.
- Female characters in stories are often restricted to traditional, stereotyped roles: playing at home, doing the housework, helping with the housework, and so on.
- In information books, women's experiences and their contributions to society are often unacknowledged or undervalued.

Children's Rights Workshop (1976) contains three studies of children's books carried out in the early 1970s. Other studies from the same period are reviewed in Sara Goodman Zimet, 1976, and a further selection, up to 1981, is summarized in Rosemary Stones, 1983.

These early studies led to an increased awareness of gender

imbalances, and there have been some attempts by writers and publishers to correct the more obvious examples. More recent work, however, shows that gender imbalances persist in children's books. I shall look at one or two studies as examples of the range of work that has been carried out.

5.3 Studies of Children's Books – Some Examples

There have been several initiatives to interest girls in the physical sciences, since girls have tended to opt out of these in the later stages of secondary schooling (I mentioned the GIST initiative in chapter 3). Alongside such initiatives have come studies that scrutinize books and other materials to see if the images they contain might deter girls from studying science.

Therese Hardy, a primary school teacher in Nottingham, analysed the *Look* primary science scheme, developed in 1981 but still in use when she wrote (1989). She found that only slightly more boys than girls were represented in illustrations, and that both girls and boys were shown carrying out a wide range of tasks. When adults were shown, however, the picture was somewhat different; there were many more examples of men than women; women were shown in non-stereotyped occupations – for instance, a scientist and a pilot – but they were also frequently shown to be incompetent or silly. Furthermore, animals and objects that were personified tended to convey male images. Hardy comments:

The dominance of males combined with the 'silliness' and incompetence of those females represented may be reinforcing the message which girls are already receiving, that science is not for them. (Hardy, 1989, p. 30)

Hardy also felt that the applications of scientific concepts discussed in the *Look* scheme tended to appeal to boys' interests and experiences more than girls'. The applications for 'Trapped Air', for instance, included items such as car tyres, air-cushion vehicles, inflated balls (footballs), and aircraft cab-ins (p. 31).

Continuing gender imbalances have been found in other areas of the curriculum, including areas in which girls tend to do well. Carolyn Baker and Peter Freebody (1989) analysed a corpus of 163 beginning reading books currently used in schools in New South Wales, Australia. Many of these books were identical to, or adaptations of, books published in other English-speaking countries: the UK, the USA, Canada, and New Zealand. Baker and Freebody's analysis is wide-ranging, covering several aspects of the text of the reading books, but not the illustrations. Much of their analysis concerns the frequency of occurrence of different words and the associ-ations of different words (that is, which other words they go alongside). These are taken as indicators of the way in which females and males are represented in the corpus of books. In terms of gender, they found that the word *boy/s* appeared more frequently than the word *girl/s*, by a ratio of three to two. There was a similar discrepancy in the appearance of boys' and girls' proper names. Furthermore, whereas a girl was equally likely to appear singly or with other girls, a boy was more likely to appear as an individual character. Mothers and fathers were more or less equally represented, fathers only slightly more than mothers; and there was a high number of grandmothers (but not grandfathers). Girl and boy characters were associated with different activities. Baker and Freebody identify what they term 'the cuddle factor': 'the portrayal of females as being associated with more emotional and less physically energetic activities' (p. 54). Girls are more fre-quently described as *little*, and they are associated with *young*, *dancing*, and *pretty*. Boys, on the other hand, are associated with *sad*, *kind*, *brave*, *tiny*, and *naughty*. Mothers and fathers, while they appear in almost equal numbers, are associated with rather sterotyped activities: fathers with *paint*, *pump*, *fix*, *drive* (a car), *pull*, *start* (a car), *water* (the garden), and *light* (a fire); mothers with *bake* (a cake), *dress* (a child), *hug* (a child), *kiss* (a child), *pack* (bags), *pick* (flowers), *set* (the table), *splash* and *thank* (a teacher) (p. 55). Baker and Freebody comment:

With the possible exception of *splash* and *thank*, these gender-exclusive activities demonstrate first the cuddle factor, and second a fairly stereotyped presentation of the mothers' chores in the house. Mothers are more firmly located in emotion-related activities, through this set of verbs, while the only gender-exclusive verb of a vaguely emotional nature associated with fathers is the verb *pat* (the dog). (Baker and Freebody, 1989, pp. 55–56)

Linda Harland (1985) analysed two reading schemes in use in many British classrooms: *Ginn 360* and *One Two Three and Away*. She looked at the numbers of female and male characters and at the activities they were depicted as carrying out. In *Ginn 360* she found the following representation of female and male activities:

Women's/girls' roles	*Men's/boys' roles*
washing clothes	playing football
housework	driving a car
preparing food	cleaning a car
skipping	out at work
teaching	piloting helicopters
in a wheelchair	playing with a train set
rescuing	gardening
	working with animals
	policeman
	demolition crane-driver
	building-site workers
	playing with spaceship
	making signs
	forester
	postman
	inventors
	airport workers
	bulldozer-driver

(Harland, 1985, p. 32)

Harland gives a closer account of four stories from one of *Ginn 360*'s books, *Across the Seas*:

The first story is about an Indian boy, Ram, a wise and talented older brother, with a younger sister, Deepti, whose only role in this tale is to think 'he was the best artist in all India'. Story two is about a boy and girl living on the coast of France. The girl is rescued from the perils of the sea by the boy's astuteness. In the third story no women appear at all, and in the fourth story, featuring a boy and his relationship with a male animal, human and animal mothers are mentioned incidentally. (p. 32)

The picture in *One Two Three and Away* is no better. In the original series, the main characters are three white boys and one white girl, the sister of one of the boys. More recently, three Asian characters have been added, two boys and a girl. Of the twelve books that constitute the core of the scheme:

We find that in four of these books no women appear at all; in six of these books women appear either as mothers providing tea or scolding the boys after their adventures, or as onlookers. Jennifer [one of the main characters] is to be seen occasionally holding her skipping rope, hovering on the edge, and staying out of trouble. The only book in which she takes a leading role is one where she looks, listens, and follows a cat through the wood at night, while wearing a nightdress – hardly the kit for action. (p. 33)

Harland claims that reading such books has a negative effect on children; it affects how they see themselves as girls and boys; it hampers their 'fullest intellectual and social development' (p. 33).

In parallel with studis of science books, reading schemes, and other series, there have been attempts to document the selection of books and other materials that are available in particular schools and classrooms. Julia Hodgeon (1985) analysed the 50 most popular books in a nursery. The imbalance in numbers of female and male characters and the stereotyped portrayal of characters were similar to what other studies have found – though Hodgeon identified nine books she felt had gone some way towards presenting alternative images. Bridget Baines (1985) followed up a complaint from some girls in her third-year secondary English class that they only ever read books about boys. She looked through her third-year stock and found that, apart from *Jane Eyre*, 'No other book in the whole of the third-year stock had even one major female character – girls and women might almost not have existed'

(p. 47). Baines charted the books that had been provided by the school, which her class had read since their arrival at the school and found that not one child had read a book with a female leading character, most books had male leads, and a few had male and female leading characters.

A further problem with respect to older pupils who have begun studying 'literature' is the dearth of books by female writers that are selected for study. Heather Morris carried out an analysis of authors included in the 1988 GCSE English 'Advisory book lists' (looking across all six examining boards). She found that 79 per cent of all prose writing and 98.68 per cent of drama was written by men (cited by National Association for the Teaching of English (NATE) Language and Gender Committee, 1988, p. 9). NATE Language and Gender Committee also analysed the representation of women poets in 14 school anthologies (see table 5.1 overleaf).

The Language and Gender Committee comment on their findings:

The table . . . does reveal a startling imbalance, not only in the poets chosen for study, but also in the editorial voices who have compiled the selections. Women have very rarely been given the opportunity to select such anthologies. It is important to bear in mind how much taste can account for the lack of inclusion of women's work, rather than any lack of intrinsic merit, or even the availability of work by women. (1988, p. 10)

5.4 Girl-Friendly Problems?

'If it takes three men two days to dig six holes . . .'

The SAT materials will be as free as possible from overt and covert gender bias. Every effort will be made to ensure that the materials avoid ethnic and cultural bias and do not disadvantage children from the ethnic minorities.
SEAC, 1990, *Specification for the Development of Standard Assessment Tasks in the Core Subjects for Pupils at the End of the First Key Stage of the National Curriculum*, p. 2)

Table 5.1 *Analysis of 14 school anthologies of poetry*

Anthology	Men	Women	Total	% Women
Here Today, Modern Poems introduced by Ted Hughes (1963)	44	1	45	2.2
Poets of Our Time, ed. F. E. S. Finn (1965)	11	0	11	0
Nine Modern Poets, ed. E. L. Black (1966)	9	0	9	0
Poetry 1900–1965, ed. G. Macbeth (1967)	21	2	23	8.7
Voices 3, ed. G. Summerfield (1968)	83	9	92	9.8
Touchstones 4, ed. M. and P. Benton (1971)	59	3	62	4.8
Touchstones 5, ed. M. and P. Benton (1971)	64	5	69	7.2
Dragons Teeth, ed. E. Williams (1972)	59	2	61	3.3
Worlds, Seven Modern Poets, ed. G. Summerfield (1974)	7	0	7	0
Telescope, ed. E. Williams (1974)	70	4	74	5.4
The New Dragon Book of Verse, ed. M. Harrison and C. Stuart-Clark (1977)	92	6	98	6.1
Strictly Private, ed. R. McGough (1981)	50	16	66	24.2
Rattlebag, ed. Seamus Heaney and Ted Hughes (1982)	127	10	137	7.8
Speaking to You, ed. M. Rosen and D. Jackson (1984)	43	19	62	30.6

Source: NATE Language and Gender Committee, 1988, p. 9

In sections 5.2 and 5.3 I have focused on the representation of girls and boys and women and men in children's books. But concern has been expressed about other resources available to children in school, where there are similar imbalances in female and male images. One particular interest has been in the wording and examples used in assessment tasks, because of the assumption that gender bias may have a detrimental effect on girls' or boys' performance. Predictably, given the direction of imbalances in school resources generally, much of the concern centres on subjects in which girls tend to lack confidence, such as the physical sciences and mathematics; but gender imbalances in assessment tasks have been found across subject areas.

The Fawcett Society carried out a study of 1986 GCE examination papers for a wide range of subjects. They found that one or two examining boards were attempting to construct papers that avoided sexism, but that, despite this, the papers examined had an 'overpoweringly masculine flavour'. It was rare for papers to achieve a balance in the inclusion of males and females; people were often represented in terms of stereotypes; and male interests predominated (Fawcett Society, 1987, p. 38). The specific forms of gender imbalance differed according to the subject-matter of the paper. For instance:

- Mathematics questions were frequently abstract; but when examples were given, these tended to be male.
- Physical science and computing questions, like those in mathematics, were frequently abstract and 'impersonal'. The applications of science were felt to relate mainly to boys' interests and not to draw enough on girls' experiences.
- In English literature, it was rare for texts by female authors to be assigned for detailed study. There were few questions focusing on female characters.
- In modern languages, set books were almost entirely by male authors. The portrayal of both adults and children was stereotyped – in terms of occupation and also of activities. Males were more active and more often in control of events. In pictures 'the overall

impression is of men doing and women watching'
(p. 24).

'Male bias' in papers is associated by those involved in the
Fawcett Society survey with girls' underachievement:

If there are practices in mathematics, including examination papers,
that disadvantage women, these will keep women out of skilled,
well paid, respected jobs. (Fawcett Society, 1987, p. 7)

Statistically girls do well in [English literature], and generally enjoy
their work. How much better might they do if the content of their
courses was more sympathetic to their gender. (Ibid., p. 15)

5.5   Images In and Out of School

Such disparities in the images of girls and boys and women
and men have to be considered alongside images that appear
in other resources available to children in school, including
those that do not constitute curriculum resources: posters,
brochures (such as those regarding careers information), topics
for assembly, and so forth. The following extract comes from
a guide to providing equal treatment for girls and boys in
careers literature:

Far too often men and boys are depicted as independent, active,
strong and interested in their work. They could be portrayed as
sensitive and caring. Similarly girls and women should be shown
as having ambition as opposed to being exclusively money or family
orientated - men also have domestic commitment. Basically, attributes should be linked to the occupation, not the sex of the job-
holder. All members of one sex do not have the same characteristics
and it is misleading to make generalisations which assume that they
do. (EOC, undated, p. 3)

Analyses of images in the 'mass media' available outside
school (including television, films, advertisements, magazines,
newspapers, and computer software) tell a similar story: there

are fewer females than males in important or leading roles, and people of both sexes are often portrayed in a stereotyped way. In children's television, for instance, there are many more male than female characters, and virtually all leading characters are male. Female characters also occupy a much narrower range of occupations than male characters.

As well as looking at the number and type of female and male characters in children's television, studies have looked at their attributes: at how females and males are portrayed. Kevin Durkin (1985) discusses various studies, many of which show males to be more active and aggressive. Durkin points out, however, that findings aren't consistent across all studies, perhaps because public concern about television violence has affected programming decisions.

There are also differences in the formal properties of television images aimed at girls and boys. One early study (Welch *et al.*, 1979) documented such differences in television adverts: girls' adverts had frequent fades and dissolves, and soft music formed a background to the narration; whereas adverts aimed at boys had more cuts and abrupt shifts of view, the music was louder, the toys used were involved in more activity, and characters were frequently aggressive. There seems to be a parallel here with linguistic studies, discussed in chapter 2, which documented differences in the *language* used towards women and men (women receiving more terms of endearment and compliments, for instance).

Tuchman *et al.* 1978 and Durkin 1985 review several studies of gender imbalances in television.

Rosalind Coward points out that our understanding of media images, both print and audio-visual, depends on the associations such images have for us. Advertisements, for instance, often depend on a whole set of cultural assumptions. Readers or viewers who don't share these would miss the point of the advert. Meanings of adverts, and no doubt of other media images, depend on the interplay between verbal and visual components. Coward argues:

We can call an advertisement sexist when it actively produces meanings which play into a whole spectrum of oppressive attitudes.

One infamous example was the hoarding hailing the advantages of orange juice with the caption, 'Juicy, Fruity, Fresh and Cheap'. The visual image was an illustration of a fat woman exposing parts of her body in the style of a naughty seaside postcard. In order to understand this poster, we are required to share its meanings whether we like them or not. At the visual level, we immediately associate the illustration with a certain kind of stereotyped 'vulgarity', the culture of Brighton promenade. The woman's brash exposure is, by association, also surrounded by these connotations. She too is vulgar, cheap. The linguistic level fixes these associations. It decides how we must read this advert. Juicy, fruity – a ripe sexuality; fresh – bold and sexually suggestive; cheap – vulgar, working class, and, like a prostitute, sexually available for a small price. (Coward, 1984, p. 67)

Children are surrounded by media images from a variety of sources, verbal and visual, both inside and outside school, that carry more or less consistent messages about females and males and their respective attributes and activities and that rely on certain cultural assumptions for their interpretation. Any consideration of gender bias in reading materials available to children in school needs to take into account that these are only one source, albeit an important one, of images of girls and boys and women and men.

5.6   Identifying Imbalances in Books and Resources

Research such as that mentioned above underlies concerns about the unequal representation of females and males in books and other resources. The close documentation of gender imbalances has also given rise to books and resources that aim to redress the balance, to provide alternative 'non-sexist' images.

Any research study makes certain assumptions about the nature of the problem it's investigating. In this section I shall look at the methods employed by different studies. Considering what has been investigated, and how, can reveal assumptions about what counts as sexist (and, by implication, non-sexist) representation of girls and boys and women and men. These assumptions aren't just of academic interest; they are relevant to those who wish to monitor resources in schools, or to select new resources.

Studies have focused on different aspects of books and resources. Some have been concerned with authorship, particularly of literary texts studied by older pupils. Others have focused on the content of resources. Baker and Freebody (1989) looked at the language used in books, at how often male- and female-referring terms occurred and what other words these terms were associated with. Several studies have examined the characters in children's stories and the examples and illustrations used in textbooks and assessment tasks; they have noted the activities carried out by females and males, as well as their attributes (that is, *how* they were depicted). One study (Hardy, 1989) also commented that the presentation of the subject-matter of science books was likely to appeal more to boys than to girls; and a similar comment was made by the Fawcett Society about the applications of science in examination questions. Analyses of female and male images may involve printed text or visual images or both.

As well as focusing on different aspects of resources, studies have used different methods to investigate gender imbalances:

- Some studies have focused on numerical imbalances in the representation of females and males; it's possible to count the number of female and male authors represented in a syllabus, the number of female and male characters in books, the frequency with which females and males are mentioned in texts or shown in illustrations, or the number of different activities female and male characters engage in. Documenting numerical imbalances is a relatively straightforward exercise, and it's reasonably objective, in that two people carrying out the same analysis would be likely to agree on the results.
- Studies have also attempted to categorize various aspects of subject-matter, plot, or characterization. For example, female and male characters may be classified

as 'active' or 'passive'. The activities they engage in may be 'stereotyped' or 'non-sterotyped'. The subject-matter may be said to reflect 'girls' interests' or 'boys' interests'. It's possible to count how many characters, activities, and so on fall into each category; for example, how many female characters in a reading scheme are 'active' and how many 'passive'. While enumerating activities and the like is a reasonably objective exercise, further classifying these is less straightforward. Different readers may disagree on what counts as 'active' or 'passive', 'stereotyped' or 'non-stereotyped', 'female interest' or 'male interest'.

Counting or categorizing and counting various features of children's books is useful because it allows you to make comparisons between different contexts; you can compare two different science, maths, or reading schemes or investigate changes over time. But such methods don't say anything about the contexts in which images occur. Imbalances, of themselves, are hard to interpret (there may be a justifiable reason why a particular book contains more male, or more female examples).

An analysis that focuses on numerical imbalances may also miss important, but more subtle, aspects of representation. The *Look* science scheme analysed by Hardy seemed to have made an attempt to include girls and to give examples of women in 'non-stereotyped' activities, but Hardy felt that the women often appeared incompetent or silly. Reducing human behaviour or attributes to a set of categories obscures the meanings such behaviour or attributes convey on specific occasions.

• Context-specific meanings may be salvaged in studies that provide a 'qualitative' account of how characters are portrayed. Some studies have attempted to give a more complete picture of a character, or characters: what they do, and how they are depicted in context (Harland's account of *One, Two, Three, and Away* did this to some extent). Coward, in her analysis of an advertisement, focussed on the interplay between verbal and visual imagery, what cultural meanings this evoked, and how the verbal and visual components worked together to create meaning. I know of little work of this detailed nature that has been carried out on images in children's books.

Qualitative analyses can be very revealing. They illustrate how relationships between women and men or girls and boys are represented in quite subtle ways. But they are subjective. Two people may very well disagree over the associations of a particular visual image or verbal description.

Research studies of gender imbalances in children's reading materials don't provide a complete account of sexism; they tend to focus on a particular aspect or aspects of the material under consideration. Nor is any research method perfect; there are pros and cons attached to each. Knowing how a piece of research was carried out will affect how it is interpreted, and may provide ideas for those who wish to monitor books and resources available in school.

5.7 Conclusion

Studies of children's reading material have claimed that, like other aspects of schooling, it is discriminatory: women and girls tend to be less 'visible' than men and boys, and characters and examples often conform to gender stereotypes. I have looked at evidence for these claims in this chapter. The main points I have made are:

- Several studies have documented an imbalance in the representation of males and females in children's reading materials: there are more male characters than female in children's stories, more male examples than female in textbooks and other non-fiction, and more male authors of literary texts studied by older pupils.

- Females and males are frequently represented in stereotyped ways: males more often take a leading role, they are more active, they feature in a relatively wide range of activities; whereas females, when present, frequently take a more passive role and engage in a narrower range of activities, such as those related to domestic life.

- Gender imbalances, of the sort mentioned above, have concerned those trying to encourage girls to take non-traditional subjects; but similar imbalances are found in different types of book (for example, fiction and non-fiction) and across the curriculum.

- Some studies have suggested that the subject-matter of print materials takes account of boys' interests more than girls'. This has also been a matter of particular concern in subjects in which many girls lack confidence.

- Studies of gender imbalances may take their evidence from the printed text or visual images or both. While the language used in reading materials does convey sexist images, it operates alongside other (non-linguistic) forms of representation.

- Earlier research (including several 1970s studies) alerted people to the presence of gender imbalances. There are now many books with more positive images of girls and women; but studies throughout the 1980s have found continuing evidence of gender imbalances.

- Patterns of gender imbalance found in print resources available in school are consistent with those found in other (non-print) media and with print materials (for example, comics, magazines) likely to be read out of school.

- Studies have used different methods to investigate gender imbalances in print materials; I contrasted methods that involve counting, or coding and counting, various aspects of female and male representation, and qualitative methods that try to take account of the meaning of images in context. There are pros and cons attached to different methods. Methods also make different assumptions about what counts as sexist.

Teachers and researchers have been concerned about imbalances in children's reading materials because of their potential immediate and local effects: they may affect the way pupils respond to a particular book and the subject with which it is associated; they may also affect pupils' performance on assessment tasks. There is further concern that, in the longer term, such imbalances may help to reinforce gender differences and inequalities: they may influence children's perceptions of what are appropriate attributes, activities, occupations, and so forth for females and males. Introducing alternative images may redress the balance, and also have a disruptive effect, causing pupils to question accepted views of girls and boys and women and men.

This chapter has considered different types of research that have been carried out to investigate gender imbalances in reading materials. The following chapter considers children's writing, where there is evidence of further, complementary gender imbalances. The implications of gender imbalances in reading and writing for teaching, learning, and assessment are considered in chapter 7. Chapter 8 gives suggestions for those who wish to monitor resources in schools and classrooms, and chapter 9 considers attempts to promote equal opportunities in images of females and males.

6

The Literate Female

It is well known that girls and boys tend to choose different books, and indeed that teenage boys tend to drop
voluntary reading altogether. If this difference is simply
accepted it will only serve to strengthen stereotypes. All
teachers should therefore enable and encourage both girls
and boys to read a variety of genres by a variety of
authors, including those which challenge stereotypes of
the roles of the sexes and of different cultural groups.
DES/WO, 1989, *English for Ages 5 to 16* (the 'Cox Report'),
para. 11.8

6.1 Introduction

Girls tend to enjoy reading and writing activities. Surveys
carried out in the UK show that girls often perform better
than boys at reading and writing. Traditionally, if there has
been a concern in the UK about gender and literacy, it has
been with the number of boys requiring additional support.
But differences in girls' and boys' reading preferences and the
different types of writing often produced by girls and boys
have given rise to further concerns: that girls' and boys' reading and writing choices are unnecessarily restricted and often
conform to popular stereotypes; both girls and boys could
benefit from undertaking a wider range of reading and writing
activities. There is a further concern that girls' aptitude for
school-related reading and writing tasks may actually disadvantage them in the longer term.

This chapter first considers some of the evidence for girls'
and boys' ability in literacy, using surveys carried out by

the Assessment of Performance Unit as an example. It then considers girls' and boys' attitudes to reading and writing and their reading and writing preferences. Finally, it looks at arguments that schools have a role to play in promoting gender differences in reading and writing.

6.2 Girls' and Boys' Ability

Girls tend to be thought of as highly able readers and writers. This is consistent with their performance on tests of 'verbal ability' and, in school, with the fact that many girls enjoy English and achieve good results in the subject in 16+ examinations (see chapter 1). As a way of considering girls' and boys' ability in literacy, I shall look at evidence from another source: the monitoring carried out in the 1980s throughout Northern Ireland, England, and Wales by the Assessment of Perfomance Unit (APU), using tasks similar to those found in schools. (I have already mentioned the APU's work in monitoring spoken language.) The APU monitored children's performance in reading and writing at ages 11 and 15. The surveys covered not only ability, but also children's attitudes towards and preferences for reading and writing activities.

The APU surveys found that girls tend to do better than boys on reading and writing tasks – though not on oracy, where there are no overall differences (see chapter 4). For writing, the degree of difference between girls and boys varies somewhat in different years, on different tasks, and at different ages, but the overall pattern is clear and consistent: in each survey, girls have performed significantly better than boys. For reading, the pattern has fluctuated more. Girls generally perform better than boys, but the differences are less extreme and have not always been statistically significant (that is, greater than what might be expected to occur by chance).

The APU surveys can be used to illustrate some general points about tests of girls' and boys' literacy:

- Differences between girls and boys are not enormous,

and they are always average ones. There is a lot of overlap between the sexes in terms of reading and writing ability, as in other gender differences. Figure 6.1 illustrates the performance in writing of 11-year-olds tested by the APU in 1982. In this survey, girls performed significantly better than boys, but the difference between girls' and boys' average scores was small: girls scored, on average, 50.7, and boys 49.2. The graph shows that girls' scores are distributed higher up the scale than boys,' but there is also considerable overlap between the sexes.

• Test results depend on exactly what is tested. The APU has surveyed performance on a range of reading and writing tasks, conflating the results to give a

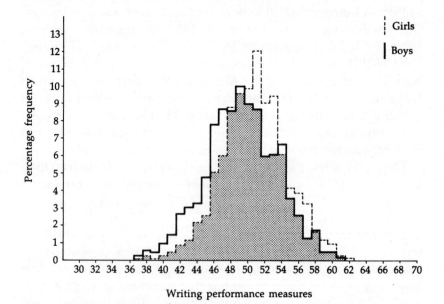

Figure 6.1 *Distribution of writing performance measures among 11-year-old girls and boys surveyed by the Assessment of Performance Unit. The horizontal axis shows the range of scores obtained and the vertical axis shows the percentage of pupils who obtained each score. The dotted line shows the distribution of girls' scores and the continuous line the distribution of boys' scores. The shaded area indicates the amount of overlap between girls and boys. From Gorman et al., 1984, p. 185.*

gender difference. But, as I mentioned above, performance varies on different tasks. One might also expect individual pupils to do better or worse at reading or writing, depending on how these were tested.

- For any test, results will apply to the population from which the sample of people tested was drawn. The APU test results were based on a large sample of children in Northern Ireland, England, and Wales: children within particular age ranges, from a range of geographical locations, and a range of social backgrounds. The average differences between girls and boys found in the APU surveys may not be replicated in any particular school or classroom. Furthermore, such average differences cannot be used to predict the performance of any individual.

Bearing in mind these qualifications, it remains the case that girls, on average, do somewhat better than boys on reading and writing activities. Related to this is girls' preference for reading and writing over certain other classroom activities and girls' and boys' preferences for different types of reading and writing. These are topics I turn to below.

6.3 Reading and Writing Choices

'They're so different. Anna's always got her head stuck in a book, but the two boys – they hardly ever read, except for comics.'
Parent talking about her three teenage children

Girls tend to enjoy language-related activities, including reading and writing. Girls and boys also express different views about reading and writing. The APU, as part of its language monitoring, documented girls' and boys' perceptions of reading and writing at ages 11 and 15. The results below come from one or more of the surveys carried out between 1979 and 1983.

While most pupils said they enjoyed reading,

- Girls were more positive than boys about school activities associated with reading, such as studying novels, plays, and poetry.
- More girls than boys endorsed statements saying that they obtained a great deal of pleasure from reading – for instance, that they liked to read 'long thick books', or that they enjoyed reading by themselves for hours.
- On the other hand, boys were more likely to agree with statements expressing reluctance to read – such as that they got bored reading by themselves or that they read only when they had to.

(Gorman *et al.*, 1988, pp. 173–174)

Similar patterns occurred in girls' and boys' perceptions of writing. For instance:

- A greater proportion of girls than of boys agreed with positive views of writing such as 'I enjoy writing'.
- A greater proportion of boys than of girls agreed with negative views about writing, such as 'I hate writing' and 'Whenever I have to write something I try to write as little as possible'.

(Gorman *et al.*, 1988, pp. 176–177)

- At 15, more girls than boys contemplated studying English as an A level subject and more girls than boys were willing to consider a career that involved writing on a daily basis.
- However, at 15, more girls than boys expressed a lack of confidence in their abilities as writers. Girls were more likely than boys to feel that they did not write as well as others, and that they weren't creative enough to do well at writing.

(Gorman *et al.*, 1987, p. 58)

The APU surveys also documented the types of reading and writing preferred by girls and boys. For reading:

- The majority of pupils indicated that they enjoyed

reading fiction. But more boys than girls enjoyed reading non-fiction, such as books related to hobbies or books which involved finding out how things work.

- At age 11, a higher proportion of boys than girls preferred to read comic books and annuals at home, rather than stories, the 'Beano' being the comic preferred by most.
- Although questions weren't designed to elicit information about different types of fiction, one distinction that emerged for 15-year-olds was that six times as many girls as boys liked reading 'love stories'.
- More boys than girls had negative views about poetry (more pupils of both sexes expressed negative attitudes to poetry at age 15 than at age 11).

(Gorman *et al.*, 1988, pp. 171–173)

For writing, the pattern was similar:

- When asked what types of writing they most enjoyed, the largest proportion of 11-year-old pupils (girls and boys) said story/imaginative writing. But when mentioning other types of writing, boys were inclined to favour 'factual writing arising out of a specific project' and girls 'letter writing' and 'writing poetry'.
- When asked, at 15, what piece of writing they had most enjoyed doing, boys' preferences were approximately equally distributed between imaginative writing and factual writing. More girls, however, expressed preferences for imaginative writing and fewer for factual writing.
- A greater proportion of girls than of boys enjoyed writing about their families and writing from personal experience.

Gorman *et al.*, 1988, pp. 176–177)

Janet White, in a later comment on the work of the APU, claims that there were differences in the samples of writing produced by girls and boys for the APU surveys, but that these were not highlighted in the APU reports. This is because the APU categorized work in terms of different genres (letters of request, literary criticism, describing how something works, and so on). Such categories hide the subject-matter of the writing, which tended to conform to different spheres of interest:

Thus, a girl writing a procedural description will tend to choose a dress-making/cooking operation, a boy a mechanical/'hard-tooled' one; a girl's strong opinion is quite likely to relate to questions of social welfare, a boy's to current political debates; observational reports written by girls tend to give prominence to aesthetic characteristics rather than those which can be measured or calculated, and so on. (White, 1990a, p. 149).

6.4 Studies of Reading and Writing - Some Examples

Several teachers and researchers have investigated pupils' reading and writing choices in the classroom. They have found differences between girls and boys that are consistent with those documented by the APU surveys.

Even in nursery and infant classes, boys and girls gravitate towards different activities. Some teachers and local co-ordinators involved in the National Writing Project monitored nursery and infant children's choices of activities, including writing. Three sets of observations are written up in the NWP booklet *What are Writers Made of?* (1990). Georgina Herring looked at children's choices in two Manchester nurseries over a three-week period. She found that more girls than boys took part in writing activities. In one nursery, girls averaged twice as many appearances as boys in the 'writing area', and every girl made at least one appearance, whereas half the boys did not use the writing area at all. Boys, however, made more appearances than girls in the 'construction' area. In the other nursery there was an attempt to encourage greater take-up of a range of activities, including writing, and almost all boys used the writing area to some extent. Even here, however, girls made (on average) twice as many appearances as boys.

Mary Foley observed infant children writing in a Manchester school over a school term. She found that, in a 'free choice' area, many more girls than boys selected writing activities. In the classroom, boys' writing from choice was limited to writing labels for objects to be put on display. Foley comments on the 'very high rate of avoidance' of writing on the part of boys (1990, p. 19). She decided to ascertain children's ideas about the desirability of some of the activities on offer in school, using a 'smiley face' drawing that represented a girl (when she talked to girls) and a boy (when she talked to boys). When asked what the 'smiley face' figure might choose to do in class, many more girls than boys selected writing activities.

Norah Arnold worked with a class of Year 5 pupils. She noticed that when they came to write, girls and boys chose to focus on rather different aspects of a topic. She analysed pieces of writing produced by her class as a follow-up to a radio series on the story of Odysseus. She found that, even when writing about the same events, girls and boys treated these differently. Girls were more likely to focus on the emotions characters were feeling; boys focused on power struggles between characters and on bloodthirstiness and violence. She gives several examples of this – for instance, Odysseus's encounter with Circe:

When writing about Odysseus forcing Circe to return his men to human form after she had turned them into swine, one girl concluded, 'Circe asked Odysseus to stay with her but Odysseus told her that he had to get back to his wife.' Another girl wrote, 'Circe said to Odysseus, "Stay with me and be my love."' On the other hand, the boys (writing about the same happening) emphasised the power and strength of Odysseus and wrote such things as:

Then suddenly Odysseus raised his sword.
'Don't kill me,' cried Circe. 'Who are you really?'
'I am Odysseus, the sacker of cities. Set my men free!'

Many of the boys' illustrations showed Odysseus as a powerful figure with his sword raised above Circe and one boy had the words,

'Change my men back or I'll cut your head off!' in a balloon coming from Odysseus' mouth. (Arnold, 1990, p. 22)

There were similar imbalances throughout the children's writing (see also figures 6.2 and 6.3).

One very popular activity in National Writing Project schools involved older children writing stories for younger ones. This provided older children with a real audience; it encouraged them to pay attention to genre and to their final presentation; and it was an activity pupils enjoyed. Janet White, however, has suggested that gender was an important but frequently ignored factor in such work. She reviewed

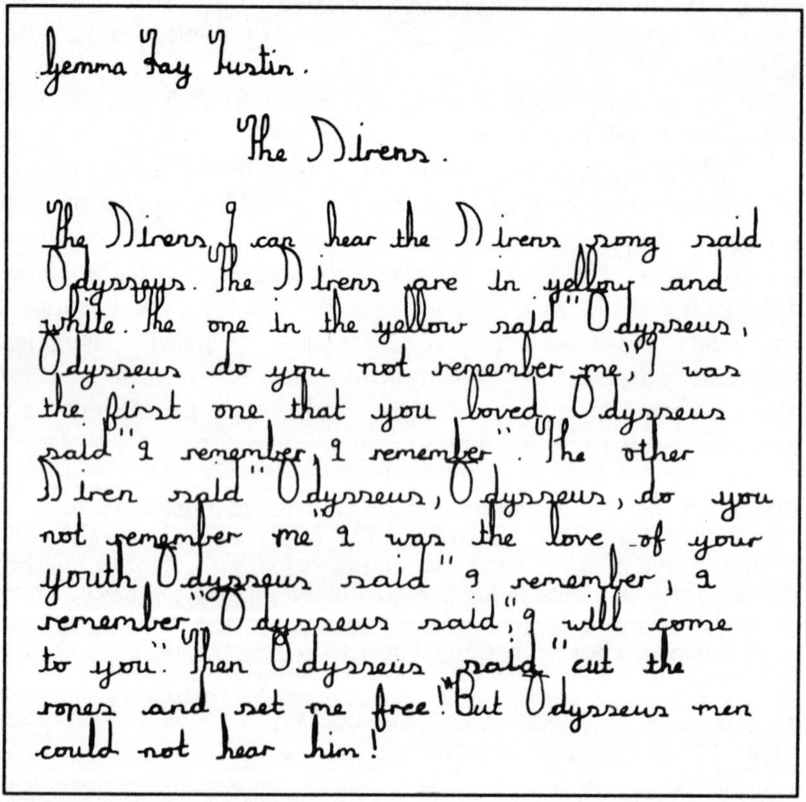

Gemma Fay Austin.

The Sirens.

The Sirens. I can hear the Sirens song said Odysseus. The Sirens are in yellow and white. The one in the yellow said "Odysseus, Odysseus do you not remember me, I was the first one that you loved. Odysseus said "I remember, I remember". The other Siren said "Odysseus, Odysseus, do you not remember me I was the love of your youth. Odysseus said "I remember, I remember. Odysseus said, "I will come to you." Then Odysseus said "cut the ropes and set me free!" But Odysseus men could not hear him!

Figure 6.2 *Sample of writing from a girl in Norah Arnold's class. From Arnold, 1990, p. 23.*

Ishani Mantri
Cylla and Caryldis

"I can see rocks captain," said Eurylochus. "Now keep close to Cylla and row as hard as you can. Cylla will not do anything But Corybdis is the danger, she sucks in any living thing and then spits them out again in a bath of blood so the blind prophet in hell told me to keep to Cylla." said Odysseus

"Whats that captain I heard something" said Eurylochus.

"That must be Cylla." said Odysseus. Ahhhhh."

"Look at that captain! a 6 headed monster. Look out, Polites," said Eurylochus

"You tricked us captain. you tricked unuss!" said Polites

"6 good men, gone. What Polites said was true.

Figure 6.3 *Sample of writing from a boy in Norah Arnold's class. From Arnold, 1990, p. 25.*

several stories produced by older children (9–10- or 12-year-olds) for 7–8 year-old readers. In this case, the younger child would provide an idea for a story, which would then be written up by the older partner. The older child would present the finished story to the younger child. White claims that one of two things tended to happen: when stories were written by a child for another child of the same sex, they tended to be more conventional and gender-stereotyped than the original idea, whereas when stories were written for a child of the opposite sex, 'gender skewing' was common. By the latter, White means that writers 'skewed' the portrayal of cross-sex actions and events towards something with which they were more familiar. Thus a girl would introduce domestic concerns and sanctions into an adventure story, whereas a boy would introduce tomboyish characteristics into a story about a girl.

White concedes that writing stories for a younger audience often produces 'good' writing; but she argues that possible adverse consequences merit examination:

Writing which has many of the hallmarks of success (attentive to a specific audience, carefully executed and presented) can nevertheless be the vehicle for a world view which is restrictive, conventional and ultimately depowering. (White, 1990a, p. 164)

Differences in writing choices made by secondary school pupils have also attracted some comment. The NATE (National Association for the Teaching of English) Language and Gender Committee provide the following caricature of girls' and boys' GCSE coursework folders:

	Jill's assignments	*Jack's assignments*
Narrative:	Boy meets girl	Raid on the bank
Discursive:	Letters to an agony column on relationships with parents	Two speeches for and against smoking
Descriptive:	My grandmother	My dream car: the Porsche 925
Own choice:	About myself	Alien landing

The Language and Gender Committee concede that 'Jill' and 'Jack' are fictions and reflect extremes. However, they contend that there are discernible patterns in girls' and boys' folders:

Jill's writing is more confessional and reflective, dealing with people and emotions, using more private forms. Jack likes facts and action, he uses more public forms. Both would grow as writers if they met the challenge of breaking the mould. Folders which share these limitations are submitted for assessment in uncomfortably large numbers. (NATE, 1988, pp. 15–16)

The work I've mentioned has focused on writing, but differences have also been found in girls' and boys' reading choices and reading behaviour in the classroom. Pip Osmont made observations of girls' and boys' reading in two infant and three junior classes in London schools. In each case, the teachers involved were aware of gender issues (and of 'race' and cultural issues). They tried to provide books that included people from a range of cultures and that showed non-stereotyped images of girls and boys. Osmont found that while most girls and boys in these classes enjoyed reading, more boys than girls had negative responses. She also observed some differences in girls' and boys' reading behaviour. During quiet reading sessions in one class,

The girls read together in groups using 'take-part' books, and became so involved that they did not want to stop when the reading time had finished. The boys, on the other hand, tended to read either individually or in pairs – and took much longer to settle, and lost interest much more quickly. They read information books with many pictures and diagrams, and spent most of their time looking at, and discussing these pictures with their friends. Many of the boys moved around during the 'reading-time', and quite a few looked at their books whilst standing. (Osmont, 1987, p. 27)

Osmont found differences in the kinds of books girls and boys preferred to read. When asked what kinds of books they would like to have in school, girls tended to choose the kinds of books already available. Boys, however, often chose *He-Man*- and *Superman*-type books, as well as comics and comic-style books. They wanted more photographic books, books about sport, 'action' books, space adventure books, and funny books (ibid., p. 33).

I mentioned earlier that differences in girls' and boys' abilities were always average differences. This applies also to girls' and boys' preferences for reading and writing: there are many similarities between girls and boys. (A general point in relation to research on gender is that people may be more inclined to notice and report differences than similarities.) To summarize those average differences I have mentioned in sections 6.2–6.4:

- Girls tend to do well in reading and writing in school, often better than boys.
- Girls tend to have positive feelings about reading and writing; more boys than girls express negative feelings. But, by the age of 15, girls have lost confidence in their abilities as writers.
- When surveyed, girls and boys express preferences for different types of reading and writing; for instance, more boys than girls say they prefer factual writing; girls express a more consistent preference for imaginative writing and for reading fiction, including, among older girls, love stories.
- In the classroom, girls and boys make different reading and writing choices: among younger pupils, girls tend to choose reading and writing activities more often than boys; girls and boys also choose different types of books, and write about different topics.

It is likely that several aspects of girls' and boys' pre-school and out-of-school experiences will affect their developing perceptions of literacy. For instance, different types of reading material are aimed at girls and boys. And girls and boys see the reading and writing engaged in by their parents and others in the community. A survey sent to parents and other adult caretakers by Manchester schools involved in the National Writing Project revealed that women tended to do writing that would be seen by children at home: letters, messages, and shopping lists. Men's writing was more likely to be work-related, so often less visible to children (NWP, 1990).

While out-of-school experiences no doubt play their part in children's perceptions of which reading and writing activities are more appropriate for females and which for males, many educationists have attempted to relate gender differences in reading and writing to the associations these activities have in school. This is not to deny the importance of out-of-school experiences, but to concentrate on factors that have more immediate practical implications – those that teachers can more readily address.

6.5 The Impact of Schools

Educationists have suggested several factors that may be related to girls' greater aptitude and liking for reading and writing. I shall look at three suggestions, relating to the passivity of reading and writing, the types of reading books used in schools, and how girls and boys view themselves as learners.

Quiet Reading

An argument is frequently made that primary schools have a 'feminine' atmosphere; for instance, there are many more female than male teachers. This might encourage girls to perform well in several activities at this stage in their school career. Reading and writing are perceived as particularly feminine. They are also associated with 'quietness' and 'passivity', which might appeal less to boys than to girls. In a brief review of how girls and boys respond to reading in the primary school, two reading advisory teachers comment:

Traditionally the approach to teaching reading and writing has required passive co-operation. There has been much filling in of worksheets, sitting still to listen to stories, reading quietly, phonic drills and language exercises, sitting quietly (and alone) to write a story, learning spellings. So, if girls do better than boys at these activities, it should not surprise us, but this approach leaves both sexes as the losers. (Kelly and Pidgeon, 1986, p. 61)

Books for Girls?

The types of early reading material that are available in schools are also said to appeal less to boys than to girls. This may appear inconsistent with the evidence cited in chapter 5 that there is a predominance of male images in school-books across subject areas. The point being made here, though, is less to do with the numbers of female and male characters than with the types of stories that make up school reading books; there is said to be a greater correspondence between the stories girls read from choice and the content of school reading books. This is consistent with the evidence I mentioned in sections 6.3 and 6.4: that girls tended to like the available selection of books in school, whereas boys would have preferred more comics, adventure books, and suchlike.

There is some evidence that the types of reading books used can affect girls' and boys' performance in reading. For instance, in an early study carried out in the USA, Stanchfield (1973) compared the reading performance of two sets of pupils. One set had been using the existing State reading scheme, which was said to have a low 'male interest'. The other set had used alternative reading books, judged to be of high 'male interest'. The alternative books had male heroes, who were also very active; they used an 'active instructional method'; they were attractive, with many coloured illustrations. Not only did both boys and girls perform better with the high 'male interest' scheme, but boys performed as well as girls, whereas they performed less well with the low 'male interest' scheme. Sara Zimet (1976), in a review of Stanchfield, attributes gains in test scores to the whole reading programme, including the teaching methods used, and not simply to the male images in the books. She refers to the programme as a 'total motivational package'. Zimet also comments that, while there is evidence that girls are less handicapped by 'dull' books than boys, children of both sexes will learn to read better with books related to an area in which they are interested (1976, pp. 39–42).

Girls and Boys as Learners

Girls and boys are said to have different 'achievement orientations', different views of themselves as learners and different beliefs about their own current and potential academic achievements. Two US researchers, Barbara Licht and Carol Dweck (1983), have proposed that girls' achievement orientations are more consistent with an aptitude for language-related activities, including reading and writing, whereas boys' achievement orientations are more consistent with success in certain other subjects, for example, mathematics.

It has been shown that girls tend to have less confidence than boys in their academic abilities. They attribute academic failure to lack of ability, but academic success to factors such as luck. They tend to underestimate their success on new tasks, and are more easily deterred by initial failure. They prefer easier tasks over those that they see as more difficult. Boys, on the other hand, have greater confidence, and are more likely to persist in the face of initial failure. Licht and Dweck suggest that girls' lack of confidence leads them to prefer language-related work, including reading and writing, in school.

Language work, argue Licht and Dweck, is not regarded as difficult or challenging by pupils. They see English as a subject in which you could do well even if you weren't bright, and in which non-intellectual factors such as handwriting contribute to success. Teachers' evaluations are also likely to be subjective; English isn't a subject in which there is only one right answer to questions. Subjects such as mathematics are seen to be harder. In secondary school several novel concepts are introduced, and pupils will probably experience at least some confusion and failure. This is likely to deter girls, but boys are more likely to retain their confidence and persist in such subjects.

Although teachers have high expectations of girls in the primary school, Licht and Dweck argue that the feedback actually given by teachers may still contribute to girls' lower confidence in their academic abilities. In one study, for instance, boys received more negative feedback than girls; but much of this was concerned with non-intellectual matters (such as neatness in the case of their written work). Girls received fewer criticisms of their work than boys, but 90 per cent of these criticisms were directed at the intellectual quality of their work.

Licht and Dweck suggest that girls should be given more experience with challenges and errors in the early years of schooling, before they have developed a stable achievement orientation; they should be encouraged to view difficulties as 'challenges to be overcome'. Licht and Dweck's stated goal is not to encourage all girls to pursue careers in 'harder' areas such as mathematics, but 'to increase the range of choices that girls consider and to encourage choices based on interests and values, not on fear of failure' (1983, p. 93).

I have mentioned three school-related factors that may help explain girls' aptitudes and preferences for reading and writing activities and, by contrast, boys' lesser success in these areas: pupils' perceptions of reading and writing as feminine, perhaps encouraged by the quietness and passivity with which reading and writing have traditionally been associated; the low 'male interest' of some school reading materials; and girls' and boys' different 'achievement orientations', which may arise in part from the types of feedback girls and boys receive on their work.

These three factors do not constitute competing explanations; they may operate in combination with one another. I think there is some value in each of them, but there is one unfortunate thing that they have in common. They are all explanations of failure. The passivity associated with reading and writing and the low 'male interest' of reading books are explanations for boys' relative lack of success. The implications that have been drawn from these explanations are that a more 'active' approach should be taken to teaching reading and writing (involving, for instance, reading in groups, collaborative writing, discussing reading choices and pieces of writing with others) and a wider range of books made available. While these strategies are meant to compensate for boys' lack of success, it is argued that their adoption will benefit girls as much as boys. Achievement orientation, while a somewhat different explanation, is also an explanation of failure; it explains girls' failure in mathematics, and sees them as opting into English by default. What is striking about each explanation is that the solution it proposes involves girls moving into 'boys'' territory and adopting 'boys'' strategies. Less attention has been paid to identifying, and setting a higher value on those aspects of language work that positively appeal to girls.

6.6 Identifying Imbalances in Reading and Writing

The teachers and researchers whose work I discussed in sections 6.3 and 6.4 identified several imbalances in girls' and boys' reading and writing choices. But researchers have investigated different aspects of reading and writing, and used different methods to identify imbalances. Some researchers have tried to ascertain pupils' reading and writing preferences, using questionnaires in the case of the APU's large-scale surveys or more informal methods in the case of individual teachers (for example, Mary Foley's use of a 'smiley face' figure with infant children). Others have observed pupils' behaviour – for example, the activities pupils engage in when given a free choice and how many of these involve writing (as opposed to other activities, such as construction activities), or how pupils behave as they read and write. There has also been considerable interest in the writing produced by girls and boys. This may be in terms of different genres or types of writing (for example, labels, descriptive or factual writing versus stories); but teachers/researchers have also looked closely at the content of children's writing (for example, Norah Arnold's focus on themes of emotion, violence, and power struggles that recurred in writing on a particular topic).

Studies designed to monitor imbalances in children's reading and writing activities have something in common with the studies of classroom interaction that I mentioned in chapter 3. Similar distinctions can be made between different types of study:

- I mentioned, in chapter 3, that many observational studies of classrooms have employed ethnographic methods in which researchers used open-ended observation to gain insights into classroom life. Some observations of children's reading and writing behaviour have employed broadly ethnographic methods. Pip Osmont used such methods, at least in part, to look at the organization and 'ethos' in five London classrooms, and then to focus more narrowly on children's approaches to reading. This kind of observational study allows one to see children's reading (or writing) in context and to look out for anything that happens that may be of interest. But the observations are necessarily subjective, and there is a danger of focusing on behaviour that supports any points the observer wishes to make and ignoring counter-evidence.

- Other studies have documented numerical imbalances in the activities engaged in by girls and boys. Georgina Herring counted the number of appearances girls and boys made in nursery school writing areas; Mary Foley counted how often girls and boys wrote in a free-choice area. There are parallels between quantitative methods of collecting information about the writing (or reading) activities children engage in and quantitative studies of classroom talk. Quantitative studies allow systematic comparisons to be made between girls' and boys' activities, but they also separate children's behaviour from its immediate context, and they may fail to take into account interesting aspects of reading or writing that cannot be counted.

- There are also different approaches to analysing the content of children's writing. It is possible to use qualitative methods to investigate a sample of writing by looking through it to gain a general impression, then focusing on aspects that are of particular interest. It's also possible to use quantitative methods, assigning pieces of writing to different categories, then counting how often girls' and boys' writing falls into each category. Norah Arnold used a combination of these methods in her study of a sample of writing produced by her junior school class.

Qualitative and quantitative analyses of the content of children's writing have similar costs and benefits to qualitative and quantitative observations of children's behaviour: a qualitative analysis of a piece of writing allows the researcher to look out for anything that is of interest, but is necessarily subjective. A quantitative analysis permits systematic comparisons to be made between girls' and boys' writing, but interesting (non-quantifiable) features may be missed. There is some virtue in using a combination of methods, as in Norah Arnold's study.

Studies of examples of writing concentrate on the product of children's work. Such studies, of themselves, say nothing of the process by which the writing was produced, which may be as important as the content of the final product.

I've focused in this section on the costs and benefits of different methods of monitoring children's reading and writing. As in earlier chapters, this seems important because such considerations affect how published studies may be interpreted. They are also important for teachers who wish to monitor reading and writing in their own classrooms.

6.7 Conclusion

This chapter has looked at girls' and boys' aptitudes for reading and writing, at the reading and writing choices they make, and the views they express about reading and writing. The chapter has also considered some aspects of schooling that might be related to girls' and boys' perceptions of themselves as readers and writers. The main points I have made are:

- Girls perform better than boys, on average, on tests of reading and writing.
- Girls tend to enjoy school-related reading and writing activities. More boys than girls express negative views of reading and writing.
- Girls and boys have different reading preferences: for example, more boys than girls say they prefer non-

fiction; many boys express preferences for the sort of reading that isn't available in school, whereas girls' reading preferences are more consistent with school-books; older girls express a preference for love stories.

- Girls and boys have different writing preferences: girls have a more consistent preference for imaginative writing; more boys than girls enjoy factual writing.
- Girls and boys also produce different types of writing. Even when engaged upon similar writing tasks, the subject-matter of girls' and boys' writing often differs.
- Differences in girls' and boys' aptitudes and choices may be related to several factors. I mentioned three explanations that related gender differences to aspects of schooling: perceptions of school reading and writing as 'quiet' and 'passive' activities, which may make them appeal more to girls than to boys; the lack of appeal of many school reading books for boys; girls' relative lack of confidence in their academic abilities and their perceptions of English as an undemanding subject.

There has been understandable concern about those boys who face problems with reading and writing. But there has also been concern about the patterns of choices made by girls and boys: about curricular imbalances (boys opting less frequently for language-related activities or subjects and girls opting less frequently for scientific and technological activities or subjects) and imbalances within the range of reading and writing undertaken by girls and boys.

Girls' and boys' choices are felt to be too restricted. There is a belief that younger children need experience of a wide range of activities in order to make an 'informed choice' of subjects at a later stage in their school careers and that in language work they should be encouraged to read a wide variety of books and engage in a wide variety of writing tasks, rather than being restricted to the forms of writing or subject-matter associated with their sex. This seems to be the position of the Cox Committee, cited at the beginning of this chapter.

A further concern has been to do with a theme that runs right through this book: namely, that language use contributes to the establishment and maintenance of gender identity. Making gender-appropriate reading and writing choices is part of learning how to behave appropriately as a girl or a boy. And the messages contained in girls' and boys' reading help to confirm children's sense of gender-appropriate behaviour. Such patterns of gender differentiation might see both girls and boys as 'the losers' when reading and writing choices are restricted. But it's been argued that, in several respects, girls are more disadvantaged than boys – even by their success in reading and writing. I shall consider some of these arguments in chapter 7.

The evidence I have discussed here will be drawn on in subsequent chapters. Chapter 7 considers some of the implications of girls' and boys' reading and writing choices. Chapter 8 discusses ways of monitoring the activities in which girls and boys engage in the classroom. And chapter 9 considers strategies teachers have employed to broaden the range of reading and writing undertaken by girls and boys and to explore issues of gender through reading and writing.

7

Literacy Issues

7.1 Introduction

This chapter brings together some of the concerns about gender imbalances in reading materials discussed in chapter 5 and gender imbalances in pupils' reading and writing choices discussed in chapter 6. I shall consider the implications of these concerns for teaching, learning, and assessment.

To summarize the position so far: chapter 5 highlighted several imbalances in reading materials available in school, such as a preponderance of male images and frequent recourse to gender stereotyping, a preponderance of male authors of 'literary' texts, and the tendency to draw on boys' experiences or topics that might interest boys – something that particularly concerned teachers of subjects in which many girls lack confidence, such as science and technology.

Chapter 6 discussed imbalances in girls' and boys' reading and writing preferences: girls' tendency to choose reading or writing activities more often than boys, girls' and boys' preferences for different types of reading and writing (for example, girls' more consistent preference for fiction), and girls' and boys' choices of different subject-matter (for example, girls' preoccupation with stories about people and emotions and boys' preoccupation with stories about action, and often violence).

Many teachers and researchers whose work I have discussed argued that such imbalances were damaging, and should be rectified. Areas of concern included the following:

- Girls and boys don't have access to a wide enough

range of reading and writing. All pupils need a more 'balanced diet'.

- Gender imbalances in materials used for assessment may adversely affect girls' or boys' performance.
- Imbalances in the reading materials available in school and in girls' and boys' reading and writing choices can affect children's perceptions of school subjects, thereby contributing to subject choice and eventual career opportunities.
- Such reading and writing imbalances contribute to children's perceptions of what is appropriate for girls and boys in a more general sense. In the longer term, they contribute to the development of gender-differentiated identities.

I shall look at these issues separately below. I shall then consider an argument that runs counter to some of those I've listed: namely, that girls and boys are 'resistant readers and writers'.

7.2 Balancing the Books

We are all aware of the importance of having non-sexist books in our classrooms and libraries, but it is worth noting that many books that are disguised in schemes of various sorts are sexist, and also that not all books describing themselves as anti-sexist are good. After all, the first criterion for judging a book is quality. Children need to read and have read to them a wide range of books spanning different subjects and genres, from fantasy to real life stories, from historical fiction to animal stories. They need opportunities to choose books that appeal to their interest, and someone who will talk about and guide their choice.

Kathy Kelly and Sue Pidgeon, 1986, 'Girls, boys and reading - an overview', pp. 61–2

It has been argued that gender imbalances, of themselves, are unjustified if not unjust. In terms of books available to children, the absence of women from many information books, the depiction in books for young children of women in the kitchen and men reading the paper, doing the garden, driving a car, and so on, and the frequent portrayal of boys as outward-bound adventure-seekers and girls as passive onlookers constitute an unnecessarily restricted set of images. They are inaccurate; they don't present a realistic picture of the range of activities in which women and men and girls and boys actually engage. Furthermore, the absence of female authors of literary texts in schools doesn't take account of the many books by women that would be suitable for study by older pupils. In terms of the types of reading and writing engaged in by girls and boys, the argument runs that pupils need access to a wider range of texts. The NATE Language and Gender Committee, commenting on the restricted nature of much girls' and boys' writing at GCSE level, argued that both girls and boys would 'grow *as writers*' (my italics) if they broadened their choices (1988, p. 16). And the Cox Committee took it as axiomatic that all pupils should read 'a variety of genres by a variety of authors' (DES/WO, 1989, para. 11.8). This is rather similar to the Cox argument in relation to speaking and listening (mentioned in chapter 4); here, too, pupils needed access to a range of 'communication skills', free from the restrictions imposed by gender.

Feminist concerns about the narrowness of girls' and boys' choices are consistent with a more general concern among English teachers and advisers that children should have access to a wide range of reading and writing. Just as pupils need to be able to use spoken language effectively in different contexts, so they need to be able to cope with a variety of texts and to write in different ways for a variety of purposes and audiences in order to be considered 'effective' communicators in the written word. This idea has become embodied in National Curriculum statements of attainment and programmes of study (and in curriculum documents in Scotland such as *English Language 5–14*). The notions of 'breadth' and 'balance' are important ones in the National Curriculum. The non-statutory guidance for English asserts confidently that 'breadth *will be achieved* by covering all that is identified within the attainment targets and the programmes of study' (NCC, 1990, p. C1; my italics). But, predictably, little direct guidance is given on this in relation to gender.

'Breadth' seems to be considered at the level of genre in reading and writing. To give an example, the requirements of the programmes of study for writing at Key Stages 1 and 3 are summarized as:

KS1 Breadth: Children should have opportunities to write in different contexts and experiment with written forms, both chronological (diaries, stories, letters, accounts of tasks or personal experience) and non-chronological (lists, captions, labels, invitations, greetings cards, notices, posters) as well as word play.

KS 3 Breadth: Pupils become familiar with many written forms: notes, diaries, personal letters, pamphlets, book reviews, advertisements, stories and playscripts. Understanding the difference between written and spoken forms and the functions and value of an impersonal style will develop. (NCC, 1990, p. B6)

These requirements could be satisfied by pupils who produced writing conforming to gender stereotypes. Norah Arnold's (1990) study (discussed in chapter 6) showed that girls and boys focused on different aspects of a story (boys on bloodthirstiness and power struggles and girls on emotions) even when tackling the same topic. And Janet White (1990) noted that the types of writing collected by the APU (letters of request, describing how something works, and so on) obscured gender differences. These still operated at the level of subject-matter, so that girls' 'observational reports' highlighted 'aesthetic characteristics rather than those that can be measured or calculated'.

The absence of relevant 'official' guidance suggests that teachers need to devise their own policy on what constitutes an appropriate range of reading and writing for girls and boys. Inevitably, the issue is not straightforward. First, as I've mentioned, there is the level at which 'breadth' is achieved: it seems that it is not sufficient to ensure that girls and boys write within a range of genres. Other aspects of a text, such as the subject-matter covered, are also likely to be gender-differentiated. Teachers also need to balance (possibly conflicting) criteria in selecting reading materials and writing tasks. In her account of older children writing for younger ones, Janet White (1990a) mentioned that writing which embodied stereotypes that she viewed as 'depowering' would nevertheless be thought of as good according to several criteria (well-thought out and attentive to a particular audience). Conversely, everyone will have come across writing that is 'ideologically sound' but rather boring. Saying what constitutes 'good writing' (or good reading material for children) is, of itself, problematical, and depends upon subjective judgement; but it's likely that there will always be competing criteria to take into account.

There remains the question of pupil choice. Gender-differentiated choices are often made precisely when pupils have a free choice of what to do. Teachers may be able to 'guide' pupils towards alternative 'choices' ('non-sexist' books, a different topic to write about), but how far should they intervene in this way? Teachers who remove 'sexist' books from the library have been accused of censoring children's reading. Censorship and choice are issues to which I shall return in chapter 9.

'Breadth' and 'balance' in children's reading and writing have been seen as ideals in their own right. But there have also been concerns that gender imbalances in images in children's books and other resources and in the reading and writing choices made by children have specific educational and social effects. This is an issue I turn to below.

7.3 Reading, Writing and Assessment

The Fawcett Society report on examinations (see chapter 5) found several examples of gender imbalances in the content and wording of examination papers. Papers often relied on male examples; females and males were often portrayed in terms of stereotypes; and boys' interests and experiences were better represented than girls'. The report suggested that 'male

bias' in examination papers might adversely affect girls' performance. In so far as girls' and boys' choices lead them to
have experience of different types of writing, one might also
predict that the type of written response required in an assessment task would affect girls' and boys' performance.

There is evidence that girls and boys tend to do better on
different forms of assessment. Patricia Murphy has identified
four ways in which assessment may show a gender bias:

- The *content* of a test item may relate more to the
  experiences of girls or boys, thereby favouring one
  sex or the other. Thus, when reading from graphs and
  tables pupils' performance is very similar. However,
  if the table to be read is concerned with traffic flow
  boys overall achieve a higher score than girls. For a
  similar question based on the day in the life of a
  secretary, girls achieve a higher score than boys.'
- Girls and boys tend to *perceive problems* differently,
  girls taking more account of the context of the problem, boys abstracting the main issues and dealing
  with them in isolation. Boys therefore tend to do
  better on those practical science problems in which
  the context is simply a kind of 'window dressing' to
  make the problem more interesting.
- Girls' and Boys' *styles of expression* often differ, girls
  tending to 'express their feelings about phenomena',
  boys providing more 'episodic, factual and com-
  mentative detail'. Questions may favour either girls
  or boys, depending on which style of expression is
  regarded as appropriate.
- Certain *features of the task* set may favour either girls
  or boys. For example, boys tend to do better than
  girls on multiple-choice questions.

(Murphy, 1988, pp. 167–170)

These factors may combine to load an assessment more or less
heavily in favour of girls or boys. They need to be taken into
account whatever subjects are being assessed and whatever
type of assessment is being devised.

While the way information is presented, as well as the tasks required of pupils, can affect girls' and boys' performance, it is harder to come by evidence that the use in assessment tasks of female or male examples or stereotyped portrayals of females and males directly affects children's performance. The Fawcett Society report on examinations found evidence of a consistent male bias in this respect; but this existed in subjects favoured by girls and in which they do well, as much as in those in which girls traditionally have less confidence. In Patricia Murphy's study, questions were equally balanced with regard to the inclusion of female and male examples (for instance, there was a balance in the use of female and male names). Whether an example in a question was female or male did not emerge as a significant factor affecting girls' and boys' performance (Murphy, 1990, personal communication). This does not mean that such aspects of representation are unimportant, but that in this survey they were outweighed by other factors such as whether the question drew on girls' or boys' interests and experience.

Considerations of 'gender bias' are as relevant to teachers assessing pupils as to those compiling standard assessment tasks. The issue needs careful discussion, because finding that the form and content of assessment tasks can affect girls' and boys' performance does not, of itself, tell us what to do about 'gender bias'. One might argue that the examples used to illustrate a problem (for instance, 'a day in the life of a secretary' as opposed to 'traffic flow') are irrelevant to the concept being tested – in which case it would be important to choose examples that didn't discriminate against one sex or else to balance items favouring girls against those favouring boys. On the other hand, the format of the assessment may be relevant to what is being tested: we may wish to know whether a student can communicate scientific knowledge effectively in writing, rather than simply demonstrate this knowledge by completing multiple-choice questions. In this case it would be important to ensure that all students had experience in carrying out the task we felt was important and that we wished to assess, but it would seem unreasonable to change the format of the assessment because it discriminated against one sex or the other. It may not always be straightforward to decide whether an aspect of assessment is incidental or relevant to what is being tested. Does it matter, as Janet White says of the APU surveys, that girls' 'observational reports' give prominence to 'aesthetic characteristics' rather than to characteristics that can be measured or calculated? We may want to set an equal value on both forms of observation, yet also ensure that both girls and boys can write competently about a range of characteristics.

7.4 Subjects with a 'Male' Image

Concern has been expressed, particularly by those who wish to encourage girls to take non-traditional subjects, such as the physical sciences, that the content of books and resources available in school may discourage girls from participating in these areas. Therese Hardy, in her study of the *Look* science scheme (mentioned in chapter 5), expressed concern at the dominance of male images, the 'silliness' of the women who were portrayed, and the fact that applications of scientific concepts tended to appeal to boys' interests rather than to girls'.

Set against the 'male imagery' argument is the fact that this is rife even in subjects liked by girls and in which they do well. Furthermore, it is not possible to separate the contribution of female and male images in curriculum materials from everything else that gives subjects such as science a 'male image': the predominance of male teachers, male scientists who are interviewed in the media as experts, teachers' attitudes, the attitudes of parents and others in the community, and so on.

This is not to suggest that the content of books and other resources is unimportant or that it isn't worth changing these to include positive female examples and to reflect girls' interests. Unbalanced representations of females and males undoubtedly play a part, along with other factors, in giving a subject an overall male image. Pupils are also likely to be aware of gender as an issue, and girls may be more dissatisfied with male imagery than they would have been a few years ago (it was pupils in Bridget Baines's English class who alerted her to the virtual absence of books about girls (Baines, 1985)). If male examples are still regarded as 'the norm', then female examples may stand out more, and by their very salience cause pupils to question the 'male image' of subjects such as science.

Related to concerns about the representation of boys' interests and experiences in science books and resources is an argument put forward by Janet White: that boys' preferred leisure reading helps to prepare them for scientific texts. White points out that, just as girls' preferred reading is more compatible with courses in English literature, so boys' reading is more closely related to scientific and mathematical areas of the curriculum. She suggests that this is not only because of preferences amongst boys for factual books (about hobbies, and how things work). Certain features of science fiction and heroic tales that occur in books and comics for boys are also compatible with features of school science texts:

The fantastic world of science fiction with its attendant tales of mythical quests introduces a distinctive and at times untranslatable vocabulary: Blusteroids, Chelnov, Excisus, Shinobo, Gryznov, The Monad, etc. Such vocabulary, however ludicrous to the adult eye, has a pedigree of scientism about it, and arguably plays its part in familiarising the young reader with a whole range of textbooks in which the vocabulary is similarly opaque but just as authoritative. Even when there is resistance to reading such textbooks, we might assume they will be more tolerable to readers accustomed to depersonalised uses of language than to those who have been led to anticipate meaning and relevance from the printed page. Very helpfully, the writers of boys' comics print in bold their 'technical terms': 'My **mystic explosion** has trapped the fool on that plant world. The plants have no machines so he-man will not be able to **rebuild a teleportation machine**.' Conventions of capitalization are used in standard expository texts to highlight key words and concepts: on this level too, reading comics may be a useful preparation for learning some of the conventions of school textbooks. (White,1990a, pp. 151–2)

White argues that such out-of-school reading experiences may confer a long-term advantage on boys, helping then to cope with 'a mass of texts, literary or not, in subjects other than

English and in the world beyond school'. In the short term, however, boys 'swell the ranks of remedial readers' (p. 152).

White's argument is interesting and persuasive. It provides a further reason for giving girls and boys access to a wide range of reading and writing, though it also raises questions about the value we set on different types of reading and writing. I mentioned in section 7.2 that several (often competing) criteria had to be balanced in selecting reading materials for children. *He-Man*-type books may prepare pupils for certain scientific conventions, but some may question whether they provide an entirely positive reading experience.

There is also a danger in seeing boys and girls as homogeneous groups. I have emphasized that the differences reported between girls and boys are always average ones. Some girls do well in the sciences and some boys do well in arts subjects. It would be interesting to look at the reading and writing experiences and preferences of girls who do well at science to see how far they coincide with those 'typical' boys' experiences and preferences that, White argues, are associated with scientific success.

Seeing boys as a homogeneous group leads White to relate boys' experiences with certain types of text (comics, adventure stories and so on) both to early reading failure and to later academic success. But there is no evidence to suggest (and indeed, it seems unlikely) that it is the *same* boys who 'swell the ranks of remedial readers' but later cope magnificently with a range of non-literary texts.

7.5 Is School Literacy Harmful to Girls?

If certain people are not supposed to have the ability to produce 'great' literature, and if this supposition is one of the means used to keep such people in their place, the ideal situation (socially speaking) is one in which such people are prevented from producing any literature at all. But a formal prohibition tends to give the game away . . . In a nominally egalitarian society the ideal situation (socially speaking) is one in which the members of the 'wrong' groups have the freedom to engage in literature (or equally significant activities) and yet do not do so, thus proving that they can't. But, alas, give them the least real freedom and they *will* do it. The trick thus becomes to make the freedom as nominal a freedom as possible and then – since some of the so-and-so's will do it anyway – develop various strategies for ignoring, condemning, or belittling the artistic works that result. If properly done, these strategies result in a social situation in which the 'wrong' people are (supposedly) free to commit literature, art, or whatever, but very few do, and those who do (it seems) do it badly, so we can all go home to lunch. (Joanna Russ, 1983, *How to Suppress Women's Writing,* pp. 4–5)

Just as science subjects have a male image, there have been concerns that English (along with other arts subjects) has a female image. This is consistent with evidence that boys are often less positive than girls towards reading and writing in school and towards English as a subject.

Concerns about boys in English seem quite understandable; but one might expect to find few concerns about girls, who tend to enjoy English and do well in the subject. Yet English teachers take as great an interest as teachers of other subjects in 'male bias', the predominance of books about boys, the predominance of literature written by men. Janet White (1986) has argued that girls' very aptitude for English-related activities (she focuses on writing) is harmful to them. She is concerned both that girls are channelled into English at the expense of their success in other subjects and that girls' success in school English isn't reflected in their subsequent achievements: 'Few [girls] ever make it to positions of power based on the strength of their apparent "giftedness", their facility with written language' (1986, p. 561). Women write novels, but make up only a small proportion of writers studied on literature courses; they write as journalists, particularly in magazines, but are less often promoted to top jobs; they work in advertising, but more often behind the scenes. White comments:

We need to ask why it is that thousands of able girl writers leave school and go into secretarial jobs, in the course of which they will patiently revise and type the semi-literate manuscripts of their male bosses, or else return in droves to the primary classroom, there to supervise the production of another generation of penwise girls. (White, 1986, p. 562)

White claims that certain aspects of the English curriculum contribute to girls' eventual 'underachievement'. She draws partly on evidence from Barbara Licht and Carol Dweck (1983) that English is perceived as an 'easy' subject, in which feedback given to pupils on their written work is subjective and often focuses on surface features. White's argument runs as follows:

- The absence of women authors in English literature syllabuses in schools and in higher education, while a symptom of women's underachievement, also reinforces the impression that language and literature are 'practised by women' but 'professed by men'. White comments: 'For girls coming through such a system, the implicit messages must be that though women may write, they rarely write Literature' (1986, p. 562).
- The feedback given on English written work seems arbitrary. This, along with a concentration on 'relatively minor surface features', is disadvantageous to girls in the long term: '[Girls] already have most of the stigmatised features under adequate control when they arrive at secondary school, and must seriously wonder what further development in the subject comprises' (ibid., p. 566)

  For boys who are 'uncommitted' writers in schools, arbitrary and trivial feedback confirms them in their attitude that success in school writing (though not necessarily in later life) is a matter of luck.

- The association of 'good' writing with English, along-side pupils' perceptions of English as an easy subject, may help persuade those who are good writers that they are not suited for harder areas of study. However, girls' writing abilities *could* confer a clear advantage in subjects other than English.
- The association of writing with English and the concentration within the English curriculum on certain *types* of writing also inhibits girls from using their literary skills to their advantage in 'non-literary' subjects, such as science and technology. White comments: 'The English Department which operates with a punctilious view of "good" writing (a matter of prescriptive correctness) and enshrines only a few types of writing as the "best" (fictional narrative, varieties of "creative" description) is ultimately doing as great a disservice to its predominantly female students as are the overtly "unfriendly" male-dominated subject areas. (1986, p. 570).

These factors, in combination, mean that girls do not use their writing abilities to their full advantage, either within the areas in which they traditionally do well in school or in other subject areas such as science and technology, where being a 'good writer' might be equally useful.

There is a danger in such arguments of identifying writing as a discrete skill, separate from the content of what is written. White emphasizes that girls are good *writers* and interested in *writing*. This argument suggests that girls might become more successful in scientific subjects if more writing in continuous prose were introduced into science and if the conception of writing in English were widened to include more 'non-literary' genres. There is some evidence to support these points. I mentioned earlier that girls tend to do better in assessment involving a written response, whereas boys do better in formats such as multiple choice. But one needs to consider also the *content* of what is written. It is at least as important to introduce content that interests girls into science subjects as to try to utilize girls' writing ability in the narrower sense.

In her effort to improve the position of girls, White is inclined to accept the low value often set upon activities associated with girls and women – for instance, in her rather dismissive reference to primary school teachers. But many feminists have questioned such values: *are* primary teachers less important than, say, advertising executives? Is the job itself less important, or is it the association with women that lowers its status and brings fewer financial rewards? Should we be encouraging girls into male areas or setting a higher value on what they already do (or both)? Many of those concerned about girls' 'underachievement' have paid less attention to the need to encourage boys into literary subjects.

7.6 Reading, Writing and Gender Identity

[Early reading books] are significant elements in a con-
stellation of sources informing young people not only of
the aspects of their gender and age that are of general
interest to the culture but also of those aspects specifically
relevant to a child's place in the enterprise of schooling.
Baker and Freebody, 1989, *Children's First School Books*,
p. 56

Books are an important avenue through which children
learn what is expected of them. Many children's books
present their readers with a narrow range of options, by
showing girls and boys in stereotyped ways.
Catalogue for *Letterbox Library*, a non-sexist and
multicultural book club for children)

A major concern about gender imbalances in reading and writing has been that the reading and writing available to pupils will affect their beliefs about, and attitudes towards, girls and boys and women and men. Educationists have been concerned that:

- The stereotypical portrayal of female and male characters in children's stories, school-books and so forth
  will cause children to have restricted views of
  appropriate female and male behaviour and restricted
  aspirations for themselves and others. This concern
  is represented in most of the work reviewed in
  chapter 5.
- Girls and boys select different types of reading
  material. The rather different messages contained in
  girls' and boys' preferred reading in and out of
  school may contribute to the development of gender-
  differentiated attitudes and behaviour. Jane Leggett
  and Judith Hemming comment on teenage magazines
  and comics aimed at girls and boys:

  The messages [in comics and magazines] are about
  what to think, what to like and how to imagine
  yourself behaving, as a boy or as a girl - and they
  are extremely stark when you start to see them. For
  girls, the message is *accept passivity* (and you get
  bonus points for anxiety, humility and innocence);
  for boys, the message is *enjoy activity* (with bonus
  points for aggression, trickery and chauvinism).
  These messages are carefully, but not deliberately,
  manufactured; they permeate practically every page,
  pictures as well as text; and any English teacher
  committed to tackling sexism in the popular media
  cannot ignore their influence. (Leggett and Hemming,
  1984, p. 74)

- Children reproduce values they have imbibed from
  their reading in their own writing. With respect to
  older children writing for younger ones, Janet White
  has commented:

  They [older children] are imbibing a lesson in
  conformity: far from learning that writers – sometimes
  – have power because they are able to challenge the
  way linguistic artefacts structure the world, they are

instead doing their best to replicate those structures. The conformism is to my mind exacerbated by the very fact that these children are commissioned to write for readers younger than themselves. (White, 1990a, p. 154)

White suggests that we need to ask how children can be helped 'to understand, practise and question the forms of language which currently hold sway in our society' (p. 165).

Most research on the effects of reading and writing has been directed at the images of girls and boys and women and men portrayed in children's books. Researchers have carried out experiments in which they have tried to measure the effects of particular reading materials on children's attitudes or behaviour. Typically, some sort of measure will be taken of a sample of children (for instance, they may be observed carrying out certain activities or they may answer certain questions about girls and boys). Half the sample, termed the 'experimental' group, will then read selected books or extracts from books, which it is thought might affect their behaviour or attitudes. The other half acts as a 'control' group; they won't read the selected books, though they may read something else. The two groups will then have gone through similar experiences except that only the experimental group will have been exposed to the target reading. A further measure is then taken of each group, to see whether the experimental group has changed relative to the control group. If it has, the change will be attributed to the reading activity. Such experimental work has shown that:

- Specific stories, reading schemes, and so forth can have an immediate effect on children's behaviour or expressed beliefs. For instance, pre-school-age boys who had heard a story about 'achievement behaviour' in a male character persisted longer in a task than those who had heard a similar story about a female character; there was a trend in the opposite direction for girls (McArthur and Eisen, 1976). And pre-school children increased the number of jobs they thought women could do after hearing and discussing stories about working mothers (Barclay, 1974).

- Books can also affect attitudes to other social groups. For instance, studies have shown that reading certain stories can produce short-term changes in attitude towards ethnic minority groups, though changes may not be maintained in the longer term. It's been suggested that reading combined with discussion is more effective in changing attitudes.
- People believe that they have been affected by books they have read, but effects are quite variable, and sometimes people claim to have been affected differently by the same books.
- Readers tend to read from choice books with which they can identify. They are also likely to interpret books in the light of their own ideas and attitudes: 'Just as the writer may be unable to avoid bias, so may the reader be limited by his or her pre-existing ideas' (Zimet, 1976, p. 17).

Many studies of the effects of reading on children's beliefs and attitudes were carried out in the 1970s. Rosemary Stones (1983) discusses one or two studies that have investigated the effects of books on their readers' perceptions of females and males. Sara Goodman Zimet (1976) reviews a larger selection of studies. Although I'm focusing here on children's reading, similar concerns have been expressed about the effects of images in other media. Kevin Durkin (1985) discusses the possible effects of television on children's developing gender identity.

Research on the effects of images in children's books sometimes appears to view readers simply as victims of 'hidden messages'. The last two points listed above are therefore important. Children come to reading not as 'blank slates', but as individuals with beliefs and values that are, to some extent, already formed. They need to make sense of what they read, according to their own frames of reference. I discovered this to my cost when, after an afternoon spent fruitlessly searching for a new picture book with an adventurous girl, I bought *Whatever Next,* in which a (male) bear travels to the moon. I read this to my 4-year-old daughter, substituting *she* for *he.* She corrected me: 'It's a he, look, he's got a space helmet, it's *he.*' Similarly, if girls and boys reproduce particular sets of values in their own writing, this means they are *aware* of conventions within the genre in which they are writing (for instance, they are trying to produce 'appropriate' stories for young children). It doesn't *necessarily* follow that they have become totally imbued with such values. This is not to suggest that books do not affect their readers, but one cannot assume that books have a single and inevitable effect, that a particular image will have an identical effect on whoever encounters it.

Research using experimental methods can isolate the specific and immediate effects of a story (or whatever) on a group of readers; but experiments necessarily take place in rather artificial conditions. They 'control' for anything else that might affect the reader. In practice, however, readers approach books in differing ways and in differing contexts. They also encounter images from sources other than print media. (I mentioned this point above in relation to the 'male image' of science.)

Kevin Durkin discusses similar problems in assessing the 'real life' effects of television. He suggests a hypothetical experiment that might isolate the effects of television over a period of years. This is based on the idea that television contains highly stereotyped representations of females and males and so would be likely to encourage strong gender differentiation in viewers.

It would be convenient to be able to divide a random sample of children into two groups, one of which would receive ten years' worth of TV input, and the other would never see a set and, assuming other environmental factors held reasonably constant, to test the children's sex role development at predetermined points throughout the period. Unfortunately, practical and ethical constraints in the real world obstruct the elegant investigations that we might desire. (Durkin, 1985, p. 55)

This quote from Durkin points up the difficulties of using experimental methods in the 'real world', but it makes a curious assumption. It assumes that whatever the non-television-viewers were doing when they weren't watching television would have no effect, or at least limited effect, on their developing gender identity. The assumption is unlikely to be valid. There is no evidence that, in the days before television, women and men and girls and boys were much more similar than they are today. It is likely that girls and boys learn about social values, including attributes and behaviour that are appropriate to their sex, from a variety of sources. When television is available, it will be an important source of information about society's values. When it is not, there will be plenty of other sources.

Similar points can be made in relation to other media, including children's books. It would be unreasonable to suggest that children's books were *responsible* for children's developing sets of values and beliefs. One can only suggest that they *contribute* to this, along with other factors.

One final point here is that female and male images are not undifferentiated. While male characters tend to be more prominent, individualized, active, and so on in children's stories, males are not everywhere depicted in identical fashion. There may also be inconsistencies between images from different sources: between men portrayed in certain books/other media and the men children encounter in and out of school, for instance. In so far as images from various sources are consistent, they are likely to reinforce one another. But inconsistencies can be exploited by those who wish to challenge gender stereotyping.

Children are faced, then, not with a homogeneous set of images, but with a range of images that is more complex, that is in some respects consistent, but that also contains inconsistencies and contradictions. From this they need to make sense of their own position as girls and boys in relation to other girls and boys. If you accept the likelihood that images in books do make some contribution to children's beliefs and values, it is legitimate to be concerned about the (overall) unequal representation of female and male characters and examples and to provide alternative images. These may have a disruptive effect, as in the provision of female images in science (if pupils are used to seeing images of passive girls, the presence of an adventurous, outgoing girl may be particularly salient). But there is a danger that they may be rejected because they do not conform to expectations.

7.7 Resistant Readers and Writers

Many of the concerns raised in this chapter about girls and boys as readers and writers seem to suggest that girls and boys (and particularly girls) are 'dupes' or victims of what they read and write, that girls' and boys' reading and writing are not just restricted, but restrictive. They are seen to limit girls' and boys' subject choices and to construct an appropriate set of social values for girls and boys, an appropriate gender identity. I've already qualified some of these claims, and argued that 'effects' operate in rather more complex ways. But anti-sexist concerns about girls' and boys' reading and writing have also been challenged on other grounds. It's been argued that such concerns are, in themselves, damaging, particularly to girls.

Gemma Moss (1989) is critical of the way teachers *respond* to pupils' stereotyped writing choices. She focuses on teachers' negative responses to popular fiction, and particularly the virulent criticism directed towards romance, by teachers with an 'anti-sexist' perspective, as well as by others:

[Romance] is disdained on the grounds that it reproduces stereotyped images of women, reinforces the powerful status of men, provides dangerously false pictures of the world and is self-evidently rubbish anyway. (Moss, 1989, p. 54)

Moss argues that there is a danger in seeing girls as in need of constant intervention and support:

By worrying about all the negative pressures on girls and their ability to cope, whilst insisting on the importance of our help, aren't we turning them into the passive, helpless victims we came to save? Meanwhile, the security of boys' identity is not subject to the same sort of scrutiny, the same doubts. (Ibid., pp. 54–5)

She concedes that, in their fictional writing, girls and boys do continually return to gender-specific genres. She feels that this is because such genres offer spaces to explore gender identity. Children are not simply reproducing meanings, but establishing meanings as they write; the romance genre, like others, is 'open to manipulation, exploration' (p. 110).

Moss illustrates this claim with an analysis of three texts written by secondary school pupils, each of which borrows themes from popular fiction. The first, a girl's story that Moss reads as an oppositional text, borrows much from the genre of romance. It is about a girl out for the day with her boyfriend and other friends. The heroine refuses to take her boyfriend back after he has left her to be with another girl who had fallen out with her boyfriend. At the end: 'In Angelique's hands the romance and all its attendant clichés turn the text upside down, confound our expectations. She ends the story with her heroine sad, but in control; alone, but determined to be so' (p. 70).

Moss argues that the writer, Angelique, is doing various things in her story: using it to explore relationships between girls and between girls and boys, for instance. She is aware of conforming to a genre, and also aware that there isn't a neat fit between this genre and her own experiences. She doesn't come across as 'duped' by romance.

Moss then analyses two more conventional texts, one by a girl (a romance) and one by a boy (a fight and a bike/car chase). She wants to investigate whether the fact that the writers have taken on board appropriate conventions means that they are locked into the 'world view' assumed by each genre (p. 81).

The first (boy's) story is action-packed and violent. The hero is challenged by a skinhead. There is a fight, which the hero wins. The hero is chased by other skinheads, and escapes, whereas his pursuers crash into a lorry and are killed. Moss sees the text not as monolithic, but as embodying certain contradictions – principally between the hero as all-powerful 'macho' man and as uncertain adolescent.

Moss seems to find it more difficult to analyse the second (girl's) story. She confesses to feeling 'hemmed in' by her possible readings. The story is about a girl buying clothes and getting ready for a party, where she meets and agrees to go out with a boy she has been attracted to for a long time. Moss finds it hard not to condemn the 'frivolous' preoccupations of the girl (for instance, with choosing clothes). Her way out is (temporarily) to change the sex of the heroine to male. Once read as 'he', the purchase of clothes becomes a 'neutral' activity (p. 93). At a later point in the story, when the heroine approaches the boy in the shopping arcade, she seems to be overwhelmed by her feelings. Moss comments: 'Her actions are no longer her own. They disappear as the object of my study. How can I retrieve them, give them back to her?' (p. 95). Again, Moss changes the sex of the heroine, and finds that 'his' actions are read differently – as more purposeful: a 'straight pick-up' (p. 95).

This text, for Moss, provides a means of exploring ways of 'acting as a female in a world defined by male power'. Like the boy's text, it embodies certain contradictions and uncertainties. The girl heroine experiences desire, but feels the need to conceal it. She needs to be, but can't be, sure of the boy's feelings towards her.

Moss argues that children are not trapped by the genres in which they choose to write. Nor are they passive imitators. They bring together material from different sources (other genres and other texts, for instance) to assemble their own texts.

If meaning has to be re-established in any one context, I do not consider that the rehearsal of a particular form brings with it for the writer a firm grasp or the outright acceptance of a particular set of values. Writing alone does not shape what we think. We bring what we know to the text and try to push it into shape. (p. 105)

In Moss's view, teachers should have a broad conception of 'useful and interesting writing', which should include writing based on popular fiction. She also feels that teachers should make explicit the conventions of different types of writing and the ways these can be used to produce meaning. The aim of this would be to help children 'manipulate the rules of the text's construction for themselves' (p. 118). Moss also suggests that contradictions in children's writing should be exploited in order to explore questions about power and about masculinity and femininity. But teachers shouldn't adopt a fixed position on gender issues. They should set the agenda for discussion, and then be prepared to support girls.

Pam Gilbert (1988), like Gemma Moss, is interested in popular fiction, and particularly in romance. Also like Moss, she rejects the notion of girls as passive consumers of romance. She argues that girls show some resistance to romantic images. Gilbert analyses two stories written by 10-year-old girls. She claims that these draw from traditional genres but demonstrate signs of resistance. In the first story a young woman on holiday in Italy with a female friend is followed by a man. On her return home, the man is revealed to be her fiancé's friend, keeping an eye on her. Gilbert claims that the young author has tried to write about adventure and suspense for her heroine (resistance), but has been forced back upon conventions of male ownership, protection, and restriction. The second story features a princess on a quest to find a husband. The princess is independent, spurns the offers of two princes, and eventually returns home with a third. Gilbert finds this more 'resistant' than the first story, although the princess's quest is still rather restricted.

Gilbert's position is similar to that of Moss, but she emphasizes that the forms of resistance open to girls are restricted, and that girls are seduced by romance. She also claims that girls' attempts at resistance need to be supported by teachers; they often go unrecognized. Girls need

a source of alternative stories to challenge the gendered generic forms of the classroom, support from their teacher readers to push their challenge further, and opportunities (and language) in which they can talk together about their resistance to romantic ideology. (Gilbert, 1988, p. 18)

Gilbert, then, supports intervention by teachers to encourage and extend girls' resistance. This would include the provision of 'alternative' stories and the opportunity to analyse 'gendered' texts.

7.8 Some Implications

I have tried to indicate the problematical nature of many educationists' concerns about gender imbalances and inequalities in reading and writing. Gender inequalities do not operate in a straightforward way, and it is not possible to provide simple 'recipes' to counteract them. It is, however, possible to suggest points to consider, that teachers may wish to discuss. I shall list those that occur to me under two headings: selecting resources for teaching, learning, and assessment and focusing directly on girls' and boys' reading and writing.

Selecting resources for teaching, learning, and assessment

- What criteria should one use to select an appropriate range of reading material for the classroom? How should one resolve conflicts of interest between, say, books considered to be of high quality and non-sexist books?
- What do you do with sexist books, especially those that children like? Do you allow *He-man, My Little Pony*, comics, and such like on the shelves, and how do you handle such books?
- How can assessment tasks be balanced so that they relate to girls' and boys' experiences, but without resorting to stereotypes of these?
- How do you decide what is relevant to assessment

and what is irrelevant, so that you know what to
change to accommodate girls and boys?

Focusing on girls' and boys' reading and writing

- How do you broaden the range of reading and writing
  engaged in by children? What counts as a wide range?
  Should girls and boys engage in an identical range
  of reading and writing?
- What value is it appropriate to set on the different
  types of writing produced by girls and boys? How
  should teachers respond to girls' and boys' writing
  that they feel conforms to stereotypes?
- Can writing in English be expanded to include non-
  literary genres? And can other subject areas use a
  range of writing tasks to appeal to both girls and
  boys – for example, more continuous writing in
  science?
- How can gender issues be opened up for discussion
  without appearing to blame girls (in particular) as
  victims? How can we support girls? Does anything
  go as a strategy? How interventionist should teachers
  be?

7.9 Conclusion

This chapter has considered several concerns raised by
educationists about the content of reading materials and other
resources and the different reading and writing activities
chosen by girls and boys. There are fears that these conspire
to restrict girls' and boys' access to the curriculum, that they
may result in 'gender bias' in assessment, and that they have
more long-term effects on relations between girls and boys
and on their developing gender identity. The main points I
have made are:

- There is some agreement that pupils need access to
  a wide range of reading and writing activities. While

the notion of 'breadth' underlies reading and writing in the National Curriculum, gender imbalances that might limit 'breadth' receive little attention. In selecting an appropriate range of activities, teachers need to balance (possibly conflicting) criteria: for example, 'good quality' (already a highly subjective judgement), 'something that will motivate pupils', 'non-stereotyped'.

- Gender imbalances in the content and format of assessment tasks may constitute a 'gender bias' by favouring one sex or the other. The different types of writing favoured by girls and boys may also work to their advantage or disadvantage in assessment. There is a need to monitor assessment tasks to check that these do not discriminate unfairly against girls or boys, but also to ensure that girls and boys have sufficient experience to cope with a range of writing tasks.

- There is a fear that gender imbalances in resource material and differences in girls' and boys' preferred reading and writing are related to girls' and boys' subject choices; for instance, the 'male image' of science and the greater continuity between boys' preferred reading and scientific texts may combine to attract boys to the subject and to put off girls. Clearly, resources and reading choices are only two among many factors to be taken into account when considering girls' and boys' subject choices.

- Girls' success in reading and writing in school isn't reflected in their achievements after they leave. It's been argued that the narrow view of writing taken in school, particularly in English departments, contributes to girls' later 'underachievement'.

- A major concern of educationists has been that the values inherent in children's reading, which they reproduce in their own writing, contribute to their developing gender identity. There is some evidence that books read by children may have an immediate and specific effect on their behaviour and expressed attitudes. In the long term, the picture is more complex. Children encounter a range of images, sometimes conflicting, from different sources. They do not passively 'imbibe' messages, but actively seek to make sense of what they read within their own frame of reference.

- Some of those who express concern about girls' and boys' reading and writing choices have seen girls, in particular, as the unwitting 'dupes' of sexism. There is a counter-argument that girls' (and boys') adoption of a particular genre does not indicate their whole-hearted acceptance of an associated set of values; they are, to some extent, 'resistant' readers and writers, and their resistance may be supported and strengthened in school.

The issues raised in this chapter have implications for teachers who wish to introduce equal opportunities in reading and writing. I have mentioned one or two points to bear in mind when selecting resources or thinking about how to broaden girls' and boys' reading or writing choices. These points are very general ones, because what teachers actually decide to do depends very much on the context in which they work. Chapter 9 provides examples of equal opportunities initiatives that involve reading and writing.

It is necessary to monitor girls' and boys' reading choices and the types of writing they produce as a precursor to any attempt to introduce equal opportunities, and to evaluate the effectiveness of whatever strategies are adopted. Suggestions for making observations in the classroom, and for looking at resources and children's writing are given in the next chapter.

8

Monitoring Language Experience

8.1 Introduction

Earlier chapters have surveyed an area of research on gender and language use or have considered the implications of such research for teaching and learning. This chapter takes a different approach. It provides guidance for those who wish to monitor girls' and boys' language experiences in schools and classrooms. The chapter is rather like a handbook: it does not review a content area, but describes practical methods of inquiry which teachers can use, and discusses their advantages and disadvantages.

The chapter will build on methodological points raised in chapters 3, 5, and 6. These chapters reviewed the (considerable) evidence of gender differences and inequalities in girls' and boys' educational language experiences. They also stressed the diverse nature of the evidence that is brought to bear on gender differences and inequalities: different aspects of language count as evidence, and studies employ a variety of methods to collect evidence. The earlier chapters referred to studies that employed a 'quantitative' approach – that is, that produced numerical comparisons between girls' and boys' speech or female and male images in written texts – and studies that were 'qualitative' and produced a more open-ended account of spoken and written texts. This broad distinction between quantitative and qualitative approaches is maintained in this chapter, although I shall also suggest that a mixture of methods may provide a more complete account of language use.

There are several reasons for wishing to monitor spoken or written language:

- to inform teaching, to find out more about individual pupils, and as an aid to planning future work;
- to carry out an investigation of girls' and boys' language use, perhaps as part of an action research project;
- to provide information for colleagues, for a staff meeting, or for school governors;
- to inform school policy making – for example, to help in the development of an equal opportunities policy or with policy on assessment or with the purchase of books and other resources;
- to evaluate current policy and practice.

These and other purposes will affect the selection of an appropriate method; they will affect what is monitored (what counts as evidence) and how. What you wish and are able to monitor will depend upon several other factors: school and classroom organization, the amount of time available, and other teaching priorities. This chapter illustrates several ways of monitoring language, but these need to be adapted to fit individual circumstances.

There remains the question of what to do with the evidence you collect. How do you respond if you find that certain children are dominating class discussion or that the books on the library shelves contain relatively few stories with girls and women in leading roles? It is difficult to provide general rules for positive action, but there are several examples now available of strategies teachers have adopted. These are discussed separately in the following chapter.

I shall begin this chapter by looking at ways of getting a general impression of classroom activities. Later sections concentrate on classroom talk and on written texts (pupils' writing and print resources).

8.2 Monitoring Classroom Activities

A useful first stage is to get an overall impression of what is going on in the classroom or in other areas of the school. How do different pupils spend their time? Who engages in which activities? Such observations can feed into curriculum planning. They can be shared with colleagues or pupils. They may suggest some specific aspect of school or classroom life to target more closely.

It is hard to combine detailed observations with teaching, and it is virtually impossible for teachers to observe their own behaviour. What you are able to observe will depend on how the class is organized. If children are working independently or in small groups, it is often possible to spend a short time making notes on one group or one or two children. You will need to make very rough notes and write these up later. An alternative strategy is to complete a simple checklist regularly. If noting things down on the spot interferes too much with teaching, try focusing your attention on particular children or events or whatever, but keep all note taking until as soon as possible after the lesson. More detailed observations can be made if you're able to collaborate with a trusted colleague by observing in one another's classes. Or children can be asked to help with observations.

Brief observations of a class provide useful information about teaching and about pupils' activities. Because you don't need to make any special arrangements, you can probably observe over several lessons without disrupting your routine too much. Involving a colleague does mean making special arrangements; you will get more information (and the benefit of someone else's point of view), but observations will be harder to set up and are likely to be less frequent.

Observing with a checklist

Simple checklists enable you to record different pupils' participation in activities: to keep a check on who contributes to 'show and tell' sessions, to class assemblies, and so forth. Checklists can also be devised to allow systematic comparison of girls' and boys' participation in a range of activities. Georgina Herring's account of children's behaviour in Manchester nursery schools (mentioned in chapter 6) was based on a checklist completed by nursery school staff. The checklist identified all available activities. Staff were asked to observe for 15 minutes three times a day over a three-week period. They noted which activity each child was engaged in during the observation period. An 'M' was recorded for children who were unsettled and moved around. Such a checklist can be devised relatively easily. Figure 8.1 shows an example, based on some of the categories identified by Herring.

Such checklists provide quantitative information about pupils' choices. They allow a comparison to be made between activities that are preferred by girls and boys; they also allow one to produce a profile of activities preferred by individual

	Writing activities	Painting	Home corner	Construction	etc.
Gemma					
Anne					
Lisa					
John					
Simon					
Nicky					
etc.					

Figure 8.1   *Checklist to observe girls' and boys' behaviour in nursery school classrooms, based on some of the categories identified by Georgina Herring (1990).*

pupils. The checklist in Figure 8.1 gives general information. More specific checklists may also be devised. Chapter 6 mentions observations made by Mary Foley, who looked at the extent to which girls and boys participated in different writing activities.

Not all checklists produce quantitative information. Figure 8.2 overleaf provides a framework for making brief open-ended notes about pupils' activities in groups. This schedule is one of a series reproduced in *Genderwatch!*, a publication I shall refer to at various points in this chapter. (A revised version of this publication, entitled *Genderwatch after the Education Reform Act*, is now available; see Further Reading.) The scheme is meant to allow 'instantaneous' sampling of pupils' behaviour (looking at one group, jotting down what each pupil is doing at that moment, then moving on to the next). Kate Myers suggests the following procedure:

When you start your observation, pick one group of pupils – the farthest away from you to your left. Note the time, what activities the female pupils are engaged in, and the names. Note anything about behaviour and record any teacher intervention. Then, using the same group, repeat the observations for the male pupils in the group.
When you've written notes on your first group, move round the room repeating the observations for each group. Go round the groups as many times as you can during the lesson. (Myers, 1987, p. 25)

Myers's schedule provides qualitative information. This can be translated into quantitative information by 'coding' children's behaviour after the event – identifying categories of behaviour, such as 'writing', 'talking to another pupil', 'talking to the teacher', 'mucking about', or whatever is appropriate – and seeing how often girls and boys participate in each type of behaviour.

Observation schedules rely on teachers being able to sample children's behaviour regularly. Georgina Herring asked nursery teachers to complete her schedule three times a day (regular observations proved difficult in practice). With schedules such as Myers's, there is an assumption that observers

CLASSROOM INTERACTION/OBSERVATION

FORM A – SMALL-GROUP WORK

Name of school .... Filled in by .... Date completed ....

	FEMALE PUPILS					MALE PUPILS			
Time	Activities	Names	Comments	Teacher intervention		Activities	Names	Comments	Teacher intervention

Figure 8.2 Checklist to observe pupils' activities in groups. From Myers, 1987, p. 28.

will develop a regular rhythm as they go round each group of pupils. A similar sampling technique can be used to look at the behaviour of one or two pupils, perhaps observing each every 10 minutes and jotting down the activities he or she is engaged in at that moment and what you can tell about the nature of the activities.

If you aren't able to complete schedules systematically, there is a danger of biasing observations. For instance, if schedules are completed whenever there is a free moment, this may always coincide with certain parts of the day and so not give a representative picture of the day as a whole.

Using Field Notes

> The girls tended to sit at their tables and raise their hands when they needed help but the boys approached the teacher, so gaining attention more quickly. More boys tended to fool around when the teacher wasn't looking and indulged in activities such as throwing rubbers whereas the girls just sat and talked to their friends.
> Jill Mountain, 1986, 'Patterns of classroom management',
> p. 42

> When they came into the classroom, girls sat around the edge, usually with one side to a wall. Some sat at the front and a few at the back, but very few braved the middle. They seemed to place themselves as far as possible from the louder boys. In mixed groups, boys tended to dominate and the girls experienced both verbal and physical harrassment, and ridicule, often of a personal nature.
> Sheelagh Harris, 1991, 'A girl-friendly approach to oracy',
> p. A113

Jill Mountain (1986) describes observations she made in the infant classrooms of four colleagues. These showed that, although the classes were organized differently, in each case boys were more demanding of the teachers' time, and teachers themselves often unwittingly reinforced gender stereotyping. Sheelagh Harris (1991), a deputy head of English, identified aspects of the behaviour of children in her own secondary 4th-year class which gave rise to some concern. Both teachers adopted a 'field notes' approach, jotting down observations about pupils' behaviour, then looking through these notes and trying to identify patterns. Such observations can provide the basis for discussion with colleagues, or they can provide ideas for more detailed monitoring. In Harris's case they led her to try out a 'girl-friendly' approach to the curriculum, which is discussed in chapter 9.

Field notes have been used in several pieces of research referred to in earlier chapters. For instance, Sara Delamont used field notes to observe interaction between teachers and pupils (examples are cited in section 3.2). Pip Osmont (referred to in section 6.4) used field notes to observe young children's reading behaviour.

To be informative, field notes need to be kept systematically. It is useful to develop a consistent format for noting the date and time of observations and relevant contextual information such as the type of lesson, teacher and pupils involved, and so on.

Field notes have the advantage over observation schedules that you can note down anything of interest as it occurs. They are still selective, however, in that you cannot, and will not wish to, note down everything that is going on. There is a danger of bias, of systematically distorting observations. Bias can be introduced at the point of making observations, by observers noting points that support their preconceptions about girls and boys. Bias is also a danger when analysing and interpreting information; evidence may (quite unconsciously) be selected so as to favour a particular interpretation.

One way of minimizing bias is simply by being aware of it: by constantly looking out for counter-evidence (evidence that does not support a point you wish to make). When making observations, try to note down (or remember and note down) events as precisely as possible, and note separately how you interpret these events. Try to combine observations with information obtained from another source – for example, through discussing lessons with pupils or a colleague who was present. It is also useful to discuss your interpretations with others – for example, by showing the pupils concerned or a colleague your field notes and asking how they interpret the events you describe.

8.3   Looking at talk

I have been aware for quite a while of the differences in behaviour between girls and boys in the classroom, but had no clear picture of who I interacted with, or of the type and length of that interaction. I needed someone to come into my classroom to observe this for me. It was difficult at the time to get another teacher to do this, so I asked one of the girls to do it for me. I gave her a seating plan of the class and she marked it every time I spoke to a pupil. This became a regular feature of the maths lesson, always with different pupils responsible for each lesson's observation, and for feeding the information back to the class.
Geraldine Scanlan, 1986, 'Was your mother good at maths?', p. 16

Although I readily accepted that girls might remain quiet and passive in *other* teachers' classrooms, I was convinced that the girls in *my* classroom did participate actively in whole class discussions. I was sure that I, as their teacher, was aware of the strengths and the needs of the girls in my class.

My complacency was jolted only by the gathering of 'hard' evidence. I began last year to tape a Year 15 mixed-ability class who were working on a play.

An analysis of the speaking turns taken in one class discussion revealed the following results:

Speaking turns taken in class discussion about a text

Speaking turns taken by the teacher	20
Speaking turns taken by boys	12
Speaking turns taken by girls	0
Speaking turns allocated by the teacher to boys	4
Speaking turns allocated by the teacher to girls	2

Only half the boys in the class (five out of ten) achieved speaking turns in the discussion about the text. These boys, however, had an almost complete monopoly on student talk and contributions. I discovered that what I thought of as 'Whole class discussion' was in fact small group discussion with the teacher's participation. The rest of the class (twelve girls and the other five boys) became the audience for the speakers in the discussion.

Mary Bousted, 1989, 'Who talks?', pp. 41–2

Perhaps, like Geraldine Scanlan and Mary Bousted, you need 'hard evidence' about pupils' talk to inform your own teaching, or class or group organisation. Or you may need evidence for more formal reasons: to contribute to the development of school policy on assessing speaking and listening or to provide the basis for an INSET day for staff on oracy. The reasons you have for observing classroom talk will affect what you choose to observe and whether this includes

- whole-class talk between teacher and pupils,
- small-group talk,
- one or two individual pupils who are causing concern, perhaps because they are particularly vocal or particularly quiet.

There is a range of methods available to observe classroom talk, but, as I mentioned in chapter 3, each has its own limitations. There isn't a perfect method; what is most appropriate depends upon the context and the purposes of the observation. I shall spend most time on observations that can be made on the spot. These are less time-consuming than making audio or video recordings, but they provide useful information. I shall try out different forms of observation on the same extracts of talk in an attempt to make a comparison between methods, to see what different methods can and can't do. Towards the end of this section, I shall look at the value of audio and video recordings and give an example of an analysis involving transcripts.

Observing Whole-Class Talk

Whole-class talk – for instance, a discussion led by the teacher – is more straightforward to observe than talk in many other contexts. It is usual, in whole-class discussion, for one person to speak at a time, and pupils are often nominated by the teacher to speak. It's relatively simple to make a checklist showing which pupils obtain speaking turns, as in figure 8.3. It is possible to devise a coding system for different types of speaking turn – for example, speaking when nominated by the teacher, making a spontaneous contribution, and so on.

In *Genderwatch!*, Kate Myers sets out a more complex obser-vation schedule based on one devised for the Girls into Science and Technology project. Such structured observations of whole-class talk, based on a checklist or observation schedule, allow an observer to detect general patterns in classroom talk. Comparisons can be made between different contexts (for example, different classes or different types of lesson). And

Girls		Boys	
Lisa	///	Ian	//////
Anna	//	Matthew	//
Fiona	////	Jonathan	/
Liz		Ben	//////
etc.		etc.	

Figure 8.3 *Checklist showing number of speaking turns obtained by different pupils.*

CLASSROOM INTERACTION/OBSERVATION

FORM B – WHOLE-CLASS WORK (based on GIST schedule)

Name of school .... Filled in by .... Date completed ....

		FEMALE PUPILS						MALE PUPILS						
Time	Name M/F	T asks F Q	F ans. Q	F comm. spontan.	T helps F	TRF	FRH	T asks M Q	M ans. Q	M comm. spontan.	T helps M	TRM	MRH	Notes

Female pupils .... Male pupils .... Name of class ..... Subject ..... Date .... Time ...... Teacher ....

Figure 8.4 Checklist to observe teacher–pupil talk. Key: T asks F/M Q = teachers asks a female/male pupil a question; F/M ans. Q = female/male pupils answers question (whether directed at them or not); F/M comm. spont. = female/male pupil comments spontaneously; T helps F/M = teacher helps a female/male pupil (e.g. in practical lessons); TRF/M = teacher reprimands female/male pupil; F/MRH = female/male pupil requests help. From Myers, 1987, p. 29.

the observer can focus on contributions from individual pupils or from girls and boys as a group. The *Genderwatch!* schedule allows comparison between different parts of the same lesson (for example, group investigation followed by a teacher-directed plenary). It enables the observer to look at the role of the teacher and pupils in managing classroom turn taking. But observation schedules necessarily restrict the observer: they allow you to observe only certain types of language behaviour.

Field notes are frequently used to observe classroom talk, as they are to observe other aspects of classroom life. Sara Delamont's field notes, cited in chapter 3, contain information about pupils' and teachers' talk. Field notes don't allow you to make a numerical comparison between features of girls' and boys' talk, but they do enable you to record talk in its context and to note down non-verbal behaviour and contextual information that add to your understanding of what is going on.

Observing Group Talk

Observing pupils' talk in small groups is less straightforward than observing talk between a teacher and pupils. Talk in groups is often informal; it is more rapid; speaking turns are less clearly delineated; and there is more overlapping speech. I shall illustrate different methods of observing talk by applying these to the same extracts of group discussion. The extracts come from video recordings made in two secondary school humanities lessons. A class of 12-year-olds was carrying out 'Cluedo'-type activities in groups of four. Each pupil in the group had some clues to a murder. The group had to piece together evidence on the basis of all their clues, and work together to decide who might have committed the crime. The clues were such that there were several plausible culprits. Similar activities were carried out in the two lessons, with the pupils working in different groupings. The extracts I'll look at show the same two girls working once with two other girls and once with two boys. I looked at these data to see how the composition of groups might affect the number and the type of pupils' contributions to discussion. In my account of the observations I have used pseudonyms to refer to the pupils.

While I've had to resort to video recordings here to compare different methods of observing the same interactions, the observations I describe immediately below could be made by a teacher on the spot.

The groups were seated as in figure 8.5. I first tried an open-ended approach, making rough notes on the interaction. Then I tried out two simple observation schedules.

Field notes on the interaction After playing parts of each video to get an impression of what was going on, I selected 10-minute extracts and simply jotted down everything I could about the talk that was going on. Rough notes made under these conditions are *very* rough, but can be supplemented by comments or interpretations made immediately after the observation:

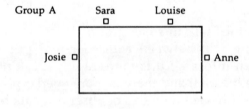

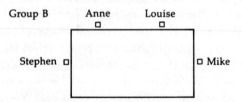

Figure 8.5 *Seating arrangement of two groups under observation in two secondary school humanities lessons.*

Notes	*Comments*
J: 'I reckon', etc.	J makes hypothesis
S: to group: 'let's all pick one person'	S suggests how group might proceed
L: idea: reads from card	L is responding to suggestion
J to L: 'Have you got anything?'	
J & S talk together - J: 'We've got to suss out why she wanted to kill him'	J & S form a pair - seem to direct things
J & S ask qns – 'What was the girls' name?' L answers etc.	L responds to suggestions from J & S etc.

I wrote up the full sets of notes and comments as the following characterizations of the talk in the two groups:

GROUP A (all girls)

The girls seem to constitute two pairs (Josie and Sara + Louise and Anne), but this doesn't mean there's a complete split – they do work collaboratively as a group. Josie and Sara are the main instigators of the action. They put forward more ideas, they request information from others.

Josie puts forward her own ideas, but also questions others – a way of keeping the conversation going.

Sara sometimes brings together ideas from different sources. She also organizes the group – directs the search for clues, suggests things that might be focused on.

Louise is involved in the conversaton but tends to respond rather than initiate. She also acts as a mediator between Josie/Sara and Anne.

Anne is very quiet – it is hard to notice her in the presence of more vocal contributors. She seems involved most of the time, though occasionally turns her attention elsewhere. She contributes to the general discussion when asked for information. Otherwise, a few contributions are made as an aside to Louise.

GROUP B (girls + boys)

The group is 'on task' most of the time, but the boys in particular are more concerned to reach a quick solution to the problem than to discuss their various clues. The pupils do not operate well as a group. A clear 'us and them' distinction emerges. The boys face one another and direct talk to one another. When they direct a question or a comment towards the girls, it's often scathing. The girls look towards one another but rarely say anything.

Stephen tries to direct talk towards the topic in hand – particularly when Mike goes off course or mucks about.

Anne reads out some of her clues initially, but is talked over by the boys. Thereafter she makes only a one-word contribution to the discussion - to side with Louise in a disagreement about the identity of the murderer. She attracts open ridicule from the boys.

Louise does make one or two contributions – once to disagree with the boys. She recognizes that her disagreement creates a problem, since the group is meant to reach a common decision on the murderer's identity (perhaps she intends to create a problem?). On one occasion she acts as a mediator for Anne, reading out one of her cards.

Mike doesn't take the task entirely seriously, and sometimes mucks about. He is drawn into the task by Stephen, but is keen to reach a quick solution.

Rough notes, made on the spot by an observer, can be quite informative. They provide a general account of pupils' talk and the roles pupils adopt in discussion – although they are necessarily rather subjective. It can be quite hard to focus on all pupils, even in a group of four. I found I'd got 6 minutes into Group A's interaction and hardly noticed Anne. An alternative technique is to focus on each pupil in turn, perhaps for 2 minutes at a time.

Table 8.1 *Number of speaking turns taken in two group discussions*

Group A	Josie	Sara	Louise	Anne
	26	35	16	4
Group B	Stephen	Mike	Louise	Anne
	55	52	10	1

Using a checklist or observation schedule   An alternative to making notes about pupils' talk is to use a checklist or observation schedule similar to those used for whole-class discussion, to note down systematically specific features of the talk. The simplest thing to note is the number of speaking turns taken by participants. My counts of the speaking turns in Groups A and B are shown in table 8.1.

Counting turns provides one measure of the distribution of talk in a group. It can be carried out on the spot, but in this case it is a very rough and ready measure. Limitations of the technique include the following:

- Unless everyone operates a 'one person at a time' rule (rare in informal talk) it isn't straightforward to say when one person's turn ends and the next person's turn begins. If one speaker is interrupted but then regains the floor and continues where they left off, does their contribution count as one turn or two? I counted a new turn whenever someone *began* speaking (whether they had been interrupted or not) because I was trying to make the count on the spot, and under these conditions, I wasn't able to make any finer distinctions.
- Turns vary enormously in length. The turn count for Group B masks the fact that Stephen and Mike spoke almost continually, with only very short interventions from Louise.
- Counting turns doesn't provide information about the nature of the talk engaged in.

Having counted the number of speaking turns, I tried to make a distinction between different types of turn. For Group A I distinguished between initiating (making a statement, expressing an opinion, or making a suggestion), questioning (asking another person for information), and responding (to a request for information). Table 8.2 shows how the talk broke down.

These distinctions are very rudimentary, and I would probably wish to revise them if I were able to listen to the video

Table 8.2 *Types of talk produced in a group discussion*

	Josie	Sara	Louise	Anne
Initiating Statement	11	24	8	1
Question	12	6	2	0
Response	3	5	6	3
Total	26	35	16	4

recording several times or use a transcript. They confirm some of my initial impressions when making notes on the talk, although Louise's 'initiating' total is higher than I would have expected.

The *Genderwatch!* observation schedule for whole-class interaction distinguished different types of talk, and there are schedules for group observation that make these sorts of distinctions. In *Gender Issues in English Coursework*, NATE reproduces a schedule for group observation that distinguishes the categories 'initiates talk', 'interrupts', 'helps another to speak', 'supports another's point of view', 'offers opposing view', 'adds to what has been said', 'challenges' and 'breaks off' (NATE Language and Gender Committee, 1988, p. 25). Given the considerable variability of talk in different contexts, many observers prefer to devise their own categories, depending on the purposes of the observation and what is suggested by the data. The categories I applied to Group A's talk did not work at all well for Group B, for instance.

Making Audio and Video Recordings

The types of observation I've mentioned so far can all be carried out on the spot. Recording pupils' talk on audio or on video allows similar observations to be made more reliably. Different types of analysis can be tried out, and observers can check one another's observations. A video or audio cassette recording is also useful for stimulating discussion with colleagues – for instance, in a staff meeting or an INSET session. Making and analysing recordings of talk is a time-consuming process, but the same extract of talk may be recorded for more than one purpose, and pupils can audio-record and discuss their own talk.

There are one or two practical points to bear in mind when using an audio or a video recorder:

- Video and audio cassette recorders are intrusive, at least initially; their intrusiveness is lessened, however, if pupils are used to being recorded or recording themselves.
- When recording whole-class talk, there will be a lot of background noise (scraping chairs and such like), and this, coupled with the fact that a single microphone or camera cannot be equally close to everyone, means that not all contributions will be picked up. Audio- or video-recording whole-class talk is a useful way of focusing on the talk of the teacher, but less useful if the main focus is pupils' talk.
- Small-group talk is easier to record, but even here it will help to have a quiet corner of the classroom for recording. If not too disruptive, try withdrawing groups to a quieter area or withdrawing other members of the class.
- Audio recordings necessarily lose important non-verbal information, so it is helpful to make field notes to accompany an audio recording.
- Video recordings, while they retain non-verbal information, are necessarily selective; even in a small group it's impossible to record everything that is going on. There is also the possibility of introducing bias; for clearly, a camera can pick up information only from where someone chooses to point it. It is best to place the camera where it records the most relevant information and then to leave it running.

Staffordshire Oracy Project have provided a set of 'Tips for taping', including suggestions for setting up a simple recording area:

Do not place a cassette recorder directly onto a desk or table top. Place the recorder on top of something such as a piece of carpet, felt or foam to absorb sounds picked up from the desk or table.

Try to use a recorder which has an automatic record level. This avoids having to worry about altering the volume settings. If your recorder has an ALC switch, make sure that it is on. This will help to prevent distortion.

If pupils are operating the recorder for themselves, use a battery operated machine. This is not only safer, it is less obtrusive than a machine which is wired to the mains.

If pupils are operating the machine for themselves, use a machine which requires only one button to be pressed for recording (on some machines record and play have to be pressed simultaneously).

Using a recorder with a built-in microphone is the most convenient method. Using a recorder with an extended microphone may produce a superior quality recording, depending upon the type and quality of the microphone and the recording context.

You can obtain a far superior recording by using tie (neck) microphones and a junction box. However, this involves extra equipment, trailing wires and things that can and do go wrong!

Choose a classroom, or an area within school which is carpeted, curtained and which has more 'built in' or existing soundproofing qualities. Plan to use this area when you know that you are going to be recording children at work.

Making a 'recording area' within your classroom can help to improve the quality of recording by cutting down the extraneous noise level. A recording area can be made by:

> Choosing an area in the classroom where least disturbance is likely to occur – i.e. in a corner away from the door.
>
> The placing of tables as far away from other pupils as possible.
>
> Arranging the pupils to be recorded so that they form a natural soundproofing barrier.
>
> Arranging movable partitions around the pupils to be recorded.
>   If all else fails, locate the pupils to be recorded into another room, small annex, cubby hole, or cupboard.

(Staffordshire Oracy Project, 1989, pp. 8–9)

Transcribing Talk

Transcription is an incredibly time-consuming process, but can be quite revealing. It permits detailed analyses of extracts from a video or an audio recording. Teachers have sometimes found that close examination of a transcript reveals evidence of pupils' understanding or language use that was not apparent from earlier observations. Transcripts also provide evidence that can be quoted if you are writing up an account of your observations (for example, for colleagues or some other professional audience).

Having carried out 'on the spot' observations of two girls working in a single-sex and a mixed-sex group (Groups A and B above), I wanted to look more closely at Anne, the very quiet girl. There were two occasions in Group A and one in Group B when Louise announced that Anne had relevant information on one of her cards. This focused the group's attention on Anne, and gave her the opportunity to make a contribution. I wanted to compare what happened in each case. The extracts, two from Group A and one from Group B, are transcribed in figures 8.6, 8.7 and 8.8 below. I have used column transcripts in these figures, rather than the more usual type that is set out as a play script, because I find column transcripts more useful for group talk. 'Play' transcripts suggest that turns follow one after another in sequence, but this isn't always the case, particularly in informal contexts. With column transcripts it is easier to show the relationship between different turns. It is also possible to look down the columns and check the number, length, and type of each speaker's contributions.

The transcripts show that, in the extracts from Group A's talk, Anne is taking an active part although she rarely speaks. In figure 8.6 (Group A, extract 1) Josie asks Anne for information, whereupon Anne searches through her cards. She eventually finds what is wanted, and makes this known through Louise. On this occasion it is Louise who reads out Anne's card. Shortly afterwards (in extract 2, shown in figure 8.7) Louise points out that Anne has relevant information. This time Anne herself reads out her card. The others pay attention to her and encourage her to contribute.

Josie	Sara	Louise	Anne	Comment
Who's who's where where was the blood found outside somebody's flat (... who's flat that was)				J. looks round table. A. catches her eye and begins searching through cards
	Hold it what's this one for 'Mrs Jones had made an appointment with the bank manager to try to bo(.)			S. reads from card
	to go and	Borrow		S. looks up from card
What's it say	see if he could go into business			J's question addressed to S. J. and S. talk to each other. L. looks on. A. still leafing through cards.
mmh	I don't think it would have been him then that killed him			A. pulls out card.
			[touches L. on arm]	

				Comment
who	if he was going to the bank manager			
			(..... Smith's garden)	A. makes an aside to L. L. question towards A.
Say that again	Mr Jones	huh		A. aside to L. again L. takes A's card
got to keep his business going			(.... knife ....)	L. reads from card S. looks over L's shoulder
Yeah (he's going to) the bank manager		Anne's Anne's got 'A knife with Mr Kelly's blood on it was found in Ethel Smith's garden'		
	That has got it's got Mr Scott's fingerprints on I think			S. To L. points to table decisively J. sits back, hands on table.
Oh he's got (.....) It's the whole lot of them				L. looks towards J. A. looks towards J. smiles. S. leafing through cards.

Figure 8.6 *Transcript of girls' talk in a single-sex group: extract 1. Conventions:* One column is allocated to each speaker, and a fifth column gives non-verbal and contextual information. Where words are aligned across columns, this means the speech is overlapping. Words that are commented on in the 'Comment' column are underlined in the transcript. Also, [nods] refers to a non-verbal signal that forms a turn of part of a turn; (he's going to) refers to words that are unclear and are a guess; (......) refers to words that could not be transcribed; and (.) means a brief pause.

Josie	Sara	Louise	Anne	Comment
		What are you looking for		Question to S.
	The knife wounds			
		Oh that		L. looks through cards. S. looks on
	I mean the knife finger bits on it finger			
		She's got that one		L. points towards A.
	No the one with the finger prints on			
		Finger prints on the knife		L. question to S.
	Yeah			
		She's got it		L. points to A.
	Come on what's it say Anne (.) does it say any finger prints on the (. .)			
	Louise		[muttering under breath]	All look at A. A. looking at cards L. peering to look at A's cards Exclamation. S. pulls L. back
			('The knife . . . .')	A. reads but can't be heard.

			Notes
What's it say about the <u>gun</u> knife (.) go on carry on carry on	The (n ....)		J. question to A.
		'A knife with Mr Kelly's blood on (.) it was found in Ethel Smith's garden'	A. reads from card. Others pay close attention
	Yeah		
So both of the weapons were found in Ethel Smith's garden			
	No		
	Yeah		
	The gun wasn't		
Yes it was she just said it was			
That was the knife she just said			
	[laugh]		
	Oh		
Right have you got any more (.... ....)			S. question to A.
			J. general question?
Where was the gun found	(......)		
		'The knife found in Ethel Smith's garden had Mr Scott's fingerprints on it'	A. begins in quite a loud voice. S. holds up finger to J. and points to A. to indicate they must listen
	It's Mr Scott I reckon		
	(No 'cos he ....)		
Well Mr Scott had something to do with it			

Figure 8.7 *Transcript of girls' talk in a single-sex group: extract 2. Conventions as in Fig. 8.6.*

Stephen	Anne	Louise	Mike	Comment
Let's look at the facts 'Mr Stone refused to let Mrs Stone sell any of her jewellery'			Well man	S. reads from card
		She's got one about refused	So see she nicked it	
Get it out get it out			Well say it then	
[spitting noise]			Spit it out [spitting gesture to floor]	
			[finger to eye] ah lovely	M. uses high voice (girlish?)
		There you go		L. speaks to A. Takes card
			(what's .....)	M's speech unclear
		'The maid had asked Mrs Stone for a loan to pay Mr Lowe. Mrs Stone refused.'	(don't ever see	L. reads from A's card. A. has hand over mouth.
			.... any ...)	
			why	L. puts down card and leans back in seat. M. speaks in funny, whiny voice
		How do I know why work it out		
mmh			Stephen why	whiny voice question intonation, whiny.
I don't know (.) Well I still reckon it's Barrett.				

Figure 8.8 Transcript of girls' talk in a mixed-sex group. Conventions as in Fig. 8.6.

The Group B extract (figure 8.8) shows a similar occurrence, in which Louise announces that Anne has relevant information on one of her cards. This seems to be at Louise's own instigation rather than Anne's. The boys want the information, but make silly comments that put down the girls. When Louise eventually reads out the card, the information is discounted.

8.4 Looking at Written Texts

This section provides suggestions for those concerned to monitor the range of writing produced by pupils in class and for those with a more formal interest in children's writing - for instance, teachers developing some aspect of school policy, such as a cross-curricular policy on writing. The section also looks at printed texts - at techniques that have been used to monitor imbalances in children's books and other resources, to inform discussion about the use of existing resources, or the purchase of new ones. While there are different reasons for looking at children's writing and printed texts, the methods used to detect imbalances are similar enough, in general terms, for them to be considered in the same section.

A preliminary decision is needed about which aspect(s) of the texts to focus on. Chapter 5 (on books and print resources) and chapter 6 (on children's written work) suggest a number of possibilities, including:

- the range of topics covered in factual writing,
- the plot and characterization in stories written for or by children,
- the ways in which females and males are portrayed.

I mentioned in the earlier chapters that portrayal of female and male characters may be linguistic or non-linguistic; moreover, it is often quite subtle. Illustrations may show girls standing or sitting as they watch boys carry out some activity or following boys who are 'in the lead'. Or the fact that boys instigate action may be conveyed linguistically: for example, 'It's starting to rain,' cried Timothy. 'Let's shelter in the old house!'

It's possible to use qualitative or quantitative techniques to monitor print resources or children's writing. Making open-ended notes on the treatment of female and male characters has some similarities with making field notes on classroom interaction. Categorizing and counting different types of character (or subject-matter or whatever) is similar to using an observation schedule or checklist to monitor talk. Teachers/researchers mentioned in chapters 5 and 6 sometimes used a mixture of qualitative and quantitative techniques. Therese Hardy counted girls and boys and women and men represented in illustrations in a primary science scheme. She also provided a more open-ended account of the types of females and males who appeared as examples. In chapter 6, we saw how Norah Arnold looked at the subject-matter of children's writing, and began to divide this into different categories so that she could make a numerical comparison between girls and boys, combining this with a qualitative account of girls' and boys' writing.

Using a Checklist to Monitor Written Texts

Several published checklists are now available for those who wish to monitor gender imbalances in print resources. Figure 8.9 (pp. 192–3) shows a checklist that was devised for modern language textbooks and is reproduced in *Genderwatch!*. It is one of the most detailed checklists I have seen.

This checklist has been carefully constructed. It allows comparison of the representation of female and male characters along several dimensions. Some parts of the checklist are straightforward to complete; there would probably be little disagreement between two readers about the number of female and male characters in a text, for instance. Other parts require some degree of judgement; when noting down numbers of women and men in high-status jobs one must first decide which jobs count as 'high status'. The constructors of the checklist sometimes give examples where there is a danger of ambiguity; – for example, 'dependency' is exemplified as 'Peter's secretary', 'John and his girlfriend', 'so-and-so's wife'.

Some published checklists are less satisfactory. Checklists may contain rather 'loaded' questions or questions that are loose and difficult to interpret. The question below comes from a checklist to analyse children's literature.

		Almost always	Occasionally	Rarely
Do both girls and boys have a variety of choices and are they encouraged to aspire to various goals, including non-traditional ones if they show such inclination?	Females Males			

(Reproduced in The English Centre, 1984, p. 57)

This kind of question serves to raise awareness of the sorts of bias that have been found in books, but I suspect that it is hard to use reliably. It is rather inexplicit, and there are too many questions bundled into one. It may be interpreted very differently by different readers.

The modern language schedule provides a lot of information, which will take time to analyse. It is useful for those who wish to look in detail at imbalances in a set of textbooks or to compare books from different schemes – perhaps as part of a piece of action research or to stimulate discussion within a department. Not everyone will require such detail, however. A checklist to help in the selection of books for a school library could be simpler – perhaps adapted from a published schedule or devised in consultation with colleagues to identify characteristics thought to be important.

Name of school ....

Filled in by.. Date completed ....

Title of book/course ....

Chapter/unit/page reference...

Publisher...

Publication date..

Name of reviewer..

	F	M

I SEXISM BY EXCLUSION OR OMISSION

(Are women or girls absent from texts or less
represented than men or boys?)

- Number of female characters or females
  mentioned in the texts
- Number of male characters or males mentioned
  in the text

ANONYMITY
- Number of nameless females
- Number of nameless males

II SEXISM BY SUBORDINATION (Who has the
more dominant role?)
- Number of females initiating a conversation
- Number of males initiating a conversation

Taking 'Turn' in dialogues
- Number of contributions made by females
- Number of contributions made by males

- Number of women dependent on men, e.g.
  Peter's secretary, John and his girlfriend,
  so-and-so's wife, etc. . . .
- Number of men dependent on women

- Number of women mentioned in their own
  right, e.g. not as so-and-so's wife
- Number of men mentioned in their own right

	F	M

Jobs and occupations
- Number of women doing a paid job
- Number of men doing a paid job
- Number of women involved in housework or looking after children
- Number of men doing housework or looking after children

- Number of women involved in intellectual activities
- Number of men involved in intellectual activities

- Number of women with a high-status job or occupation
- Number of men with a high-status job or occupation

III SEXISM BY DISTORTION
- Number of females presented as being emotional, weepy, irrational, irresponsible, etc.
- Number of males presented as being emotional, weepy, etc.

- Number of females who have a passive or negative role, e.g. doing as they are told, appearing helpless, being mentioned for their looks rather than for their actions
- Number of men who have a passive role

- Number of females involved in physical activities: leisure and work, e.g. doing sports, driving cars, decorating the house, etc.
  Number of males involved in physical activities

IV SEXISM BY DEGRADATION
- Number of women presented as sex objects
- Number of men presented as sex objects

- Number of females shown as talking too much, chatting and wasting time
- Number of males shown as talking too much, chatting and wasting time

- Number of females presented as stupid, mindless, spending money carelessly, etc.
- Number of males presented as stupid, mindless, spending money carelessly, etc.

ANY EXAMPLES where women are shown as inferior to men, patronized by, e.g. 'Not bad for a girl', or 'sponging' off men.

Figure 8.9 *Checklist to monitor modern language textbooks, devised by a group working at the Modern Language Teachers' Centre. From Myers, 1987, pp. 113–14.*

An alternative to looking at written texts with pre-specified questions in mind is to read through them to gain a general impression and to determine what sorts of features are worth looking out for. Such an open-ended approach may be a better way to begin monitoring children's writing. Norah Arnold used her initial impressions to devise three categories of subject-matter in stories written by her pupils: emotions, power struggles, and bloodthirstiness and violence (see section 6.4). It is likely that different categories would have emerged from a consideration of the same children's writing on different topics.

Figure 8.10 shows a checklist I have used for looking at the range of stories available in a set of books for young children. It is much simpler than the modern language checklist, and provides quantitative information on female and male main and subsidiary characters. But it also allows for open-ended notes on each story and so mention of whatever one thinks is of interest. In this case I have focused on aspects of the plot. While this seems to work for young children's stories, alternative formats would probably be better for non-fiction or other types of resources.

Making a More Detailed Analysis of Written Texts

In the case of *Timothy Finds a Playmate* (by Trudy Mordue), it seemed that some care had been taken to include a female as well as a male kitten joining in the day's adventures, though other minor characters were male. The illustrations seemed to give more or less equal prominence to each kitten. I felt, though, that Timothy took nearly all the initiatives and that the female kitten, Ginger, largely acquiesced. The text contains a lot of direct and indirect speech. I decided to look more closely at the ways in which Timothy and Ginger spoke. Much of the kittens' speech was concerned with initiating something – for instance, suggesting some course of action. I decided to separate out speech that made an initiative, speech that responded to an initiative, and follow-up action. Figure 8.11 (p. 196) shows an analysis of one page from *Timothy Finds a Playmate*. In this case I have put indirect speech in square brackets.

Story-book	Main character(s)	Others mentioned as individuals	Comment
The Worst Witch	F (schoolgirl/witch)	All F except two wizards, one the chief	'Girls' school' type story, featuring witches. Main character is likeable/incompetent. Gets into various scrapes.
Fancy Nancy in Disguise	F (Fancy Nancy – small girl)	Mother, father, baby brother. Various others (M & F) appear in each chapter.	Adventures of (outgoing) small girl. Shown playing with girls and boys. One nice touch is a male librarian reading story to children.
Rita the Rescuer	F (Rita – small girl)	Rita's 2 brothers, 1 sister; various others, M & F.	Rita gets left out of things as she's 'too young'. She gets a rescuer's outfit (à la Supergirl) and carries out several daring feats.
Timothy Finds a Playmate	M (Timothy – a kitten)	Another kitten (F); M hedgehog; other animals, M or sex not given.	Adventures of two kittens as they play. F kitten plays a major role, but Timothy takes nearly all the initiatives: 'Let's go outside'; 'Let's shelter in the old house'.

Figure 8.10 *Simple checklist to analyse children's stories.*

This seemed a useful way of representing the story. It preserved something of the structure of the plot, but allowed me to identify differences in the ways the kittens directed the action. It showed that both Timothy and Ginger initiated activities. Each responded positively to the other's initiatives (no attempts at subversion!). But Ginger made very few initiatives, and usually followed those of Timothy.

Timothy		Ginger		
Initiative	Response	Initiative	Response	Action
Now that we know each other, let's go and find somewhere nice to play.				
				They trotted down the lane ...
This could be a good place to play in, what do you say, Ginger?				
			Oh, yes.	
		Let's play hide and seek.		
	[T agreed]			
[and told Ginger that she could go and hide first].				
				G scampered off ... T turned his back and shut his eyes.
Don't go too far from here, I'll soon be looking for you.				

Figure 8.11 *Extract from an analysis of initiatives and responses in a children's story.*

What you look out for in analysing a text depends upon the nature of the text itself, and also on your own interests. Earlier chapters have given examples of detailed analyses of printed texts or children's writing. Chapter 5 mentioned Ros Coward's account of the meanings reproduced in a particular advert; and Gemma Moss's and Pam Gilbert's work on resistant writers (discussed in chapter 7) is based on close analyses of children's writing of romance and other 'popular fiction' genres. While these kinds of analysis are very revealing, they are also time-consuming. The time taken to do them has to be weighed against the value of the information obtained.

8.5 Interpreting Imbalances

The evidence collected about written or spoken texts can be used to inform teaching or school policy or practice. Earlier chapters have made clear, however, that the interpretation of gender imbalances is not a straightforward matter. Imbalances need to be interpreted in context. For instance, a series of books may contain more male than female characters, but how you interpret this imbalance (and what you decide to do about it) will depend upon the nature of the books, other books that are available, how you might be able to use them (given practical and other constraints), and how you think children will respond to them. Similar points crop up in relation to children's own writing or children's and teachers' talk (if boys – or some boys – monopolize speaking turns in whole-class talk, this is something to be concerned about; but it's also important to take into account the type of talk produced and the range of contexts provided for pupils' talk). Such issues are important for those who wish to counteract any form of perceived bias and redress gender inequalities. They underlie the work discussed in the next chapter.

When interpreting information, it's important to take account of the specific pros and cons of whatever method(s) have been used to collect it. In this chapter I have made a distinction between quantitative and qualitative methods. I have mentioned that, broadly speaking, quantitative methods allow you to make a numerical comparison between different groups of pupils, different contexts, and different types of talk or written text; but that they necessarily restrict the information you can collect, and tend to abstract information from its immediate context. Qualitative methods are more flexible; they allow you to make open-ended observations and to retain any information (for example, aspects of the context) that adds to the meaning of what you observe; but they are necessarily selective, and there is a danger of 'seeing what you want to see'.

Chapters 3, 5, and 6 say more about the costs and benefits of different methods (in relation to published studies); in this chapter I have also tried to specify the strengths and weaknesses of the particular methods discussed. Such methodological considerations will affect how you interpret information and what claims you can legitimately make on the basis of this.

8.6   Conclusion

I have tried to sketch out briefly a range of methods that can be used to investigate gender differences or imbalances in spoken and written texts. This is by no means a comprehensive inventory of methods; it is simply meant as a starting point for teachers and others who wish to carry out their own monitoring. Earlier chapters provide ideas for particular questions to investigate. I have discussed methods that allow an investigator to focus on different aspects of children's language experience. These include:

- Monitoring classroom activities. This allows an observer to get a general picture of what is going on or to focus on specific aspects of children's behaviour: for example, the way they behave as they read, the writing activities they select, and so on.
- On-the-spot observation of whole-class or group talk, to detect general patterns – for example, imbalances

between girls' and boys' contributions – or to provide a qualitative account of pupils' talk.

- Using video and audio recordings to examine class or group talk in more detail.
- Transcribing extracts of talk for close scrutiny and analysis.
- Monitoring written texts – children's writing or printed texts – to investigate imbalances in terms of genre, subject-matter, plot, and characterization.
- Focusing more closely on one text or an aspect of a text.

I have mentioned the pros and cons of different methods – what they can and can't tell you – and I have suggested that these need to be taken into account in interpreting the evidence you collect.

Monitoring aspects of children's spoken or written language or print resources is often a precursor to the introduction of change within the school or classroom. Chapter 9 discusses a range of equal opportunities strategies that have been developed by teachers working in different contexts.

9

Introducing Equality

The design of courses, the use of materials which avoid sex stereotyping and the involvement of girls' own perspectives on problems, issues and ideas are important factors in increasing the involvement of girls in physical science.

NCC, 1989b, *Science: non-statutory guidance*, pp. A9–10

It is up to the school to take steps to redress [gender] inequalities by promoting good classroom practice and by itself providing an example of equality in action.

SED, 1990, *English Language 5–14*, p. 20

I'm afraid gender and those sorts of issues have tended to take a back seat, with the National Curriculum.

Primary headteacher

9.1 Introduction

The 1980s have seen the development of several initiatives designed to provide equal opportunities for girls and boys in schools. Initiatives have taken place with children of all ages and in all curriculum areas. They stem from a variety of motives, and target different types of inequality between girls and boys. Language plays a part in many of these initiatives. Sometimes there is an explicit focus on language. On other occasions the focus is elsewhere, but language is necessarily involved because of its pervasiveness in schools and classrooms. Suggestions for ways of introducing equal opportunities are now widely available, in the form of case studies of practice in particular schools and classrooms; policy statements produced by schools, local authorities, and other institutions; and guidance and 'educational implications' that derive from educational research. They are therefore part of the 'literature' of gender and education. I shall give several examples of initiatives that involve language. These are presented not as models of good practice, but as a body of work that can be considered and discussed in its own right, much as the examples of research I discussed in earlier chapters.

At the end of chapters 4 and 7 I listed questions that would need to be taken into account by those who wished to introduce equal opportunities in speaking and listening, reading and writing. I grouped these under two headings: questions that related to contextual factors, such as the selection of resources and planning contexts for talk, and questions that related directly to pupils' spoken and written language. This chapter is organized in a similar way. The initiatives I shall discuss are, in part, attempts to answer the earlier questions; some tackle school or classroom contexts, while others focus directly on pupils' language use. In many cases, gender inequalities are tackled 'surreptitiously', by manipulating contexts or aspects of language use. But some teachers have felt the need to confront inequalities 'head on' by bringing these out into the open for discussion with pupils. Such initiatives are considered in a later section.

The notion of 'equal opportunities' is, of itself, problematical. I shall continue to use this term because of its general currency, but I shall return to its problematical nature towards the end of the chapter. I shall also consider the desirability of teacher intervention. I mentioned in chapter 7 that some forms of intervention have come under attack from educationists who believe that they are damaging to pupils, particularly girls.

9.2 Contexts for Equality

I have emphasized that pupils' language behaviour will vary according to context; for instance, pupils will speak in different ways in different situations. A corollary of this is that gender imbalances in reading, writing, speaking and listening may be affected by focusing not just on language behaviour itself, but on various contextual factors. I shall mention here strategies involving the selection of reading materials for children, paying attention to how children are grouped, and the tasks groups are asked to work on. Such strategies *may* be designed explicitly to affect pupils' spoken language or their reading and writing choices. More often, they have some more general motivation, such as challenging pupils' (restricted) perceptions of how girls and boys behave or increasing pupils' participation in non-traditional subjects.

Image Management: Selecting Books and Other Resources

The prime concern when planning any unit of work is to allow as many voices as possible into the classroom. This means actively searching for more balanced representation of male and female writers.

NATE Language and Gender Committee, 1988, *Gender Issues in English Coursework*, p. 20

Glyn Kendall produced a computer game called *Alien Syndrome*, in which a player has to rescue comrades who have been captured by baddies. He introduced a 'gender choice' feature, so that players could choose whether to be female or male. He also wanted to introduce female comrades, but was faced with the problem of how to identify these as females:

The female comrades [had] bows in their hair(!), to make the difference obvious, but these had to be taken out as 'it's not like the original' comments were passed. Determined that there were going to be female comrades, I (together with Tahir Rashid, graphics) arrived at the current version of the yellow tracksuit, longer hair, and less frantic arm waving than the male comrades.

Glyn Kendall, cited in *Oasis*, October 1989, p. 3

Resources, particularly print resources, are a very tangible example of inequality in schools, and an example on which much attention has been focused. It's perhaps not surprising that the selection of books may be one of the first things tackled by those concerned to introduce equal opportunities. For instance, when Jackie Hughes took over as head teacher in a Birmingham primary school, with the intention of working towards an equal opportunities policy, one of her first actions was to buy a small selection of new books to promote positive images of girls and women and Black people and to promote discussion of gender issues as well as 'race', disability, and the environment (Hughes, 1992).

I mentioned in chapter 5 that studies of gender imbalances in children's books had focused on different aspects of books. The introduction ts alternative resources may, similarly, be designed to counteract one or more specific imbalances. A need may be identified for

- more books (or stories or poems) by female authors
- books (or other resources) with more female characters or examples
- books that recognize the achievements of women (for example, in history or science)
- books that present non-stereotyped images of girls and boys and women and men and that show girls and women in a positive light
- books that use 'inclusive language' (for example, by avoiding 'generic' *he* and *man*)
- books that show girls and boys behaving competently in 'non-traditional' areas of the curriculum
- books that address issues in ways likely to interest and appeal to girls and boys.

It's difficult, if not impossible, to find books that counteract all these imbalances! Teachers' priorities in selecting alternative print resources will be determined by the type of resources involved and the contexts in which they are to be used. For instance, authorship has probably been more of an issue for those selecting fiction than for those selecting textbooks.

Because early studies uncovered gross imbalances in the numbers of females and males represented in books and gross stereotyping of female and male characters and examples (features that are still being found in later studies), 'non-sexist' strategies have often sought to introduce more females and counter-stereotypes of females and males. Examples of this strategy can be found in a collection of rhymes called *Father Gander Nursery Rhymes*:

Wee Willie Winkie runs through the town,
Upstairs and downstairs in his nightgown.
Rapping at the window, crying through the lock,
'Are the children in their beds,
For it's now eight o'clock?'

Wee Wendy Winkie stands on the stair,
Watching and guarding the townspeople there.
If she sees danger she'll ring the town bell,
When peaceful she shouts,
'Eight o'clock and all's well!'

Larche, 1986, p. 20

'Father Gander' seeks to introduce a female parallel to Wee Willie Winkie and to give her a positive image. This strategy has been used in non-fiction books and resources as well as in stories and poems. There is a danger that it will simply result in more subtle forms of sexism. There has also been a concern that widening the available images for girls some-times results in them becoming boys in all but name, with the result that girls and their interests are still disparaged.

An example of the latter problem can be seen in some educationists' reactions to Gene Kemp's well-known and popular book *The Turbulent Term of Tyke Tiler*. The story concerns the adventures of the main character, Tyke Tiler, over a school term. Tyke has a friend, Danny Price, who is 'not too bright'. Tyke gets into various scrapes trying to help Danny. The term culminates in Tyke shattering the school bell tower, falling from a roof, and ending up in hospital. The story is written in the first person, and it isn't until the climax that we learn Tyke's hated real name – Theodora – and that she is a girl.

Tyke Tiler has a female main character who engages in non-stereotyped activities. It's also a funny book, one likely to appeal to children. Yet it has come under criticism from those concerned about sexism in books. Elaine Millard, who read the story with a class of 11-year-olds, suggests that Tyke is in effect a boy, identified finally as a girl by sleight of hand. Other female characters are stereotyped and ineffectual. Millard comments:

Isn't there an implied reading that girls' actions are worth attention only when they are indistinguishable from those of their brothers? (Millard, 1985, p. 60)

Tyke Tiler is definitely a 'boyish' heroine. Many of her encounters are with boys in her class, and, as Elaine Millard points out, there is a contrast between the portrayal of Tyke and that of other female characters. This is pointed up in the illustrations, where Tyke is pictured with short hair, jeans, and a jacket or tee shirt. Other girls have longer hair and/or dresses. I suspect that the illustrations play an important part in the identification of Tyke as male. I read the book to my own daughter and came to the climax:

Mrs Somers came round the corner, stopped, spoke to Sir, looked up, saw me and shouted, her face red and corrugated: 'Get down at once, Theodora Tiler, you naughty, disobedient girl!' Kemp, 1979, p. 19)

As we talked about the book I realized that, despite this revelation, my daughter still believed Tyke to be a boy.

Such non-sexist strategies seek to create a counter balance to the preponderance of male images and the stereotyping of females and males. They seem to appeal to an androgynous world, in which anyone can do anything; but they do this by implication. They don't address the problem of sexism explicitly.

Another strategy has been to tackle sexism more directly. I shall call this an 'anti-sexist' strategy, but please note that 'non-sexist' and 'anti-sexist' aren't always used with this distinction in mind. An anti-sexist strategy would be to make it explicit that (for instance) girls can be brave (or succeed in science or maths) and boys can show their feelings (or do well in home economics or modern languages). Sometimes anti-sexist strategies may reside in the introduction of 'morals' into poems and stories. Father Gander again:

> Jack be nimble, Jack be quick,
> Jack jump over the candlestick!
> Jill be nimble, jump it too,
> If Jack can do it, so can you!
> (Larche, 1986, p. 8)

I have to confess that, while trying to remain dispassionate about all this, I cannot read such morals without a slight cringe.

In the sense in which I've used the terms, non-sexist and anti-sexist strategies aren't incompatible: one could, for instance, introduce stories with a wider range of characters and also explicitly encourage children to take part in a wider range of activities.

In the debate about how to tackle sexism in books for children there has been some suggestion that we need to move from talking about non-/anti-sexism to considering 'feminist perspectives' in children's books. (The issue was debated, for instance, in newsletters for the book club *Letterbox Library* in 1989 and 1990.) I don't think there is clear agreement on what a feminist perspective would be, except that it would involve giving a positive image of girls and women and their activities – setting a higher value on girls and women in their own right and not just in so far as they become more like boys and men. In this sense it can be seen as a reaction to 'boy-like' heroines in stories such as *Tyke Tiler*. (See Adler, 1992, for a discussion of feminism in children's books.)

Despite attempts to provide alternative images of girls and boys, there is still not nearly enough published material available. Furthermore, departmental budgets are unlikely to run to large-scale restocking. Several teachers and librarians have produced their own resources to counteract imbalances. NATE Language and Gender Committee (1988) provides suggestions for using single copies of published poems – for instance, copying these on to OHP slides for whole-class discussion – alongside unpublished poems, including poems by teachers and pupils, to counteract the very poor representation of women poets in popular anthologies. And a London maths teacher, Geraldine Scanlan, describes how two secondary school departments collaborated to produce displays to promote positive images of girls as mathematicians:

We are working, together with the English department, on producing a set of posters giving pupils a positive image of themselves and their mathematical ability. As part of their English work, pupils are writing self-description. We intend to use these on the posters and put in the odd sentence about what wonderful mathematicians they are. It's not easy to get hold of positive images of girls and black pupils e g and succeeding at maths, so we will produce some ourselves. (Scanlan, 1986, p. 16)

I mentioned in chapter 7 that images of girls and boys and women and men were available from a variety of sources, and that school-books and print resources were only part of a much bigger problem. A corollary of this is that imbalances in print resources may be tackled not only by buying, borrowing, or producing alternative materials, but also by other means. A common strategy to counteract the predominance of male images in science has been to invite women with scientific careers to talk to pupils. This was one of the strategies adopted by the Girls into Science and Technology project, which I referred to in chapter 3.

While there have been several initiatives to compensate for the under-representation of women and girls in school-books and resources or to present alternative images of girls and boys and women and men, teachers have often been loathe to dispense with any but the 'worst' examples of sexist resources from their existing stock. This may be a matter of economic necessity, but some teachers have seen a positive value in using books with male- and female-stereotyped images:

We don't just use books which present a positive view of women. It is just as important for pupils to understand how women have traditionally been portrayed. They are sometimes taken by surprise in noticing the differences between a stereotypical character and themselves. This leads *them* to question why stereotypes exist and what *they* see as being 'true' of female and male behaviour. (Bleiman and Abse, 1984, p. 59)

I don't consider it good educational policy to restrict teaching material solely to ideologically sound 'sanitized' resources I do feel that part of our job as teachers is to get children to be critically aware of the ways they are manipulated by the media, including books. (Claire, 1986, p. 63)

Classroom Organization

> Group composition should always be the result of a conscious decision. A guiding principle should be to ensure that over a period of time children learn to work harmoniously and effectively with a range of other children.
> NCC, 1989a, *English Key Stage 1: non-statutory guidance*,
> p. C4)

The way the classroom is organized affects several aspects of pupils' behaviour, including reading and writing. But classroom organization has perhaps more frequently been targeted by teachers concerned to remedy imbalances in mixed-sex talk, such as those I discussed in chapter 3.

Teachers concerned about imbalances in girls' and boys' talk have adopted strategies such as

- paying attention to how pupils are grouped for discussion work and checking how girls and boys participate in different types of grouping
- organizing the content of discussion so that this will interest girls and boys and perhaps encourage girls to participate confidently.

There has been quite a lot of debate about whether one should encourage single-sex groupings, both for everyday classroom activities and for assessment. Left to their own devices, pupils in mixed classes often elect to work in single-sex groups, and there are many advocates of single-sex schools or classes, particularly to provide support for girls in non-traditional subject areas. Dale Spender comments on such arrangements for girls:

In single-sex schools girls do not experience the same constraints upon talk. In an all-girls classroom, those who talk are girls. A range of verbal roles is available, not just the subordinate ones. (Spender, 1980, p. 153)

The question of how to group pupils is not unproblematical, however. For instance, Spender appears to be suggesting that girls, or some girls, are free to take on alternative roles ('boys' roles'?) in single-sex classes. It is not clear whether she is concerned about any inequalities there may be between speakers in an all-female class. Does it matter if some pupils dominate talk, so long as 'those who talk are girls'? A further point, often mentioned by advocates of mixed-sex classes and groups, is that girls and boys need to learn how to interact with each other. For instance (this point is also made by Dale Spender) there seems little value in female speakers being supremely confident in single-sex groupings if this confidence is lost with the appearance of male speakers.

Factors other than the quality (or quantity) of talk will affect decisions regarding how pupils are grouped; for instance, some advocates of single-sex classes are concerned to stimulate girls' uptake of, and success in non-traditional subjects such as the physical sciences. In terms of pupils' behaviour, while teachers will testify to the fact that all-girls' classes and all-boys' classes behave differently, there is a dearth of published evidence on the respects in which the same pupils' behaviour differs in single-sex and mixed-sex groups.

While single-sex groupings have usually been suggested as a strategy to help girls (for example, to promote girls' confidence), they also allow teachers to introduce changes with boys. Diane Reay (1992) worked closely with a group of nine infant boys. Five of the boys had been presenting difficulties – for instance, by not settling down to work and by disrupting the work of others. Reay worked on a book-making project with these boys and with others who were more conscientious and whom she felt might provide positive 'role models'. She encouraged the boys to work collaboratively and to consider the needs of other children in the class by making books that would appeal to girls as well as boys. The small, single-sex group, which received close attention from her did motivate the five boys to work better, and Reay was able to respond to their needs more effectively than if she had been responsible for the whole class. The motivation of some of the boys was maintained in the whole-class setting, but two boys reverted to their original behaviour when deprived of the increased attention and supervision.

Because there are so many factors to take into account when grouping pupils, decisions need to be taken on an individual basis. Development Education Centre, 1986b and Open University, 1991, provide several ideas for organizing collaborative group work.

Other contextual factors, such as the content of group discussion, will affect how pupils work together. Shelagh Harris (1991) describes a GCSE English project she undertook with her class of 14–15-year-old pupils. She wanted the class to carry out an investigative project that looked at the experiences of local women. She had monitored girls' and boys' interaction in this class, and was concerned that boys tended to dominate classroom life. She also felt that girls, and some boys, were at a disadvantage in oral assessment: 'The GCSE regulations specify that the assessor can only mark what is there, so it was hard to allocate marks to reticent pupils' (p. A113). One reason for focusing on women's experiences was 'in the hope that this would interest girls and improve their contribution to oral work as well as raising girls' and boys' awareness of gender inequalities' (p. A112).

The class decided to look at women's education. They organized themselves into groups, some single-sex and some mixed. Harris established ground rules for discussion – for example, that the roles of scribe and spokesperson should rotate within each group. Pupils interviewed family members and friends, then collated their results, producing a picture of the diverse experiences of local women and how these had changed over the years. Harris comments on the discussions that formed part of this work:

Although it isn't possible to ensure that every child contributes equally to a discussion, the level of involvement and excitement generated meant that they all had something to say. As I passed from group to group, assessing their oral contribution, I found I could intervene and draw in the quieter ones quite easily.

The group arrangement, being self selected and largely friendship based, meant that some groups were mixed while others were not. There was little noticeable difference between the two types: all members of all groups seemed equally engrossed in their discussions. There were certainly no complaints about anyone 'spoiling it' or 'mucking about'. (Harris, 1991, pp. A114–115)

9.3 Focusing on Pupils' Language

Some teachers have focused not just on the selection of reading materials, how pupils are grouped, or the content of lessons, but on pupils' own language behaviour. I shall discuss below strategies designed to affect pupils' talk and pupils' writing.

Tackling Talk

I decided to adopt a deliberate policy of asking the girls for questions and feedback first. This was by no means easy since the boys' behaviour was to shout out, butt in, demand attention, so stopping the girls from answering. Yet I persevered and the change in this aspect of classroom management was noticed by the girls. One commented that I was 'the only teacher who notices us'.
Geraldine Scanlan, 1986, 'Was your mother good at maths?' p. 15)

Several strategies have evolved for intervening directly in the patterns of talk that obtain in the classroom, paying careful attention to one's own talk as a teacher and to the quality and/or quantity of talk produced by pupils. Strategies have included

- trying not to use, or have pupils use 'sexist language'
- trying to divide one's time equally between girls and boys (for example, asking the same number of questions of girls and boys in class discussion)
- encouraging girls/quiet pupils to respond more confidently (for example, giving them more time to respond)
- trying various techniques to encourage greater collaboration between girls and boys in group work
- teaching girls to be 'assertive'

Many equal opportunities policy statements incorporate guidance on teachers' and pupils' language use:

We should try to be aware of any sexist or racist references or thoughtlessness on our own or our pupils' part and not let it pass without comment. (Extract from a science department's statement of aims, cited by Baran, 1986, p. 9)

You should have respect for yourself and other girls and women. This means you should not use words which are offensive about women. Women have fought very hard to gain respect in society; you throw this away when you call someone 'slag' or worse. (Extract from an equal opportunities policy in a girls' secondary school, cited by Smith, 1986, p. 11)

Some of the studies of 'sexist language' discussed in chapter 2 showed that children and young people are very well aware of the power of language to 'put someone down' and of discrepancies in the use of insult terms for girls and boys. Challenging these usages constitutes an attempt to intervene in the process whereby girls (in particular) are routinely disparaged. Such challenges may also draw attention to gender inequalities in a more general sense.

As well as challenging the more overt forms of sexist language, teachers have tackled gender imbalances in the way classroom talk is organized – for instance, in the amount of teacher attention taken up by girls and boys. It is sometimes claimed that it is extremely difficult for teachers to divide their time and attention evenly between girls and boys. Dale Spender (1982) suggests that a 'one-third' rule operates in mixed classes: if teachers allocate more than this amount of time to girls, it feels as though they are spending more time with girls than with boys. Judith Whyte, in her account of the GIST project (mentioned in chapter 3), is less pessimistic. She notes that after a project conference on classroom interaction, many teachers agreed to have their lessons observed and their interactions with girls and boys systematically coded. In this context, teachers discovered that they could devote equal attention to girls and boys, but only with considerable effort: 'Most believed they were giving far more than half their attention to girls and were rather disconcerted to find they had achieved only more or less equal interaction ratios' (Whyte, 1986, p. 196).

Several strategies have been suggested for teachers who wish to encourage wider participation in class or group discussion. In whole-class discussion, it has been suggested that teachers should deliberately call upon girls to speak. Clearly, such interventions need to be handled sensitively, since quieter pupils can still participate effectively in discussion, and there are those who simply wish to remain silent on a particular occasion. Mary Bousted, a secondary head of English, found that her initial attempts to involve all pupils in class discussion failed:

I tried to create the expectation within the class that everyone would quite frequently be called upon to contribute to the discussion.
I adopted the practice of calling upon particular students to answer questions and to contribute their ideas and opinions on the topic or text examined . . .

I realised very quickly, however, that quieter students were indeed often embarrassed and became tongue tied by my attempts to single them out and give them speaking rights by naming them. In many cases they did not have the confidence, borne out of long years of practice, to respond effectively and to switch from silence to a fluent, convincing expression of an idea or response to others' suggestions and ideas. (Bousted, 1989, p. 47)

Bousted's solution in this context was to introduce more formal talk into the classroom – for instance, by using written work and informal group work to support a short speech or a debate. She argues that, because they lack confidence, quiet students prepare very well, and their success boosts self-confidence and esteem. Bousted also used self-assessment to negotiate clear targets with students for their oral work; she used role play to 'give quieter students the opportunity to adopt the persona of a character who can be quite different from themselves' (p. 50); and she introduced 'buzz sessions' – regular, 1-minute breaks in whole-class discussion in which students would discuss their response to a point with their partner. After buzz sessions certain students were selected to put forward their ideas. Because they had had the chance to prepare, quieter students were then less intimidated by a whole-class audience.

While much work on whole-class discussion has focused on mixed-sex classes, quieter girls may need encouragement to speak out in single-sex groupings too, particularly in subjects in which they don't have much confidence. Graz Baran discusses how girls may be encouraged to participate, and particularly to ask questions, in a secondary science lesson:

It is useless trying to encourage discussion in class unless you are prepared to spend time explaining what it is you are trying to achieve and reassuring pupils that if they speak up and contribute they will be taken seriously by everybody. They must be constantly reassured that asking a question, rather than being a sign of ignorance, is usually a sign of understanding and involvement. You won't know what to ask when you've understood nothing at all. They must be reassured that the only person who is allowed to be laughed at, if at all, is the teacher. Also that they are not holding everybody up when they ask something. A good way of demonstrating this is to throw the question open to the whole class. It is surprising how often this demonstrates to all concerned that they are all in the same boat when other pupils try to grapple with the same problem and how this can create a supportive atmosphere among pupils. (Baran, 1986, p. 6)

It may seem easier to devise strategies to tackle imbalances in whole-class talk, for these involve, at least in part, teachers tackling their own behaviour. But teachers have also found ways of intervening in talk between pupils. Shelagh Harris, in her 'women's history' project (mentioned above), attempted to tackle secondary school pupils' talk in groups, by asking each group to have a rotating scribe and spokesperson. Hilary Claire (1986) describes some of the strategies she and a fellow teacher devised to reduce the dominance of boys and encourage participation by quiet girls in their class of 6–7-year-olds. Their initial objective was a simple one: the children should 'learn the process of talking and listening in pairs' (p. 45). This involved getting the children to work in pairs, some mixed-sex and some single-sex. Each child had to talk about a topic, listen to his or her partner, then sit in a circle with others from the class, and report what the partner had said. At first everything was tightly controlled, with strict time limits for contributions from each pupil. Eventually, pupils moved from simply telling, listening, and reporting back to discussing their views on topical issues and taking part (in role) in a formal meeting. In addition to providing equal opportunities for girls and boys to contribute to discussion, the teachers hoped to encourage a collaborative approach to learning: 'What we tried to do was to create situations in which girls and boys needed each other, and gained mutual support' (p. 45).

The teachers whose work I have discussed so far were primarily concerned with children's talk in class; but what children learn about talk in the classroom has implications for their behaviour in other contexts. Some secondary schools have introduced assertiveness training for pupils, which seeks consciously to address the issue of how they behave inside and outside school:

I think assertion training is about trying to help me in becoming more confident in myself and to help me act in a more positive way towards others. (Secondary school pupil, cited by Hordyk, 1986, p. 71)

Anna Hordyk (1986) describes her syllabus for assertiveness training in a girls' secondary school. The work, based on discussion and role play, is designed to explore what it means to be assertive, as well as to encourage assertiveness in the pupils themselves. Such work seems to be a conscious attempt at social change, in that it tackles the way people routinely behave towards each other. Changes in behaviour are by no means easy to effect; and Hordyk is aware that problems are produced when people go against others' expectations of what is normal. Some pupils have commented that acting assertively may lead to them being thought rude and aggressive by other teachers and parents. Hordyk responds that many adults need 'educating about the difference between aggression and assertion and the real skill is to know when to be assertive' (p. 71). She is in no doubt that there may be social (and physical) constraints that it is not possible for the girls in her class to overcome; that there are times when 'the best course of action is silence' (p. 69).

Tackling Pupils' Writing

> Hurrecia and Lee wanted to write a 'Love story' and a story about football. They combined the ideas and proceeded to work on their story 'Ace Team'. They started to write the first draft of the story, then switched to using a tape recorder. This was then transcribed and typed up. They decided they would like to illustrate their book using real photographs; these were duly set up, taken, sent off for developing, and eventually stuck into the book. The result was an excellent piece of children's work – even the shape of the book was that of a football. The story, however, centred round a team of boys – all from our school – who played in various football matches eventually getting through the final and winning it.
> The 'Love story' part of it consisted of:
> – *Meeting some girls at a bus stop and saying 'Do you want to come and watch US play football?'. The girls said 'Yes';*

– *After the match as supporters of the rival team were involved in football violence, two members of the school team were otherwise engaged in 'getting the kisses off the girls';*
– *At the next match the girls were told to stand a long way back so they wouldn't get hurt in any trouble that might break out;*
– *The girls were invited to join the team at their victory celebration at McDonalds.*

Throughout the story the 'girls' remained nameless.
Frances Broadway, 1986, 'Investigating children's collaborative writing', p. 66

[National Writing Project] teachers have been well versed in the inadequacies of one-shot writing (writing which is written in one session, without planning or revision). We need equally to be aware that even when the whole process of extended composition has been fulfilled, the outcome may be one-shot or incomplete in another sense – it may be writing in need of (critical) reading. It is here that the teacher's role is crucial: only by strategically and sensitively tackling stereotypes as children (or adults) present them can a teacher help meaningful and long-term change to take place. The skills of intervention demanded of the teacher far exceed those demanded of the class, group, or outside helpers; it is one of the often overlooked challenges of allowing pupils freedom to choose.
Janet White, 1990b, 'Questions of choice and change', p. 58

Teachers have sometimes been caught between their wish to allow children a greater degree of choice in their reading and writing and their wish to intervene and take children beyond the often limited choices they make if left to their own devices. Strategies for change have included

- encouraging both girls and boys to obtain experience within a range of genres and a range of topics

- reviewing, and encouraging pupils to review, their work in terms of its reliance on gender stereotypes, in the same way that one might review published sources
- using pupils' work as a vehicle for the exploration of gender issues.

The NATE Language and Gender Committee comments that, in encouraging pupils to write for different audiences,

It is important to ensure that each pupil has equal opportunity to address the full range of audiences, and that gender stereotyping does not mean that girls produce personal writing and stories for children, while the boys concentrate on writing radio scripts and more impersonal tales of the 'blood and thunder', 'cops and robbers', variety. (NATE Language and Gender Committee, 1988, pp. 14–15)

When writing within a particular genre, the tendency to adopt a 'male-voiced perspective' should be avoided: 'All letter stories do not have to be written from a soldier in the trenches to his family back home' (ibid., p. 14).

Anne Reyersbach (1986) discusses strategies she has employed to encourage children to read and write poetry – to which there was initially some resistance from boys:

Mike Rosen came to school and read to children and parents, effectively dispelling uncertainty some parents had about the place of poetry in the curriculum and showing the boys that 'Real men do write poetry!' (Reyersbach, 1986, p.68)

Reyersbach discusses the importance of the choice of appropriate poems to read to children or for children to read themselves and the importance of appropriate stimuli for children's own work. She gives examples of children's poems written in response to a picture of a man who looked as though he might be crying, commenting that the picture 'stimulated the boys to write about emotions sympathetically' (p. 68). She argues that, as well as allowing boys to write about emotions, poetry 'often gives girls a chance to excel' (p. 68).

Much of the concern about children's writing has come from teachers of English or those with responsibility for language, but an implication of Janet White's work, which I mentioned in chapters 6 and 7, is that we need to consider writing in other subjects. Graz Baran describes her (girls' school) science department's approach to writing:

Written work should always have a purpose. Accordingly, we are attempting to develop skills in more display work. This has many advantages.

1　It encourages collaborative work and purposeful writing to communicate with others about what's been learned.
2　It gives pupils a chance to take pride in their achievements.
3　It detracts from the image of science laboratories as being rather uninviting, clinical places and creates a warmer atmosphere.

(Baran, 1986, p.7)

Gender issues may also be explored through critical examination of pupils' writing. Norman Shamroth and Barbara Tilbrook (1990) provide an account of how drama was used to explore gender issues with a class of 10–11-year-olds. The class had been asked to write, in pairs, a plan for a play. All the boys' plays had female characters who were ineffectual or submissive minor characters. Pupils were asked to consider one play, written by two boys, in which the two main characters (played by the authors) became involved in a fight when two other characters tried to take their girlfriends off them in a pub. The authors/main characters accused the girls of 'dressing up sexy', which was what attracted the other boys. The class teacher asked four pupils (the authors and two confident girls) to act out a scene from the play. This was discussed with other pupils. The four actors also wrote diaries in reversed roles. Through such strategies, the teacher tried to get the two boys to see the situation they had scripted through the eyes of their girl characters. He achieved at least some success. Shamroth and Tilbrook comment: 'Clearly [the boys'] thinking had undergone a disturbance, and from disturbance comes learning' (p. 36).

9.4   Making Gender Explicit

The strategies I've discussed so far have been concerned to manipulate the range of reading materials available to pupils, the contexts in which pupils work, and teachers' and pupils' language behaviour. But many teachers also raised gender issues more explicitly. Some have argued that gender divisions are so pervasive and their influence so powerful that it's necessary to bring gender issues out into the open and discuss them with pupils. I shall consider below two ways in which gender issues have been raised in relation to language. These are getting pupils to reflect on their own spoken language and engaging pupils in critical reading and redrafting of written texts.

Talking about Talk

Encouraging pupils to avoid sexist language, as many equal opportunities policies do, and discussing the meaning of assertiveness for women, as suggested by Anna Hordyk, involve bringing the issue of gender and language out into the open. Others have also felt that inequalities in girls' and boys' talk should be tackled by discussing these explicitly with pupils and getting them to devise their own strategies to deal with them. Jackie Hughes, at the time a deputy head teacher in a primary school in Birmingham, carried out a project on Images with her class of 9–11-year-olds. Part of the aim of the project was to foster equal opportunities. Hughes had become concerned that boys were contributing more than girls to discussion and that they used techniques such as calling out to obtain speaking turns. She discussed with the pupils why some people might find it more difficult to contribute to discussion, as a result of which the talkative boys became more sensitive to the needs of others (cited Graddol and Swann, 1989, pp. 186–7). As a prelude to such discussions, pupils have sometimes carried out investigations of spoken language; for instance, monitoring the contribution of girls and boys to mixed-sex discussion.

Gender differences and inequalities in language may be tackled as an aspect of 'language awareness'. One or two language textbooks for children have included an examination of gender issues. Maura Healy, in *Your Language: Three,* has a Unit on 'Girl talk/boy talk'. She suggests that pupils tape-record and monitor girls' and boys' talk in groups, and she also raises questions pupils should consider:

Listen to your tapes and to your friends talking and answer the questions below:

1 Do boys swear as much as girls?
2 Are girls as polite as boys?
3 If they wanted to criticize something, would they use the same words?
4 Do they tell the same jokes?
5 Do they talk to teachers in the same way?
6 Are girls cheekier than boys?
7 What do you think people mean when they say 'Talk like a lady' or 'It's unladylike to talk like that.'
8 What do they mean when they say 'Boys will be boys'?
9 What *messages* are we given about girl talk? boy talk?

(Healy, 1981, p. 102)

There is a danger in presenting pupils with such questions that stereotypes may simply be regurgitated. But, with guidance, pupils may be able to explore their own and others' language use and to challenge conventional expectations.

Critical Reading for Children

What do you think?

1 Can you give any reasons why he = he + she? Why don't we use she = she + he since she contains he?
2 Does it matter that human beings are often described as men? When you read 'Man invented the wheel' do you think it means that either a man or woman invented it?

3   Do some research. Look in your library catalogue and see how many books include the word 'man' or 'mankind' in their title. Now look at some of the books. Are they really about men and women? How many of the pictures show women? Look in the index. How many women are named there? Look at the text. Is *he* or *his* always used?

Maura Healy, 1981, *Your Language: Three*, p. 98

The kind of book I really do like to read is when the women or girls in it do something really good. When they do something unusual. I especially like it when she does something that is better than the men do. I like to read those kind of books because I'm so used to hearing about all the wonderful things men do. In most books the hero is good-looking but also extremely intelligent. It is nice to read something different, like when it's about women.

Fourth-year pupil, cited by Barbara Bleiman and Karen Abse, 1984, *Gender: One Department's Practice*, p. 59

Boys Boys Boys don't you ever write for girls although saying that the description is very very good but you can tell a boy has written it because there is no words for girls.

Child's comment on another's story, cited by Bernadette Fitzgerald, 1990, 'Means to an end', p. 39

Perhaps because print forms such a central, tangible part of school life and pupils' lives out of school, an important focus of anti-sexist work with children has been getting pupils to respond critically to written texts. While designed to affect the way in which pupils habitually approach texts, this may also have the aim of making pupils aware of wider, social inequalities between girls and boys and women and men.

Pupils have looked at the extent to which written materials, including school resources, use 'sexist language' (in much the same way as they might investigate their own and others' spoken language). But an examination of written materials normally involves broader issues of representation. It may include

- analysing visual images of girls and boys, and women and men – in advertisements, magazines, birthday cards, and so forth
- investigating female and male images from a variety of sources – magazines, comics, reading books, fairy stories
- reading books with alternative images – such as non-sexist fairy stories – and using these books, often by comparison with more traditional books, as a spring-board for discussion about gender issues
- rewriting traditional stories, perhaps changing the plot or reversing the sex of the main protagonists
- reviewing books or unpublished writing (including other pupils' writing) or noting down books that are felt to be sexist (or racist or biased in some other way).

Making gender issues explicit forms part of some of the strategies I've already mentioned for tackling reading materials and girls' and boys' writing. Norman Shamroth and Barbara Tilbrook, in asking pupils to reflect on their own and others' writing, were also encouraging them to consider conventional images of girls and boys. Barbara Bleiman and Keren Abse, and Hilary Claire, in retaining 'sexist' books for use with their classes, had as an aim the development of critical reading in children.

The idea that pupils can study gender and other forms of imbalance, in both written and visual texts, has been particu-larly prominent in media education. This is perhaps why analyses have frequently been carried out on 'popular' texts of one sort or another. It still seems more controversial to subject 'literature' or 'art' to this sort of analysis.

The British Film Institute has produced packs for use in schools, to encourage pupils to explore the meanings of visual images (photographs, magazine covers, adverts, greetings cards and so on). Activities also encourage pupils to explore

Figure 9.1 *Birthday cards sent to a 5-year-old girl. British Film Institute,* Selling Pictures, *slide 36.*

the basis of their understanding of visual images, drawing on the immediate context of the image (a caption, surrounding text) and their own cultural knowledge of different types of image.

Whereas other forms of critical reading may involve pupils in looking at books and sources at a fairly general level (for example, in terms of the number and type of characters), this form of visual analysis involves close scrutiny of a single image, or perhaps contrasting different types of image. For instance, an activity on gender stereotyping intended for use with 14–16-year-old pupils asks pupils to consider images in girls' and boys' birthday cards (see figures 9.1 and 9.2).

Pupils are asked to consider what all eight images have in

Figure 9.2 *Birthday cards sent to a 5-year-old boy. British Film Institute,* Selling Pictures, *slide 37.*

common and what the four images on each slide have in common. It is expected that they will consider features such as 'dress, expression, pose, activity, setting, species of animal and predominant colours' (BFI, p. 23). While the immediate focus of the BFI pack is on the analysis of specific images, it is also meant to raise social issues such as the role of stereotyping in perpetuating unequal power relations between women and men (and other social groups); thus it has a much wider aim than simply understanding how individual images produce meaning.

At a more general level of analysis, a popular strategy has been to ask pupils to examine comics and magazines aimed at their own age-group. Jane Leggett and Judith Hemming wanted to explore and expose the values inherent in teenage magazines, but they were aware of two dangers that have concerned others and that I mentioned in earlier chapters: namely, that teenagers enjoy comics and magazines and are likely to be resistant to criticism of these by teachers, and that there is a tendency to be more critical of girls' interests than boys':

Somehow it had seemed *easier* to criticise girls' magazines for their triviality and feebleness than to look closely at what goes on in boys' comics, which seemed to have a protective shell of 'energy'. (Leggett and Hemming, 1984, p. 74)

Leggett and Hemming designed a teaching pack that first asked secondary school pupils (aged 14/15 and over) to consider their own current concerns and how far these were dealt with in comics and magazines. Pupils then analysed extracts from comics and magazines, compared magazines aimed at boys with those aimed at girls, and began to devise the kind of teenage magazine that they would like to see. In piloting their materials, Leggett and Hemming found that girls were concerned about the images conveyed in both their own and boys' reading:

The girls were particularly critical that the boys' comics offered no help and guidance on how to look and how to cope with girls. They were ready to concede the boys' criticism that the photo-stories were predictable and soppy but countered this by asserting that the issues and topics that both boys and girls had highlighted as important appeared in none of the material examined. (Ibid., p. 78)

Other teachers have focused on books for younger children. Christopher Draper (1986) describes how a general discussion about reading books with children in his primary class produced a complaint from some of the girls about the 'soppiness' of the female characters in one reading scheme, *One, Two, Three, and Away*. (An analysis of this reading scheme is discussed in chapter 5.) Draper followed up the complaint with drama and discussion work, during which the children strung together some 'sexist' scenes from *One, Two, Three, and Away*, but added a surprise ending: the girls and women caused a bus carrying the boys and men to crash into the village pond; they agreed to rescue the boys and men, but only on condition that they 'stop making them do soppy things' (1986, p. 64). Eventually, some children produced alternative reading books: *Billy Blue Hat Washes Up, Jennifer Joins the 'A' Team,* and *Roger Goes Shopping*.

Fairy stories have been the focus of a great deal of anti-sexist work. Non-sexist fairy stories often provide a stimulus for children to re-examine and discuss female and male images in traditional stories. One of the most comprehensive sources of ideas for work on fairy stories is Bronwen Mellor, Judith Hemming, and Jane Leggett, *Changing Stories* (1984). It encourages children to examine the characteristics of fairy stories and some of the motives behind fairy stories produced at different periods. *Changing Stories* builds on children's (often implicit) knowledge of fairy stories. Children are encouraged to examine plots, characterization, and 'morals' that are common in fairy stories; to compare different versions of the same story; to consider how (and why) stories might have changed through time; and to produce their own stories. As well as considering characteristics of fairy stories, the book is likely to provoke a more general discussion of gender issues (see Figure 9.3).

Frogs, Princesses

Look at the illustrations on this page. The artist has included many typical elements and characters from fairy stories and folk tales. Some parts of the picture will probably remind you of particular stories and titles that you know.

In your pair or group see how many typical elements and characters from fairy stories or folk tales you can note down. Also write down as many titles of folk and fairy stories as you can think of.

Here are a few ideas to help you get started:

TYPICAL THINGS	TITLES
Frogs	Cinderella
Forests	Rumpelstiltskin
Wicked relations	Jack the Giant Killer

You may not realise just how much you already know about stories — about what happens in them and about how the characters usually look and behave.

Complete the following sentences with as many ideas as you can think of to do with fairy stories and folk tales:

● Princesses are......................................

● Old women who live in the forest are.......

● Princes are ....

● Frogs turn in to.......................

● Animals can often ....

Figure 9.3   *Illustration from* Changing Stories *(Mellor et al., 1984), p. 4.*

9.5 Equality Issues

A common goal for all those who express concern about gender imbalances in speaking and listening, reading and writing, would probably be a situation in which girls and boys participated confidently in a wide range of activities and where activities traditionally associated with girls were not devalued. How anyone tries to move towards this goal, however, will depend on how they perceive the current problem; the pupils they are working with, the context in which they work, and what they feel able to do, given various practical constraints and other equally pressing priorities. Despite differences in the strategies adopted by teachers, there are common issues that run through attempts to introduce equal opportunities in and through spoken and written language. I shall discuss these below.

Towards Equality?

The work I have considered in this chapter has all been concerned with changes in classroom practice; changes that are meant, somehow, to redress the sorts of imbalances and inequalities that have been identified in earlier chapters. I've used the term 'equal opportunities' for such work, because that is the term that seems to have greatest currency within education as an umbrella term for a whole range of initiatives designed to counteract sexism and other forms of social inequality. It is a term that seems to have gone out of fashion and come back in again. It is respectable enough to hang around the margins of the National Curriculum. But its use draws attention to one or two problems with work designed to counteract sexism – not least of which is the extent to which 'equality' is a practical or even a desirable aim.

Equal opportunities reside in the way girls and boys are treated in schools; but this doesn't imply that schools need to treat girls and boys equally. In fact, equality of treatment

cannot be a sound basis for the provision of equal opportunities. It seems reasonable to insist that pupils should not be
treated differently on irrelevant grounds; but not all grounds
are irrelevant. For instance, it does not seem reasonable to
adopt an identical teaching approach for two pupils who have
different degrees of familiarity with a task they've been set.
The strategies I've discussed in this chapter do not seem to
depend on the notion of 'equal treatment'. They may depend
on treating girls and boys, or individual pupils, differently or
unequally.

One indicator of the success of equal opportunities would
be the outcomes they produce for girls and boys. But few
strategies presuppose that they will produce equal outcomes;
the idea seems to be, in the main, to open up choices, not to
make all pupils behave in an identical way. Sometimes, equal
outcomes may be inappropriate. I mentioned, in relation to
spoken language, that girls who use conversational styles
associated with boys may be responded to differently than
boys would be. A paradox here is that gender inequality tends
to be identified in terms of *un*equal outcomes (fewer girls than
boys study physical sciences when they have the choice; more
boys than girls contribute to whole-class discussion). A measure of the effectiveness of strategies designed to counteract
such imbalances would be the degree to which girls and boys
became more similar (more girls studied physical sciences or
spoke out in class). (Donald Mackinnon, 1989, discusses in
greater detail the relationship between equal opportunities,
equal treatment, and equal outcomes.)

Some people have responded to the problem posed by the
notion of equality by turning to an alternative notion, that of
equity. This presupposes that one behaves in a way that is
just or fair, but not (necessarily) that one metes out equal
treatment or strives for equal outcomes. It is no easier to
measure the effectiveness of equity than of equal opportunities, but the term does at least suggest that judgements about
what counts as equitable are subjective. What is equitable will
depend very much on the circumstances in which teachers
work, the types of pupils they teach, and what they perceive
as the specific needs of the moment. It is in some ways a more

difficult concept to handle than equality. But it does at least recognize the variety of ways in which what happens to girls and boys is *in*equitable, as well as the varying strategies that may be employed to counteract these (some, but not all of which, may involve greater equality). It also recognizes that what is equitable is open to discussion; that there may be disagreement about what the problem is, what counts as a solution, and what strategies are appropriate in trying to attain it.

Introducing Change through Language

Written and spoken language necessarily play a part in most equal opportunities work, though they are not always an explicit focus of such work. Because of the varying motives for equal opportunities initiatives and the different contexts in which these are carried out, such initiatives have highlighted different aspects of language. In line with much of the research in this area, initiatives that involve girls' and boys' spoken language have been concerned with the management of talk or with specific conversational features: how to encourage a more even distribution of talk, how to encourage girls to be assertive, or all pupils to engage in collaborative talk. Initiatives that have involved written language have more often been concerned with the content of what is written: how to tackle stereotyped images in reading materials, or how to widen the range of topics girls and boys write about.

The initiatives I've discussed in this chapter have shown that speaking and listening and reading and writing may be tackled indirectly, by changing contexts of language use. Changes in classroom organization will probably bring about changes in pupils' spoken language, even if this is not the teacher's intention (changes in language use may be an incidental by-product of other changes). But changing language use will also affect other aspects of classroom life. Managing talk so that more pupils contribute to discussion may create a more relaxed and informal atmosphere. Encouraging pupils to write in science lessons in a less impersonal way may change their perceptions of science.

The relationship between language and the things that surround it is very much closer than the traditional linguistic dichotomy between 'language' and 'context' suggests. The same effects may be achieved linguistically and non-linguistically: somebody may be silenced by another person making a comment or a gesture or beginning to re-arrange books on a table; a book may appear 'girl-friendly' by virtue of what is in the text or the illustrations or the cover. The very pervasiveness of language means that it is inevitably bound up with equal opportunities initiatives, whether intentionally so or not. But it also means that it is unwise, and probably impractical, to introduce changes in language without taking account of other aspects of classroom life.

Language and Social Relations

I've mentioned at various points that language is one of the key ways in which we relate to others, and that changing language use therefore brings about changes in social relationships. This applies most obviously to interpersonal language, which tends to be spoken language. I have also emphasized that what goes on in the classroom has social implications that go beyond the school: children bring some of their patterns of language use and language attitudes into school with them; in the same way, changes in children's attitudes and behaviour in the classroom are likely to affect relationships between girls and boys and women and men in other contexts. This has been recognized by many of those concerned to introduce equal opportunities. Language use may be tackled in the classroom as a way of changing relationships between girls and boys (or between other social groups), as when girls are taught to be more assertive. But the existing state of social relationships may also inhibit changes in language use (there are penalties for going against social expectations).

Reading and writing also provide avenues for challenging, and perhaps changing, the ways girls and boys conventionally relate to others. Non-sexist images in reading books are intended, among other things, to challenge conventional expectations of girls' and boys' behaviour. And pupils' writing may be used as a vehicle for exploring relations between girls and boys. Set against this is the fact that social relations are not *determined* by what we read and write (or by the ways we speak, for that matter) – and that pupils may reject 'non-sexist' images that do not conform to their expectations.

The Politics of Intervention

All the teachers whose work I have discussed in this chapter have made the decision to intervene: to attempt to introduce changes in language (or other forms of representation) or to use language/representation as a vehicle for the introduction of change in other aspects of classroom practice. But such interventions have themselves been subject to criticism. Those who do not wish to see schools involved in social change, who do not believe that gender distinctions are detrimental to girls or boys, or who simply believe that schools should devote their energies to other things might be expected to object to teacher interventions. But feminists have also questioned some of the work designed to combat gender inequalities. Gemma Moss, whose work I discussed in chapter 7, has been critical of certain anti-sexist strategies. For instance, she, like many others with very different motives, has referred to the danger of 'censoring' what pupils read.

Censorship has been the subject of frequent debate, most recently in the pages of the newsletter for the children's book club Letterbox Library. There is an argument that children do not have a real choice anyway; their preferences have come about because of their earlier experiences and the expectations of others. In providing children with alternative reading, then, the teacher may be constraining what they do, but she is also giving them a wider basis for making choices. Set against this is a view that children are more motivated to read when they are pursuing their own choices – and also that, as a matter of principle, children should have more autonomy, and the opportunity to choose and plan their own work. While 'censorship' seems particularly relevant to discussions of pupils' reading, similar issues underlie strategies designed to challenge, or change, pupils' writing or the ways they speak; in each case, there is a tension between pupil choice and teacher control.

Gemma Moss (1989) suggests that teachers' over-zealous desire to control pupils' choices arises from a concern about girls (rather than boys), but that this concern might itself render girls helpless. She argues that teachers should 'spend less time prescribing how girls should behave by devising anti-sexist strategies and more time supporting girls in what they are already up to' (pp. 123–4). 'Supporting girls', for Moss, means supporting whatever strategy they adopt to subvert sexism. This doesn't just mean when they take an active 'anti-sexist' stand, but also when they play along with sexism (for example, with boys' sexist behaviour). Different strategies will be appropriate in different contexts.

I've mentioned at several points in the book that more concern has been expressed about girls than about boys. It is often girls who are perceived to have problems (or to constitute a problem) in terms of their subject choices and their eventual careers; at a local level, it is girls who are more often seen to be disadvantaged by imbalances in mixed-sex talk or images in children's books. Some of the initiatives I have discussed in this chapter have recognized this as a problem, and have tried to focus on the restricted nature of boys' behaviour and boys' choices, as much as on girls'. But there is something of a tension between the need to value lhat girls and women do (in various respects) and the fact that less value *is* currently placed on what girls and women do, on almost every level – from boys' tendency to disparage girls in the classroom to the much lower salaries earned by women in paid employment. It is, no doubt, easier to encourage girls to engage in activities that enjoy high status than it is to encourage boys to take part in activities associated with girls that we, but not they, regard as valuable.

While many teachers recognize the danger of seeming to attach less value to girls' than to boys' activities, the initiatives

I've discussed take a more 'pro-active' stance than that which Moss seems to advocate. They are involved in rather more than 'supporting girls in what they are up to'. In this, they probably come closer to the position adopted by Pam Gilbert, whose work I discussed in chapter 7. Gilbert recognized that girls are 'resistant readers and writers', but felt that they needed active support to resist sexism.

Gilbert also emphasizes a point I've made in earlier chapters: namely, that girls' and boys' language use (she focuses on reading and writing) cannot be tackled in isolation:

Sexist children's literature is only one of the many cultural practices involved in the construction of gendered subjectivity, and while it is important that girls be offered alternative stories, with alternative messages, such changes need to be seen as part of a wider political change. (Gilbert, 1988, p. 14)

9.6   Conclusion

In this chapter I've tried to give a sense of the different ways in which teachers and other educationists have intervened to counteract gender inequalities in schools and classrooms. I've suggested that equal opportunities strategies differ in the extent to which they make gender issues an explicit focus of pupils' work, in the ways in which they involve language, and in the aspects of language they draw on. I've also given some attention to the debate about the extent to which teachers should intervene at all.

The strategies I have discussed include:

- Selecting reading material and other resources so as to counteract gender imbalances, and as a means of providing positive encouragement for girls and boys to engage in non-traditional activities.
- Focusing on classroom organization and on the content of group discussion. In this respect I mentioned

the debate about when, or whether, single-sex groupings were desirable.

- Tackling spoken language directly: for instance, using
  techniques that might encourage quiet girls to participate in discussion or boys and girls to collaborate
  together.
- Tackling pupils' reading and writing choices, by
  encouraging girls and boys to explore a range of
  genres and subject-matter and using pupils' writing
  for the exploration of gender issues.
- Discussing differences and inequalities in spoken language with pupils, perhaps as part of language awareness and encouraging pupils to observe and monitor
  their own language use.
- Encouraging pupils to read critically: to explore gender stereotyping in visual images, magazines, books,
  and other printed material. I mentioned that popular
  texts have often been the focus of such work, as have
  children's stories. 'Serious' literature and art tend to
  escape this sort of critical reading.

There are several issues that run through these attempts to
counteract gender inequalities: whether, and in what respects,
equality between girls and boys should be an aim of such
initiatives; the fact that language is necessarily implicated in
equal opportunities work, but that it is bound up with several
other contextual factors; that changing pupils' language would
probably bring about changes in the way they relate to others
in and out of school; that, conversely, current relations may
inhibit language change; the tension between pupil choice
and teacher control; and how far one should intervene and
how far this might be detrimental to girls.

The teachers whose initiatives I have discussed work in
different contexts, and have different motives for introducing
change. I have tried to preserve some of this diversity, rather
than distilling a set of 'guidelines for equal opportunities',
because I think equal opportunities initiatives need to be
planned (and evaluated) in context. This does not mean that
anything goes, but that what teachers are able to do (or what

counts as successful) depends on several factors: the type of school involved, the type of pupils, and what aspects of the curriculum or classroom life seem to require most attention.

In one sense gender, as a social division, is something that pre-exists individuals and that exists outside individual activities and interactions. But gender also needs to be constantly refashioned at an individual and interpersonal level. I have indicated throughout this book how written and spoken language play a part in the routine maintenance of educational gender divisions and inequalities. I have also mentioned a corollary of this, which underpins the work discussed in this chapter: that language may be used to subvert routine practice, to challenge expectations, and to contribute towards educational and social change.

Further Reading

There isn't space here to give a comprehensive bibliography covering all the issues discussed in this book. I have set out a few suggestions as starting points for those who wish to look further into some of these issues. I have also suggested some sources of further information. The readings are grouped into general information on gender and education and related issues (chapter 1); material exploring the relationship between gender and language (chapter 2); discussion of gender imbalances in classroom interaction/spoken language in the classroom (chapters 3 and 4); discussion of imbalances in reading materials and children's own writing (chapters 5, 6, and 7); suggestions for tackling imbalances (chapters 8 and 9).

Chapter 1

Several books on gender and education appeared in the late 1970s and 1980s. For a comprehensive list of references (up to 1988) see Gaby Weiner and Madeleine Arnot (eds), *Gender and Education Bibliography*. The bibliography was produced for Open University MA students. It is available from Kim Watts, The Open University, 527 Finchley Rd., London, NW3 7BG.

Sara Delamont's *Sex Roles and the School* appeared originally in 1980, but was revised in 1990. This revised edition provides a good general introduction to gender issues. Another book that has been revised and updated is Dale Spender and Elizabeth Sarah's *Learning to Lose*. This is an edited collection covering several aspects of schooling, including the curriculum, classroom life, women teachers, 'race' and gender, and sexuality. The bibliography is a particularly valuable source of other books and publications.

Two books edited by Gaby Weiner and Madeleine Arnot (Arnot and Weiner (eds), *Gender and the Politics of Schooling* and Weiner and Arnot (eds), *Gender under Scrutiny* bring together a number of key articles on various aspects of educational policy and practice.

For further reading on the development of gender differences and biological and social explanations of these, John Archer and Barbara Lloyd's *Sex and Gender*, although published originally in 1982, is still a good starting point. See also Diane Halpern, *Sex Differences in Cognitive Abilities*, and several chapters in David Hargreaves and Ann Colley (eds), *The Psychology of Sex Roles*.

Chapter 2

The following books contain more detailed discussion of some of the issues raised in this chapter: Jennifer Coates, *Women, Men and Language*; David Graddol and Joan Swann, *Gender Voices*; Deborah Cameron, *Feminism and Linguistic Theory*. Cate Poynton's *Language and Gender: making the difference* is also concerned with educational issues.

Jennifer Coates and Deborah Cameron have produced an edited collection of studies of women's (and men's) language use: *Women in their Speech Communities*. Barrie Thorne, Cheris Kramarae, and Nancy Henley's book *Language, Gender and Society* includes an annotated bibliography of language and gender up to the early 1980s.

A comprehensive set of guidelines for the avoidance of 'sexist language' can be found in Casey Miller and Kate Swift's *Handbook of Non-Sexist Writing for Writers, Editors and Speakers*.

I mentioned in chapter 2 that we don't have enough information about the development of gender differences in language use. Suzanne Romaine, in *The Language of Children and Adolescents*, discusses children's acquisition of communicative competence, including differences between girls' and boys' speech.

Chapters 3 and 4

Sara Delamont's book *Sex Roles and the School* (also referred to in chapter 1) is a good source of information on gender and classroom interaction. It focuses particularly on qualitative studies.

Louise Wilkinson and Cora Marrett's *Gender Influences in Classroom Interaction* includes an overview of the area and a comprehensive review of the literature, plus a selection of studies of several aspects of classroom interaction: whole class and small group, different subject areas, focusing on both teachers and pupils. All the studies are from the USA, and there is a bias towards quantitative work.

Subject journals, publications produced by subject organizations, and general education journals occasionally contain accounts of gender and classroom interaction in particular subject areas or studies that extend or qualify the notion of gender differences. An example of the former is Mary Bousted's 'Who talks?', which looks at gender and talk in English lessons. Bousted's work is mentioned in chapter 9 because she suggests strategies for changing patterns of classroom interaction. Valerie Morgan and Seamus Dunn's article 'Chameleons in the classroom: visible and invisible children in nursery and infant classrooms' provides an example of the latter category; Morgan and Dunn relate gender to the notion of (in)visibility.

Chapters 5, 6 and 7

Rosemary Stones's book *'Pour out the Cocoa, Janet': sexism in children's books* illustrates some of the concerns that grew out of early (1970s and early 1980s) studies of gender imbalances in books. It also contains a set of 'Questions to ask about children's books'.

Many studies have documented imbalances in resources associated with particular subject areas. It's worth looking through journals or publications produced by subject organizations for examples of these. For instance, NATE (National Association for the Teaching of English) has an active Language and Gender Committee. Some of the work mentioned in Chapter 5 comes from their books *Alice in Genderland* (NATE Language and Gender Working Party, 1985) and *Gender Issues in English Coursework* (NATE Language and Gender Committee, 1988).

I mentioned in chapter 5 that I knew of few detailed qualitative accounts of gender and visual images in children's books. There are publications that discuss the analysis of visual images in educational resources, but without a particular focus on gender. See, for instance, Gunther Kress and Theo van Leeuwen, *Reading Images*. This book includes analyses of visual images in children's writing.

The National Writing Project book *What are Writers Made of? Issues of gender and writing* contains accounts of teachers' investigations of girls' and boys' writing, as well as other case studies written by teachers and project co-ordinators. Janet White's article 'On literacy and gender' is a thought-provoking discussion of gender differences in writing and their implications. White questions some aspects of 'process' approaches to writing, which have been associated with the National Writing Project.

Carolyn Steedman's book *The Tidy House* provides a detailed interpretation of a piece of collaborative writing produced by three young working-class girls, which reflects their own lives as children and their expectations about adult life. Gemma Moss's book *Un/Popular Fictions* also provides an analysis of children's writing, this time from three secondary school pupils. Moss's book is also interesting because of her explicit questioning of anti-sexist approaches to dealing with gender imbalances in children's writing and in books and other reading material.

Chapters 8 and 9

If you wish to monitor gender imbalances as part of a project or a piece of action research, a number of books give general

advice on research methods. See, for instance, Graham Hitchcock and David Hughes, *Research and the Teacher*; P. Hopkins,
A Teacher's Guide to Classroom Research; and R. Walker, *Doing
Research: a handbook for teachers*. In *Investigating Classroom
Talk*, A. D. Edwards and D. P. G. Westgate discuss a range of
techniques for observing and analysing talk, and provide
advice on transcription.

There are now several books that provide more specific
guidance for teachers who wish to monitor and/or redress
gender imbalances in the classroom. I shall mention a few
books here to give an idea of what is available, then refer to
a published bibliography which provides further sources.

Kate Myers's *Genderwatch!* provides comprehensive guidance on monitoring gender imbalances in school and classroom life. It contains schedules to monitor classroom talk and
reading materials (three of these are reproduced in chapter 8).
The revised (1992) edition, *Genderwatch after the Education
Reform Act*, includes material on race and class.

Many sets of guidelines exist for those who wish to look at
bias in school texts or who would like advice on points to
consider when buying new books. For guidance on new books
see, for instance, the 'Questions to ask about children's books'
in Rosemary Stones's *'Pour out the Cocoa, Janet'*. There are also
published non-sexist book lists; a recent example is Susan
Adler, *Ms Muffet Fights Back*, available from Penguin. Another
source of non-sexist books is Letterbox Library, a children's
book club that specializes in non-sexist and multicultural
books and also produces a regular newsletter (the book club
address is Unit 2D, Leroy House, 436 Essex Road, London N1
3QP).

Subject organizations or local authority advisers may provide advice on monitoring gender imbalances in particular
subject areas. ILEA's booklet *Everyone Counts: looking for bias
and insensitivity in primary mathematics material* includes advice
on several sources of imbalance, including gender.

The Development Education Centre in Birmingham has
produced a book that discusses several forms of 'bias' in
school resources (it covers 'race', class and perceptions of
other countries, as well as gender). Entitled *Hidden Messages:*

activities for exploring bias, the book contains suggestions for exploring ideas about bias with colleagues, for devising a checklist and for discussing bias with children.

ILEA's two books *Primary Matters* and *Secondary Issues* contain case studies written by teachers that will provide ideas for dealing with gender issues throughout the school. Many of the case studies involve written or spoken language, and I have referred to some of them in chapter 9. The English Centre's *The English Curriculum: gender* contains material for discussion with colleagues on language, literature, media, and other topics relevant to the English curriculum. *Changing Stories*, also published by the English Centre, contains several suggestions for exploring the themes and motives of traditional fairy stories. (English Centre publications are available from NATE Publications, 49 Broomgrove Road, Sheffield, S10 2NA.)

The Equal Opportunities Commission publishes booklets on equal opportunities in several aspects of school life (their address is Overseas House, Quay Street, Manchester M3 3HN).

A useful bibliography containing books for teachers, as well as resources for use with children, is *Teaching for Equality: educational resources on race and gender*, by Catherine Brooking, Marina Foster, and Stephanie Smith.

References

Adler, S. (1992) 'Aprons and attitudes: feminism and children's books', in Claire, H., Maybin, J. and Swann, J. (eds) *Equality Matters*, Clevedon, Multilingual Matters.

Adler, S. (undated) *Ms Muffet Fights Back: a Penguin non-sexist booklist*, Harmondsworth, Penguin.

Archer, J. (1991) 'Testosterone and human aggression: a review', *British Journal of Psychology*, 82:1–28.

Archer, J. and Lloyd, B. (1982) *Sex and Gender*, Harmondsworth, Penguin. Rev. edn 1985, Cambridge University Press.

Arnold, N. (1990) 'A bit too close to Homer: gender and writing in the junior school', in National Writing Project (NWP) *What are Writers Made of? Issues of gender and writing*, Walton-on-Thames, Nelson.

Arnot, M. and Weiner, G. (eds) (1987) *Gender and the Politics of Schooling*, London, Hutchinson in association with the Open University.

Baines, B. (1985) 'Literature and sex-bias in the secondary school English curriculum', in NATE Language and Gender Working Party (eds.), *Alice in Genderland*, Sheffield, NATE.

Baker, C. D. and Freebody, P. (1989) *Children's First School Books*, Oxford, Basil Blackwell.

Baran, G. (1986) 'Rethinking the science curriculum', in Inner London Education Authority (ILEA) *Secondary Issues? Some approaches to equal opportunities in secondary schools*, London, ILEA.

Barclay, L. K. (1974) 'The emergence of vocational expectations in pre-school children', *Journal of Vocational Behaviour*, 4:1–14.

Barnes, D. (1969) 'Language in the secondary classroom', in Barnes, D., Britton, J. and Rosen, H. (rev. edn 1986) *Language, the Learner and the School*, Harmondsworth, Penguin.

Beattie, G. W. (1981) 'Interruption in conversational interaction, and its relation to the sex and status of the interactants', *Linguistics*, 19:15–35.

Bleiman, B. and Abse, K. (1984) 'Gender: one department's practice', in The English Centre (ed.) *The English Curriculum: Gender. Material for discussion*, London, English Centre.

Bornstein, D. (1978) 'As meek as a maid: a historical perspective on language for women in courtesy books from the Middle Ages to *Seventeen* magazine', in Butturff, D. and Epstein, E. L. (eds) *Women's Language and Style*, Deparment of English, University of Akron.

Bousted, M. (1989) 'Who talks?', *English in Education*, 23/3:41–51.

British Film Institute (BFI) (undated) *Selling Pictures: a teaching pack about representation and stereotyping*, London, BFI Education.

Broadway, F. (1986) 'Investigating children's collaborative writing', in Inner London Education Authority (ILEA) *Primary Matters: some approaches to equal opportunities in the primary school*, London, ILEA.

Brooking, C., Foster, M. and Smith, S. (1987) *Teaching for Equality: educational resources on race and gender*, London, Runnymede Trust.

Cameron, D. (1985) *Feminism and Linguistic Theory*, London, Macmillan.

Central Statistical Office (1990) *Social Trends 20*, London, HMSO.

Cheshire, J. (1982) *Variation in an English Dialect*, Cambridge, Cambridge University Press.

Cheshire, J. and Jenkins, N. (1991) 'Gender issues in the GCSE oral English examination, Part II', *Language and Education*, 5/1.

Children's Rights Workshop (1976) *Sexism in Children's Books: facts, figures and guidelines*, London, Writers and Readers Publishing Cooperative.

Claire, H. (1986) 'Collaborative work as an anti-sexist process', in Inner London Education Authority (ILEA) *Primary Matters: some approaches to equal opportunities in the primary school*, London, ILEA.

Claire, H. and Redpath, J. (1989) *Girls' and boys' interactions in primary classrooms*, Ealing Gender Equality Team Occasional Paper no. 2, Ealing Education Authority.

Clark, H. H. and Clark, E. V. (1977) *Psychology and Language*, New York, Harcourt Brace Jovanovich.

Clarricoates, K. (1983) 'Classroom interaction', in Whyld, J. (ed.) *Sexism in the Secondary Curriculum*, London, Harper and Row.

Coates, J. (1986) *Women, Men and Language*, London, Longman.

Coates, J. and Cameron, D. (eds) (1988) *Women in their Speech Communities*, London, Longman.

Coward, R. (1984) 'Underneath we're angry', reproduced in The English Centre (ed.) *The English Curriculum: Gender. Material for discussion*, London, English Centre.

Culley, L. (1988) 'Girls, boys and computers', *Educational Studies*, 14:3–8.

Cumbria Oracy Project (1988) *Talking Sense: oracy group work in primary classrooms*, Carlisle, Cumbria County Council.

Dart, B. C. and Clarke, J. A. (1988) 'Sexism in schools: a new look', *Educational Review*, 40/1:41–9.

Delamont, S. (1990, rev. edn) *Sex Roles and the School*, London, Methuen.

Department of Education and Science (DES) (1975) *A Language for Life*, London, HMSO (the Bullock Report).

Department of Education and Science (DES) (1989) *Statistics of Education: school Examinations GCSE and GCE*, London, DES.

Department of Education and Science/Welsh Office (DES/WO) (1989) *English for Ages 5 to 16*, London, HMSO (the 'Cox Report').

Development Education Centre (1986a) *Hidden Messages: activities for exploring bias*, Birmingham, Development Education Centre.

Development Education Centre (1986b) *Theme Work: approaches for teaching with a global perspective*, Birmingham, Development Education Centre.

Draper, C. (1986) 'Challenging a reading scheme', in Inner London Education Authority (ILEA) *Primary Matters: some approaches to equal opportunities in the primary school*, London, ILEA.

Durkin, K. (1985) *Television, Sex Roles and Children*, Milton Keynes, Open University Press.

Eakins, B. and Eakins, G. (1976) 'Verbal turn-taking and exchanges in faculty dialogue', in Dubois, B. L. and Crouch, I. (eds) (1978) *The Sociology of the Languages of American Women*, Papers in Southwest English IV, San Antonio, Trinity University.

Edelsky, C. (1976) 'The acquisition of communicative competence: recognition of linguistic correlates of sex roles', *Merrill Palmer Quarterly*, 22/1:47–59.

Edelsky, C. (1981) 'Who's got the floor?', *Language in Society*, 10:383–421.

Edwards, A. D. and Westgate, D. P. G. (1987) *Investigating Classroom Talk*, Lewes, Falmer Press.

Edwards, J. R. (1979) 'Social class differences and the identification of sex in children's speech', *Journal of Child Language*, 6:121–7.

Edwards, V. (1986) *Language in a Black Community*, Clevedon, Multilingual Matters.

Edwards, V. (1988) 'The speech of British Black women in Dudley, West Midlands', in Coates, J. and Cameron, D. (eds) *Women in their Speech Communities*, London, Longman.

The English Centre (ed.) (1984) *The English Curriculum: Gender. Material for discussion*, London, English Centre.

Equal Opportunities Commission (EOC) (1991) *Women and Men in Great Britain*, London, HMSO.

Equal Opportunities Commission (EOC) (undated) *A Guide to Equal Treatment of the Sexes in Careers Materials*, Manchester, EOC.

Esposito, A. (1979) 'Sex differences in children's conversation', *Language and Speech*, 22/3:213–20.

Evans, G. (1988) ' "Those loud black girls" ', in Spender, D. and Sarah, E. (eds) (1988, rev. edn) *Learning to Lose: sexism and education*, London, Women's Press.

Fawcett Society (1987) *Exams for the Boys*, London, Fawcett Society.

Fisher, J. (1991) 'Unequal voices: gender and assessment', in Open University (1991) P535: *Talk and Learning 5–16*, Milton Keynes, Open University.

Fishman, P. M. (1983) 'Interaction: the work women do', in Thorne, B., Kramarae, C. and Henley, N. (eds) *Language, Gender and Society*, Rowley, Mass., Newbury House.

Fitzgerald, B. (1990) 'Means to an end', in National Writing Project (NWP) *Responding to and Assessing Writing*, Walton-on-Thames, Nelson.

Foley, M. (1990) 'Infant children's choices and preferences', in National Writing Project (NWP) *What are Writers Made of? Issues of gender and writing*, Walton-on-Thames, Nelson.

French, J. and French, P. (1984) 'Gender imbalance in the primary classroom: an interactional account', *Educational Research*, 26/2:127–36.

Gilbert, P. (1988) 'Stoning the romance: girls as resistant readers and writers', *Curriculum Perspectives*, 8/2:13–18.

Goodwin, M. H. (1980) 'Directive-response speech sequences in girls' and boys' task activities', in McConnell-Ginet, S., Borker, R. and Furman, M. (eds) *Women and Language in Literature and Society*, New York, Praeger.

Gorman, T. P., White, J. and Brooks, G. (1987) *Language Performance in Schools 1982 Secondary Survey Report*, Department of Education and Science/Department of Education for Northern Ireland/Welsh Office, London, HMSO.

Gorman, T. P., White, J., Brooks, G., Maclure, M. and Kispal, A. (1988) *Language Performance in Schools: review of APU Language Monitoring 1979–1983*, Department of Education and Science/Department of Education for Northern Ireland/Welsh Office, London, HMSO.

Gorman, T. P., White, J., Hargreaves, M., Maclure, M. and Tate, A. (1984) *Language Performance in Schools 1982 Primary Survey Report*, Department of Education and Science/Department of Education for Northern Ireland/Welsh Office, London, HMSO.

Graddol, D. and Swann, J. (1989) *Gender Voices*, Oxford, Basil Blackwell.

Halpern, D. F. (1986) *Sex Differences in Cognitive Abilities*, Hillsdale, N.J., Lawrence Erlbaum Associates.

Hammersley, M. (1990) 'An evaluation of two studies of gender imbalances in primary classrooms', *British Educational Research Journal*, 16/2:125–43.

Hardy, M. T. (1989) *Girls, Science and Gender Bias in Instructional Materials*, Occasional Papers on Aspects of Primary Education, Nottingham, School of Education, University of Nottingham.

Hargreaves, D. J. and Colley, A. M. (eds) (1986) *The Psychology of Sex Roles*, London, Harper and Row.

Harland, L. (1985) 'Why doesn't Johnny skip? Or a look at the female roles in reading schemes', in NATE Language and Gender Working Party (eds), *Alice in Genderland*, Sheffield, NATE.

Harris, S. (1991) 'A girl-friendly approach to oracy', in Open University (1991) PS35: *Talk and Learning 5–16*, Milton Keynes, Open University.

Healy, M. (1981) *Your Language: three*, London, Macmillan.

Henton, C. G. and Bladon, A. W. (1985) 'Breathiness in normal female speech: inefficiency versus desirability', *Language and Communication*, 5:221–7.

Herring, G. (1990) 'Nursery children's choices', in National Writing Project (NWP) *What are Writers Made of? Issues of gender and writing*, Walton-on-Thames, Nelson.

Hewitt, R. (1989) 'The new oracy: another critical glance', paper presented to the annual conference of the British Association of Applied Linguistics, September 1989.

Hitchcock, G. and Hughes, D. (1989) *Research and the Teacher: a qualitative introduction to school-based research*, London, Routledge.

Hodgeon, J. (1985) 'Holding a mirror: considerations of book provision', in NATE Language and Gender Working Party (ed.) *Alice in Genderland*, Sheffield, NATE.

Holly, L. (1989) 'Teaching sex: the experience of four teachers', in Holly, L. (ed.) *Girls and Sexuality: teaching and learning*, Milton Keynes, Open University Press.

Hopkins, P. (1985) *A Teacher's Guide to Classroom Research*, Milton Keynes, Open University Press.

Hordyk, A. (1986) 'Assertion and confidence training with girls', in Inner London Education Authority (ILEA) *Secondary Issues? Some approaches to equal opportunities in secondary schools*, London, ILEA.

Hoyles, C. and Sutherland, R. (1989) *Logo Mathematics in the Classroom*, London, Routledge.

Hughes, J. (1992) 'Starting points', in Claire, H., Maybin, J. and Swann, J. (eds) *Equality Matters*, Clevedon, Multilingual Matters.

Hughes, M., Brackenbridge, A., Bibby, A. and Greenhaugh, P. (1989) 'Girls, boys, and turtles: gender effects in young children learning with Logo', in Hoyles, C. (ed.) *Girls and Computers*, London, Bedford Way Papers 34, Institute of Education.

Inner London Education Authority (ILEA) (1985) *Everyone Counts: looking for bias and insensitivity in primary mathematics materials*, London, ILEA Learning Resources Branch.

Inner London Education Authority (ILEA) (1986a) *Primary Matters: some approaches to equal opportunities in the primary school*, London, ILEA.

Inner London Education Authority (ILEA) (1986b) *Secondary Issues? Some approaches to equal opportunities in secondary schools*, London, ILEA.

Jenkins, N. and Cheshire, J. (1990) 'Gender issues in the GCSE oral English examination, Part I', *Language and Education*, 4/4:261–92.

Kelly, K and Pidgeon, S. (1986) 'Girls, boys and reading – an overview', in Inner London Education Authority (ILEA) *Primary Matters: some approaches to equal opportunities in the primary school*, London, ILEA.

Kemp, G. (1977) *The Turbulent Term of Tyke Tiler*, London, Faber and Faber. Repr. 1979, London, Puffin.

Kendall, G. (1989) 'Select Mary or Rick', *Oasis*, October 1989, p. 3.

Kramer, C. (1977) 'Perceptions of female and male speech', *Language and Speech*, 20:151–61.

Kress, G. and van Leeuwen, T. (1990) *Reading Images*, Victoria, Deakin University Press.

Lakoff, R. (1975) *Language and Woman's Place*, New York, Harper and Row.

Larche, D. W. (1986) *Father Gander Nursery Rhymes: traditional nursery rhymes updated for the 1980s*, Watford, Exley Publications.

Lees, S. (1986) *Losing Out: sexuality and adolescent girls*, London, Hutchinson.

Leet-Pellegrini, H. M. (1980) 'Conversational dominance as a function of gender and expertise', in Giles, H., Robinson, W. P. and Smith, P. M., *Language: social psychological perspectives*, Oxford, Pergamon.

Leggett, J. and Hemming, J. (1984) 'Teaching magazines', in The English Centre (ed.), *The English Curriculum: gender. Material for discussion*, London, English Centre.

Leith, D. (1983) *A Social History of English*, London, Routledge and Kegan Paul.

Lewis, C. (1986) 'Early sex-role socialization', in Hargreaves, D. J. and Colley, A. M. (eds) *The Psychology of Sex Roles*, London, Harper and Row.

Licht, B. G. and Dweck, C. S. (1983) 'Sex differences in achievement orientations: consequences for academic choices and attainments', in Marland, M. (ed.) *Sex Differentiation and Schooling*, London, Heinemann.

Loveday, L. (1981) 'Pitch, politeness and sexual role: an exploratory investigation', *Language and Speech*, 24:71–88.

McArthur, L. Z. and Eisen, S. V. (1976) 'Achievements of male and female storybook characters as determinants of achievement behaviour by boys and girls', *Journal of Personality and Social Psychology*, 33/4:467–73.

Mackinnon, D. (1989) *Egalitarianism*, Unit 22 in Open University course E208: *Exploring Educational Issues*, Milton Keynes, Open University.

Majewski, W., Hollien, H. and Zalewski, J. (1972) 'Speaking fundamental frequencies of Polish adult males', *Phonetica*, 25:119–25.

Mellor, B., Hemming, J. and Leggett, J. (1984) *Changing Stories*, London, English Centre.

Millard, E. (1985) 'Stories to grow on', in NATE Language and Gender Working Party (ed.) *Alice in Genderland*, Sheffield, NATE.

Miller, C. and Swift, K. (1981, British edn) *The Handbook of Non-Sexist Writing for Writers, Editors and Speakers*, London, Women's Press.

Milroy, L. (1980) *Language and Social Networks*, Oxford, Basil Blackwell.

Mordue, T. (1984) *Timothy Finds a Playmate*, London, Medici Society.

Morgan, V. and Dunn, S. (1988) 'Chameleons in the classroom: visible and invisible children in nursery and infant classrooms', *Educational Review*, 40/1:3–12.

Morse, L. W. and Handley, H. M. (1985) 'Listening to adolescents: gender differences in science classroom interaction', in Wilkinson, L. C. and Marrett, C. B. (eds) *Gender Influences in Classroom Interaction*, New York, Academic Press.

Moss, G. (1989) *Un/Popular Fictions*, London, Virago.

Moulton, J., Robinson, G. M. and Elias, C. (1978) 'Sex bias in language use: 'neutral' pronouns that aren't', *American Psychologist*, 33:1032–6.

Mountain, J. (1986) 'Patterns of classroom management', in Inner London Education Authority (ILEA) *Primary Matters: some approaches to equal opportunities in the primary school*, London, ILEA.

Munsch, R. N. (1980) *The Paper Bag Princess*, London, Hippo Books/Scholastic Publications.

Murphy, P. (1988) 'Gender and assessment', *Curriculum*, 9/3:165–71.

Myers, K. (1987) *Genderwatch! Self-assessment schedules for use in schools*, London, SCDC publications. Rev. edn repr. as Myers, K. (ed.) (1992) *Genderwatch after the Education Reform Act*, Cambridge, Cambridge University Press.

National Association for the Teaching of English (NATE) Language and Gender Working Party (1985) *Alice in Genderland*, Sheffield, NATE.

National Association for the Teaching of English (NATE) Language and Gender Committee (1988) *Gender Issues in English Coursework*, Sheffield, NATE.

National Curriculum Council (NCC) (1989a) *English Key Stage 1: non-statutory guidance*, York, NCC.

National Curriculum Council (NCC) (1989b) *Science: non-statutory guidance*, York, NCC.

National Curriculum Council (NCC) (1990) *English: non-statutory guidance*, York, NCC.

National Writing Project (NWP) (1990) *What are Writers Made of? Issues of gender and writing*, Walton-on-Thames, Nelson.

Nichols, P. (1979) 'Black women in the rural south: conservative and innovative', in Dubois, B. L. and Crouch, I. (eds) *The Sociology of the Languages of American Women*, Papers in Southwest English IV, San Antonio, Trinity University.

O'Barr, W. M. and Atkins, B. K. (1980) ' "Women's language" or "powerless language"?' in McConnell-Ginet, S., Borker, R. and Furman, N. (eds) *Women and Language in Literature and Society*, New York, Praeger.

O'Connor, P. (1989) 'Images and motifs in children's fairy tales', *Educational Studies*, 15/2:129–44.

Open University (1987) 'Study Guide to Block 3', in course EH207: *Communication and Education*, Milton Keynes, Open University.

Open University (1991) P535: *Talk and Learning 5–16*, Milton Keynes, Open University.

Orr, P. (1985) 'Sex bias in schools: national perspectives', in Whyte, J., Deem, R., Kant, L. and Cruickshank, M. (eds) (1985) *Girl Friendly Schooling*, London, Methuen.

Osmont, P. (1987) 'Girls, boys and reading', in Inner London Education Authority (ILEA) Equal Opportunities Team (ed.), *Stop, Look and Listen. An account of girls' and boys' achievement in reading and mathematics in the primary school*, London, ILEA.

Penelope, J. (1990) *Speaking Freely: unlearning the lies of the fathers' tongues*, New York, Pergamon.

Poynton, C. (1985) *Language and Gender: making the difference*, Victoria, Deakin University Press.

Preisler, B. (1986) *Linguistic Sex Roles in Conversation: social variation in the expression of tentativeness in English*, Berlin, Mouton de Gruyter.

Randall, G. (1987) 'Gender differences in pupil–teacher interaction in workshops and laboratories', in Weiner, G. and Arnot, M. (eds) *Gender under Scrutiny: new inquiries in education*, London, Hutchinson in association with the Open University.

Reay, D. (1992) "He doesn't like you, miss!" Working with boys in an infant classroom', in Claire, H., Maybin, J. and Swann, J. (eds) *Equality Matters*, Clevedon, Multilingual Matters.

Rennie, L. J. and Parker, L. H. (1987) 'Detecting and accounting for gender differences in mixed-sex and single-sex groupings in science lessons', *Educational Review*, 39/1:65–73.

Reyersbach, A. (1986) 'Feelings on show: poetry and anti-sexism', in Inner London Education Authority (ILEA) *Primary Matters: some approaches to equal opportunities in the primary school*, London, ILEA.

Risch, B. (1987) 'Women's derogatory terms for men: that's right, "dirty" words', *Language in Society*, 16/3:353–8.

Romaine, S. (1984) *The Language of Children and Adolescents*, Oxford, Basil Blackwell.

Rosen, H. (1969) 'Towards a language policy across the curriculum', in Barnes, D., Britton, J. and Rosen, H. (rev. edn 1986) *Language, the Learner and the School*, Harmondsworth, Penguin.

Russ, J. (1983, British edn 1984) *How to Suppress Women's Writing*, London, Women's Press.

Sachs, J., Lieberman, P. and Erickson, D. (1973) 'Anatomical and cultural determinants of male and female speech', in Shuy, R. W. and Fasold, R. W. (eds) *Language Attitudes: current trends and prospects*, Washington, Georgetown University Press.

Sadker, M. and Sadker, D. (1985) 'Sexism in the schoolroom of the '80s', *Psychology Today*, March 1985, pp. 54–7.

Scanlan, G. (1986) '"Was your mother good at maths?"', in Inner London Education Authority (ILEA) *Secondary Issues? Some approaches to equal opportunities in secondary schools*, London, ILEA.

School Examinations and Assessment Council (SEAC) (1990) *Specification for the Development of Standard Assessment Tasks in the Core Subjects for Pupils at the End of the First Key Stage of the National Curriculum*, London, SEAC.

Schulz, M. (1975) 'The semantic derogation of women', in Thorne, B. and Henley, N. (eds), *Language and Sex: difference and dominance*, Rowley, Mass., Newbury House.

Scottish Education Department (SED) (1990) *English Language 5–14* (Curriculum and Assessment in Scotland: a policy for the '90s. Working Paper no. 2), Edinburgh, SED.

Shamroth, N. and Tilbrook, B. (1990) 'Scratching the surface', in National Writing Project (NWP), *What are Writers Made of? Issues of gender and writing*, Walton-on-Thames, Nelson.

Silveira, J. (1980) 'Generic masculine words and thinking', *Women's Studies International Quarterly*, 3:165–78.

Singleton, C. (1986) 'Sex roles in cognition', in Hargreaves, D. J. and Colley, A. M. (eds) *The Psychology of Sex Roles*, London, Harper and Row.

Smith, C. and Lloyd, B. B. (1978) 'Maternal behaviour and perceived sex of infant', *Child Development*, 49:1263–5.

Smith, P. (1986) 'School policy', in Inner London Education Authority (ILEA) *Secondary Issues? Some approaches to equal opportunities in secondary schools*, London, ILEA.

Smith, P. K. (1986) 'Exploration, play and social development in boys and girls', in Hargreaves, D. J. and Colley, A. M. (eds) *The Psychology of Sex Roles*, London, Harper and Row.

Spender, D. (1980) 'Talking in class', in Spender, D. and Sarah, E.

(eds) (rev. edn, 1988) *Learning to Lose: sexism and education*, London, Women's Press.

Spender, D. (1982) *Invisible Women: the schooling scandal*, London, Writers and Readers Publishing Cooperative.

Spender, D. (1985, 2nd edn), *Man Made Language*, London, Routledge and Kegan Paul.

Spender, D. and Sarah, E. (eds) (rev. edn, 1988) *Learning to Lose: sexism and education*, London, Women's Press.

Staffordshire Oracy Project (1989) *Bulletin 1*, Staffordshire County Council.

Stanchfield, J. M. (1973) *Sex Differences in Learning to Read*, Bloomington, Ind., Phi Delta Kappa Educational Foundation.

Stanley, J. P. (1977) 'Paradigmatic woman: the prostitute', in Shores, D. L. and Hines, C. P. (eds) *Papers in Language Variation*, Birmingham, University of Alabama Press.

Stanley, J. P. and Robbins, S. W. (1978) 'Sex-marked predicates in English', *Papers in Linguistics*, 11/3–4:487–516.

Stanworth, M. (1983, 2nd edn) *Gender and Schooling: a study of sexual divisions in the classroom*, London, Hutchinson.

Steedman, C. (1983) *The Tidy House*, London, Virago.

Stones, R. (1983) *'Pour out the Cocoa, Janet': sexism in children's books*, London, Longman for the Schools Council.

Studio Publications (1988) *Cinderella*, Ipswich, Studio Publications.

Swann, J. (1991) 'Gender and talk in the classroom', in Open Univeresity (1991) P535: *Talk and Learning 5–16*, Milton Keynes, Open University.

Swann, J. and Graddol, D. (1988) 'Gender inequalities in classroom talk', *English in Education*, 22/1:48–65.

Thorne, B., Kramarae, C. and Henley, N. (1983) (eds) *Language, Gender and Society*, Rowley, Mass., Newbury House.

Trudgill, P. (1972) 'Sex, covert prestige and linguistic change in the urban British English of Norwich', *Language in Society*, 1:179–95.

Trudgill, P. (1974) *The Social Differentiation of English in Norwich*, Cambridge, Cambridge University Press.

Trudgill, P. (1983, 2nd edn) *Sociolinguistics*, Harmondsworth, Penguin.

Tuchman, G., Daniels, A. K. and Benet, J. (1978) *Hearth and Home: images of women in the mass media*, New York, Oxford University Press.

Underwood, G., McCaffrey, M. and Underwood, J. (1990) 'Gender differences in a cooperative computer-based language task', *Educational Research*, 32/1:44–9.

Walker, R. (1989) *Doing Research: a handbook for teachers*, London, Routledge.

Weiner, G. and Arnot, M. (eds) (1987) *Gender under Scrutiny: new inquiries in education*, London, Hutchinson in association with the Open University.

Weiner, G. and Arnot, M. (eds) (1988) *Gender and Education Bibliography*, document produced for Open University course E813: *Gender and Education*, Milton Keynes, Open University.

Welch, R. L., Huston-Stein, A., Wright, J. C. and Plehal, R. (1979) 'Subtle sex-role cues in children's commercials', *Journal of Communication*, 29:202–9.

West, C. and Zimmerman, D. H. (1983) 'Small insults: a study of interruptions in cross-sex conversations between unacquainted persons', in Thorne, B., Kramarae, C. and Henley, N. (eds) *Language, Gender and Society*, Rowley, Mass., Newbury House.

White, J. (1986) 'The writing on the wall: beginning or end of a girl's career?', *Women's Studies International Forum*, 9/5:561–74.

White, J. (1990a) 'On literacy and gender', in Christie, F. (ed.) *Literacy for a Changing World*, Victoria, Australian Council for Educational Research (ACER).

White, J. (1990b) 'Questions of choice and change', in National Writing Project (NWP) *What are Writers Made of? Issues of gender and writing*, Walton-on-Thames, Nelson.

Whyte, J. (1986) *Girls into Science and Technology: the story of a project*, London, Routledge and Kegan Paul.

Wilkinson, A. with Davies, A. and Atkinson, D. (1965) *Spoken English, University of Birmingham Educational Review*, Occasional Papers no. 2.

Wilkinson, L. C. and Marrett, C. B. (eds) (1985) *Gender Influences in Classroom Interaction*, New York, Academic Press.

Wolfson, N. (1984) 'Pretty is as pretty does: a speech act view of sex roles', *Applied Linguistics*, 5/3:236–44.

Wolfson, N. and Manes, J. (1980) ' "Don't 'dear' me!" ', in McConnell-Ginet, S., Borker, R. and Furman, N. (eds), *Women and Language in Literature and Society*, New York, Praeger.

Wood, J. (1984) 'Groping towards sexism: boys' sex talk', in McRobbie, A. and Nava, M. (eds), *Gender and Generation*, London, Macmillan.

Wright, C. (1987) 'The relations between teachers and Afro-Caribbean pupils: observing multi-racial classrooms', in Weiner, G. and Arnot, M. (eds) *Gender under Scrutiny: new inquiries in education*, London, Hutchinson in association with the Open University.

Zimet, S. G. (1976) *Print and Prejudice*, London, Hodder and Stoughton in association with the United Kingdom Reading Association.

Zimmerman, D. H. and West, C. (1975) 'Sex roles, interruptions and silences in conversation', in Thorne, B. and Henley, N. (eds) *Language and Sex: difference and dominance*, Rowley, Mass., Newbury House.

Index

ability (gender differences in) 5ff, 115

Abse *see* Bleiman and Abse

academic performance (gender differences in) 2–3, 75ff, 115–6

accent 24ff, 32ff, 80, 81

achievement orientation 129ff

address, terms of 31ff

aggression 5ff

amount of talk 27–8, 49ff, 74ff, 171ff, 197–8, 211ff

anti-sexist initiatives ch9 *passim*

anti-sexist language 34, 35, 212–13

Archer and Lloyd 6

Arnold 121, 139, 190, 194

assertiveness 5ff, 51ff, 79ff training 215–16

assessment
of spoken language 80ff
of written language 141ff
tasks that favour girls or boys 105ff, 141ff

Assessment of Performance Unit (APU) 78, 80–2, 115ff, 131, 139, 143

audio-recordings (of classroom talk) 180ff

authorship (of literary texts) 109, 203

Baines 103

Baker and Freebody 100–1

Baran 214, 219

bias
in assessment tasks *see* assessment tasks that favour girls or boys
in books/resources *see* imbalances in books/resources
in language *see* sexism in language
in research methods 169, 170, 181

biological and social explanations of gender 5ff

Bleiman and Abse 222, 223

Bornstein 18–19

Bousted 172, 213–14

British Film Institute (BFI) 223–4

categories
of images in books/resources 99ff, 109ff, 190ff
of reading and writing choices 120ff, 132–3, 165ff
of speaking turns 56ff, 67–8, 76, 179ff

censorship 140, 232ff

Changing Stories 226–7

checklists
for classroom observation 165ff, 173, 178ff
for written texts 190ff

Cheshire 24–5

Cheshire and Jenkins 82ff

children's television *see* television

Claire 208, 215, 223

Claire and Redpath 65–6

formant frequency 22
French and French 58, 68
fundamental frequency 22

GCSE
  girls' and boys' overall
    performance 2–3
  English *see* English at GCSE
gaze (teacher's) 61–2
gender bias
  in assessment/examinations *see*
    assessment
  in books/resources *see*
    imbalances in books/resources
  in language *see* sexism in
    language
gender identity *see* identity
Genderwatch! 167–8, 173–4, 180,
    190–3
generic masculine terms 35ff
genres (preferred by girls and
    boys) Ch 6 *passim*, 137, 139,
    148, 153, 156, 199, 218, 235
Gilbert 158, 197, 234
Girls Into Science and Technology
    (GIST) 55, 67, 99, 173, 207,
    213
Goodman Zimet *see* Zimet
Goodwin 29–30
Gorman et al. 118ff
group talk 54–5, 56–7, 62ff, 66, 76,
    79, 81, 92, 175–80, 208ff, 212ff,
    234–5

Halpern 7ff
Hardy 99–100, 110, 143, 190
Harland 101–2
Harris 169–70, 210–11, 215
Healy 221, 222
hedges (in spoken language) 28
Hemming *see* Leggett and
    Hemming, and Mellor,
    Hemming and Leggett
Herring 120–1, 166
Hodgeon 102
Hordyk 215–16, 220

hormones 6ff
Hughes 203, 220–1

identity (language and) 33, 72ff,
    135, 149ff, 156ff
images
  in books/resources Ch 5
    passim, 127, 149ff, 202ff; *see
    also* representation
  in the media 104ff, 150ff, 222ff;
    see also representation
imbalances
  in books/resources ch5
    passim, 137ff, 191ff, 202ff,
    222ff
  in classroom talk ch3 passim,
    ch4 *passim*, 171ff, 197ff, 211ff,
    220–1
  in reading and writing choices
    ch6 *passim*, 137ff, 155ff, 189ff,
    216ff, 222ff
indirect speaking styles 30
insults 44ff
interaction
  general studies 26ff
  in the classroom ch3 *passim*
interruptions 28, 29–30, 80, 83

Jenkins *see* Cheshire and Jenkins

Kemp 204ff
Kramarae 16–17, 20

language awareness 47, 221
language guidelines *see* anti-sexist
    language
lateralization 7ff
learning (talk and) 74ff
Lees 44, 52
Leggett *see* Mellor, Hemming and
    Leggett
Leggett and Hemming 150, 225–6
Letterbox Library 206, 232
lexical gaps 37ff
Licht and Dweck 129ff, 147

Lloyd *see* Archer and Lloyd, and
Smith and Lloyd

McCaffrey *see* Underwood,
McCaffrey and Underwood
Mackinnon 229
magazines (children's) 107, 150,
225–6
male bias
in assessment *see* assessment
tasks that favour girls or boys
in books/resources *see*
imbalances in books/resources
male image
of computers 53
of the physical
sciences/technology 55ff, 143ff
male images in books/resources *see*
images in books/resources
masculine
grammatical gender 35ff
speaking styles 17, 23, 29, 32ff
media images *see* images in the
media
Mellor, Hemming and Leggett
226–7
Millard 205
minimal responses (in
conversation) 28, 83
mixed-sex
groups and classes (in school)
51, 54–5, 56, 62ff, 68, 72, 75, 82,
93, 169, 175, 209–11, 212, 213,
233
talk (outside school) 28–9, 34,
47
Morse and Handley 56, 67
Moss 155ff, 197, 232ff
Mountain 169
Murphy 141–2
Myers 167, 173–4, 192–3

National Association for the
Teaching of English (NATE)
Language and Gender

Committee 103, 104, 124, 138,
180, 202, 207, 218
national curriculum 1, 49, 73, 103,
228; *see also* English in the
national curriculum
National Oracy Project (NOP) 75
National Writing Project (NWP)
120, 217
non-sexist
initiatives Ch 9 *passim*
language *see* anti-sexist language
non-standard varieties of language
24ff; *see also* vernacular speech
and working-class speech
non-verbal behaviour 33, 55, 61–2,
67, 69, 89ff, 175, 181
Northern Ireland Curriculum 1, 49

observations (of children's
language behaviour) Ch8
passim
open-ended
notes on written texts 190, 194
observation 67, 131, 162, 167,
176
oracy Ch4 *passim*, 172
Orr 2
Osmont 125, 170

Patois 24–6
peer groups 24, 43
perceptions of female and male
speech 15ff, 52ff, 72, 80; *see
also* assessment of spoken
language and teacher
expectations
physical sciences *see* science
subjects
pitch of voice 21–3
poetry 118, 119, 218
popular fiction 155ff, 197
power (inequalities between
females and males) 23, 28, 34,
37, 47, 68, 73, 147, 155ff, 224
prescriptions about female
speech 17ff

prescriptive grammarians 41
prestige varieties of language
24–6

qualitative research 63, 68, 110,
112, 132, Ch8 *passim*
quantitative research 56, 68, 132,
Ch8 *passim*
questions
female and male use of 28, 34,
54, 56, 83, 88–9
teachers', to girls and boys 48,
56, 57, 58, 61–2, 76, 124, 211,
212, 214; *see also* teacher talk

Randall 56, 67
reading material
bias/imbalances *see* imbalances
in books/resources
girls' and boys' choices *see*
imbalances in reading and
writing choices
Reay 209
Redpath *see* Claire and Redpath
Rennie and Parker 56–7, 67
representation (of females and
males) Ch5 *passim*, 143ff,
190ff; *see also* images
Reyersbach 218–19
Risch 45
romance 155ff, 197
rough and tumble 7, 9

Sachs, Lieberman and Erickson 22
Sadker and Sadker 52, 53, 64
Scanlan 171, 207, 212
schedules (for classroom
observation) 165ff, 173, 178ff
Schulz 37
science subjects 2, 55ff, 69, 76,
99–100, 105, 136, 143–5, 148,
207, 209, 214, 219
Scottish Development
Programme 1, 5–14, 49; *see
also English Language* 5–14
semantic derogation/pejoration 37

sexism, sexist bias
in assessment *see* assessment
in books/resources *see*
imbalances in books/resources
in language 11, 34ff, 223ff
Shamroth and Tilbrook 219–20,
223
single-sex groups and classes 51,
55, 56, 63, 82, 209–11, 215
Smith, C. and Lloyd 10
Smith, P. 212
Smith, P. K. 9
social explanations of gender *see*
biological and social
explanations
speaking pitch *see* pitch of voice
speaking turn 27, 28, 34, 56, 58ff,
65–6, 68, 75–6, 172, 173ff, 175,
178ff, 197, 221
Spender 27, 40, 41, 52, 75, 209,
213
Staffordshire Oracy Project 181–2
standard variety of language 24–6
stereotypes
about language use 17, 20, 27
in books/resources *see* images in
books/resources
in linguistic images 34, 39, 40
in reading/writing choices *see*
imbalances in reading/writing
choices
Stones 98, 152
Swann and Graddol 60–1, 68

tag questions 28
talkativeness *see* amount of talk
teacher
attention 52, 61, 65, 68, 92, 169,
210, 212ff
expectations 83, 129
talk Ch3 *passim*, 75ff, 172ff,
212ff
technology 55, 69, 76, 136, 148
tentative (speaking style) 28, 33,
79ff
testosterone 6ff

Index 261

Tilbrook *see* Shamroth and
  Tilbrook
transcription (of classroom talk)
  183ff
Trudgill 20, 21, 23, 32
turn taking *see* speaking turn
Tyke Tiler 204ff

Underwood, McCaffrey and
  Underwood 55

varieties of language 23ff
verbal ability *see* ability
vernacular speech 25, 32; *see also*
  nonstandard varieties of
  language and working class
  speech

video recordings (of classroom
  talk) 180ff

Welch et al. 107
White 120, 122, 139, 140, 144, 146,
  217, 219
whole-class talk 48, 51, 57, 172,
  173–5, 180–1, 197, 198, 213–14, 229
Whyte 55, 213
Wolfson 31
Wolfson and Manes 31
Wood 44–5
working class speech 32, 72
Wright 64
written texts (making analyses
  of) 189ff

Zimet 98, 128, 152